THREE CITIES OF YIDDISH
ST PETERSBURG, WARSAW AND MOSCOW

LEGENDA

LEGENDA is the Modern Humanities Research Association's book imprint for new research in the Humanities. Founded in 1995 by Malcolm Bowie and others within the University of Oxford, Legenda has always been a collaborative publishing enterprise, directly governed by scholars. The Modern Humanities Research Association (MHRA) joined this collaboration in 1998, became half-owner in 2004, in partnership with Maney Publishing and then Routledge, and has since 2016 been sole owner. Titles range from medieval texts to contemporary cinema and form a widely comparative view of the modern humanities, including works on Arabic, Catalan, English, French, German, Greek, Italian, Portuguese, Russian, Spanish, and Yiddish literature. Editorial boards and committees of more than 60 leading academic specialists work in collaboration with bodies such as the Society for French Studies, the British Comparative Literature Association and the Association of Hispanists of Great Britain & Ireland.

The MHRA encourages and promotes advanced study and research in the field of the modern humanities, especially modern European languages and literature, including English, and also cinema. It aims to break down the barriers between scholars working in different disciplines and to maintain the unity of humanistic scholarship. The Association fulfils this purpose through the publication of journals, bibliographies, monographs, critical editions, and the MHRA Style Guide, and by making grants in support of research. Membership is open to all who work in the Humanities, whether independent or in a University post, and the participation of younger colleagues entering the field is especially welcomed.

ALSO PUBLISHED BY THE ASSOCIATION

Critical Texts
Tudor and Stuart Translations • New Translations • European Translations
MHRA Library of Medieval Welsh Literature

MHRA Bibliographies
Publications of the Modern Humanities Research Association

The Annual Bibliography of English Language & Literature
Austrian Studies
Modern Language Review
Portuguese Studies
The Slavonic and East European Review
Working Papers in the Humanities
The Yearbook of English Studies

www.mhra.org.uk
www.legendabooks.com

EDITORIAL BOARD

Chair: Professor Jonathan Long, University of Durham
For *Germanic Literatures*: Ritchie Robertson (University of Oxford)
For *Italian Perspectives*: Simon Gilson (University of Warwick)
For *Moving Image*: Emma Wilson (University of Cambridge)
For *Research Monographs in French Studies*:
Diana Knight (University of Nottingham)
For *Selected Essays*: Susan Harrow (University of Bristol)
For *Studies in Comparative Literature*: Duncan Large
(British Centre for Literary Translation, University of East Anglia)
For *Studies in Hispanic and Lusophone Cultures*:
Trevor Dadson (Queen Mary, University of London)
For *Studies in Yiddish*: Gennady Estraikh (New York University)
For *Transcript*: Matthew Reynolds (University of Oxford)

Managing Editor
Dr Graham Nelson
41 Wellington Square, Oxford OX1 2JF, UK

www.legendabooks.com

Studies in Yiddish

Legenda *Studies in Yiddish* embrace all aspects of Yiddish culture and literature. The series regularly publishes the proceedings of the International Mendel Friedman Conferences on Yiddish Studies, which are convened every two years by the European Humanities Research Centre of the University of Oxford.

Published in this series

1. *Yiddish in the Contemporary World*
2. *The Shtetl: Image and Reality*
3. *Yiddish and the Left*
ed. by Gennady Estraikh and Mikhail Krutikov
4. *The Jewish Pope: Myth, Diaspora and Yiddish Literature*, by Joseph Sherman
5. *The Yiddish Presence in European Literature: Inspiration and Interaction*
ed. by Joseph Sherman and Ritchie Robertson
6. *David Bergelson: From Modernism to Socialist Realism*
ed. by Joseph Sherman and Gennady Estraikh
7. *Yiddish in the Cold War*, by Gennady Estraikh
8. *Yiddish in Weimar Berlin: At the Crossroads of Diaspora Politics and Culture*,
ed. by Gennady Estraikh and Mikhail Krutikov
9. *A Captive of the Dawn: The Life and Work of Peretz Markish (1895-1952)*,
ed. by Joseph Sherman, Gennady Estraikh, Jordan Finkin, and David Shneer
10. *Translating Sholem Aleichem: History, Politics and Art*,
ed. by Gennady Estraikh, Jordan Finkin, Kerstin Hoge and Mikhail Krutikov
11. *Joseph Opatoshu: A Yiddish Writer between Europe and America*,
ed. by Sabine Koller, Gennady Estraikh and Mikhail Krutikov
12. *Uncovering the Hidden: The Works and Life of Der Nister*,
ed. by Gennady Estraikh, Kerstin Hoge and Mikhail Krutikov
13. *Worlds of Yiddish Literature*,
ed. by Simon Neuberg and Diana Matut
14. *Children and Yiddish Literature: From Early Modernity to Post-Modernity*,
ed. by Gennady Estraikh, Kerstin Hoge and Mikhail Krutikov
15. *Three Cities of Yiddish: St Petersburg, Warsaw and Moscow*,
ed. by Gennady Estraikh and Mikhail Krutikov

Three Cities of Yiddish
St Petersburg, Warsaw and Moscow

Edited by
Gennady Estraikh and Mikhail Krutikov

Modern Humanities Research Association
Studies in Yiddish 15
2017

Published by Legenda
An imprint of the Modern Humanities Research Association
Salisbury House, Station Road, Cambridge CB1 2LA

ISBN 978-1-910887-07-3 (HB)
ISBN 978-1-78188-336-5 (PB)

First published 2017

All rights reserved. No part of this publication may be reproduced or disseminated or transmitted in any form or by any means, electronic, mechanical, photocopying, recording or otherwise, or stored in any retrieval system, or otherwise used in any manner whatsoever without written permission of the copyright owner, except in accordance with the provisions of the Copyright, Designs and Patents Act 1988, or under the terms of a licence permitting restricted copying issued in the UK by the Copyright Licensing Agency Ltd, Saffron House, 6–10 Kirby Street, London EC1N 8TS, England, or in the USA by the Copyright Clearance Center, 222 Rosewood Drive, Danvers MA 01923. Application for the written permission of the copyright owner to reproduce any part of this publication must be made by email to legenda@mhra.org.uk.

Disclaimer: Statements of fact and opinion contained in this book are those of the author and not of the editors or the Modern Humanities Research Association. The publisher makes no representation, express or implied, in respect of the accuracy of the material in this book and cannot accept any legal responsibility or liability for any errors or omissions that may be made.

Trademark notice: Product or corporate names may be trademarks or registered trademarks, and are used only for identification and explanation without intent to infringe.

© Modern Humanities Research Association 2017

Copy-Editor: Nigel Hope

CONTENTS

❖

	Acknowledgements	ix
	Introduction: Revisiting Three Cities	1
1	Jewish Geography in Three Cities: St Petersburg, Moscow, and Warsaw in 1897 JEFFREY VEIDLINGER	5
2	Missionaries of the Jewish Nation: Meeting Points between Russian and Polish Jewry before the First World War JOANNA NALEWAJKO-KULIKOV	22
3	What the Readers Think: Two Reader Surveys in the *Literarishe bleter* SIMA BEERI	33
4	Moscow Threefold: Olgin, Bergelson, Benjamin HARRIET MURAV	45
5	Sholem Asch's Moscow Sojourn, 1928 GENNADY ESTRAIKH	56
6	Der Nister's 'Leningrad': A Phantom *fartseykhenung* SABINE KOLLER	73
7	From Facts to Symbols: Space and Architecture in Der Nister's *Hoyptshtet* MIKHAIL KRUTIKOV	90
8	Did Mikhail Epelbaum Study at Warsaw Conservatoire?: The Early Years of an Eminent Yiddish Singer ALEXANDER FRENKEL	104
9	Warsaw, St Petersburg, and Moscow in the Life of the Yiddish Actress Clara Young GALINA ELIASBERG	124
10	Yiddish Music and Musicology in Petrograd/Leningrad/St Petersburg through the Prism of the City Archives ALEXANDER IVANOV	141
11	Between Ethnography of Religion and Anti-religious Propaganda: Jewish Graphics in the Leningrad and Moscow Museums in 1930s ALLA SOKOLOVA	158
	Index	194

ACKNOWLEDGEMENTS

The editors wish to thank the Mendel Friedman Fund and the Faculty of Medieval and Modern Languages, University of Oxford, for sponsoring the publication of this volume. We offer warm thanks to Jack and Naomi Friedman for their generous and extensive support of Yiddish studies at Oxford, which made possible the conference at which this book began to take its shape. Thanks are due to all participants at this conference, and to St Hilda's College, Oxford, which superbly hosted the event. Copy-editing of this book was skilfully provided by Nigel Hope. Finally, we gratefully acknowledge the help, support and expertise of Dr Graham Nelson, Managing Editor of Legenda Press, without whose expertise and patience this book would have been much poorer.

G.E., M.K., New York and Ann Arbor, August 2016

INTRODUCTION: REVISITING THREE CITIES

The idea of this volume was inspired by Sholem Asch's epic novel trilogy *Farn mabl* (*Before the Deluge*, entitled in English *Three Cities*, 1927–32), which presented a panorama of Jewish life in the Russian Empire during the tumultuous period of the First World War and the Revolution. Its publication became a landmark event in the history of Yiddish literature as well as in Asch's literary career. Praised by the *New York Times* critic Louis Kronenberger for portraying, 'in all their scope and mass, the life of three cities, three distinct societies — the wealthy Jews of pre-revolutionary St. Petersburg, the poor Jews of Warsaw, and the whole wide theatre of Moscow during the October revolution', the novel became the first international Yiddish bestseller which inaugurated a new trend in the genre of the realist novel in Yiddish. In Kronenberger's view, the novel made Asch 'a great deal more than the finest of living Yiddish writers' and established his reputation as 'a genuinely significant novelist for the whole world'.[1] The choice of the three largest cities of the Russian Empire offered Asch a trifocal perspective, which enabled him to transcend the spatial constraints of Yiddish literary imagination traditionally focused on the shtetl, and embrace the dramatic historic transformation in its totality.

It was during Asch's lifetime (1880–1956) that St Petersburg/Petrograd/Leningrad, Warsaw, and Moscow developed into the major centres of Jewish cultural, intellectual, and political life in Eastern Europe. They were sites of triumphs and tragedies, but also spaces of everyday life for hundreds of thousands of ordinary Jewish men, women, and children. Each city had its own distinct character and unique features but together they stand for the most encompassing representation of modernity for the Yiddish-speaking Jewry of Eastern Europe. On the eve of the Revolution St Petersburg was home to the most prosperous and acculturated Jewish community in the Russian Empire, which was actively searching for ways of reforming Jewish life and improving its conditions within the Russian imperial framework. Warsaw became at that time the largest city in the Empire open for Jews, and its rapidly growing Jewish community became the hub for Yiddish and Hebrew creativity as well as the stronghold of Polish acculturation. Warsaw retained its central position during the interwar period as the most diverse and dynamic community in the Jewish world. Moscow's growth as the major centre of Soviet Yiddish culture took place during the 1920s thanks to its newly acquired status as the Soviet capital, which attracted masses of Jews from the former Pale of Settlement, predominantly from its Ukrainian provinces that were ravaged by the Civil War pogroms. The centralization policy of the Soviet government created a unique situation, making Yiddish the only minority culture in the Soviet Union whose institutions, such as the Der Emes publishing house, the State Yiddish Theatre (GOSET), as well as the Department of Yiddish Language and Literature at the Moscow Pedagogical Institute, were located in the capital while the majority of the Yiddish-speaking population lived in Ukraine and Belorussia. The flourishing of Yiddish in Eastern Europe came to an abrupt and tragic end during the 1940s, with the Nazi Holocaust followed by Stalin's destruction of Yiddish culture in the Soviet Union.

Taking its cues from Asch's panoramic trilogy, our volume explores different aspects of Yiddish-related activities in the three cities at different moments of the turbulent twentieth century. But unlike Asch's novel, most of the chapters in this volume do not focus on one particular city but rather examine various forms of cultural contacts and interactions between spaces, genres, identities, cultures, and languages across geographical borders and political boundaries. Most Yiddish-speakers spent their early years in the traditional shtetl, and they were highly resourceful and creative in adapting to the new urban environment of the imperial and post-imperial metropolis. Although the German occupation separated Poland from the rest of the Russian Empire in 1915, and the subsequent emergence of the Soviet Union and the Polish Republic further deepened the division between the two countries, Yiddish-speaking Jews on both sides of the new political divide retained remarkable resources of shared cultural memory. Like the previous publication in the 'Studies in Yiddish' series, the present one interprets Yiddish in a broad sense, reaching beyond the spheres of language and literature into the areas of theatre, music, and the visual arts. As the chapters demonstrate, Yiddish served as an important vehicle for preserving and transmitting Jewish identity, sometimes working in unusual and creative ways through different media.

The volume opens with a socio-demographic survey of the Jewish population of the three capitals' dynamics at the turn of the twentieth century based on the Russian census of 1897. Jeffrey Veidlinger offers a fresh perspective on the complex issue of literacy among the Jewish population in the three cities prior to the First World War. His analysis of the population statistics helps understand the dynamics of the growing social and cultural diversity among Jews in the late Russian Empire. Joanna Naliwajko-Kulikov focuses on one significant aspect of that diversity, the distinction between *Litvaks*, i.e. Jews from the lands of the former Grand Duchy of Lithuania which largely overlapped with the imperial administrative region of the North-Western *krai*, and Polish Jews from what was known as Congress Poland, or the Kingdom of Poland, which until 1867 enjoyed a semi-autonomous status in the Empire. This division manifested itself in many apparent forms such as dress, speech, cuisine, and religious customs, and was at the root of substantial social and political conflicts, particularly in Warsaw. Polish nationalists, including some assimilated Polish Jews, considered *Litvaks* agents of Russian imperialism who were harmful to Polish culture and society. The cultural preferences and literary taste of Yiddish readers in post-First World War Poland are discussed in the chapter by Sima Beeri, who examines the readership surveys conducted by the Warsaw high-brow literary weekly *Literarishe bleter* in 1925 and 1929. Responses to these questionnaires offer a unique insight into the reading culture and tastes of interwar Poland and demonstrate a significant interest among readers, some of whom remained loyal to the paper despite their dire poverty, in literature and theatre. Among other things the surveys confirm that Sholem Asch was the most popular Yiddish author of that time. They also show a clear shift in the readers' interest from world literature to Yiddish literature, which can be interpreted as a result of the growing literacy in Polish, which enabled Yiddish readers to read world literature in Polish.

The new dynamic Soviet capital of Moscow was 'a space of aspiration' for many sympathetic visitors. Harriet Murav explores its representations by three different authors who visited the city in the mid-1920s: the leading American communist Yiddish journalist Moyshe Olgin, the Yiddish writer David Bergelson who at that time resided in Berlin but maintained close relationships with the Soviet Union,[2] and the famous German leftist intellectual Walter Benjamin. The most famous among many Yiddish celebrities who came to the Soviet Union during that relatively liberal decade was Sholem Asch. His visit was widely publicized in the Soviet Union, Poland, and the United States, to no small degree because of a scandal that broke out at a reception by Soviet dignitaries. The incident and its wide international repercussions revealed tensions within the Soviet Yiddish establishment, but also demonstrated that as late as 1928 Soviet Yiddish culture remained closely connected with its counterparts abroad, which made its position unique among other Soviet cultures, whose isolation from their foreign counterparts was more severe. Asch's visit and its background are reconstructed by Gennady Estraikh. While Soviet sympathizers perceived Moscow as a construction site of the communist utopia, Leningrad was relegated to the status of a museum city. Ghosts of the past figure prominently in Der Nister's portrait of Leningrad, which he visited for first time in 1932. As Sabine Koller argues in her chapter, this imagery reflects Der Nister's painful search for a way of return to Soviet literature after a distressing ideological attack of 1929.[3] 'Leningrad', along with 'Kharkov' and 'Moscow', appeared in the collection of reportages from the three Soviet cities, *Hoyptshtet* (Capitals, 1934), which marked Der Nister's return to creative writing. *Hoyptshtet* can be regarded as a polemic counterpart to Asch's trilogy, an attempt to assert the superiority of the new Soviet order. Yet as Mikhail Krutikov demonstrates by analysing Der Nister's representation of urban space, the emerging result is a complex, ambiguous, and often contradictory fusion of Der Nister's symbolist fantasy with the fact-oriented positivist Soviet style. But however clumsy and confusing this first attempt at appropriating socialist realist style may be, it became an important step toward Der Nister's later masterpiece novel *The Family Mashber*, which, uncommonly for Soviet literature, garnered universal acclaim across ideological boundaries.

The chapters in the last section deal with the visual arts, music, and theatre. Each one in its own way, they discover traces of continuity across time and space, drawing on a large variety of previously unknown sources. Alexander Frenkel subjects to a rigorous critique the widely circulated version of the early career of the Yiddish folk singer Mikhail Epelbaum, who was instrumental in making the Yiddish song part of the prestigious Soviet genre of 'folk art'. Galina Eliasberg reconstructs the life of the Yiddish actress Clara Young, who enjoyed considerable international success before choosing to settle in the Soviet Union in 1934. The dramatic history of suppression and resilience of Jewish musical culture in St Petersburg/Petrograd/Leningrad is reconstructed, on the basis of numerous archival sources, by Alexander Ivanov.

One of the central components of Soviet ideology was atheism, which was aggressively promoted in numerous exhibitions and museums. By meticulously reconstructing some of the landmark events and drawing extensively on the previously unknown museum holdings in St Petersburg and Moscow, Alla Sokolova reveals the paradoxical fusion of anti-religious propaganda with accurate reconstruction of Jewish religious imagery in the works of artists and curators who were commissioned to set up those exhibitions.

Notes to the Introduction

1. Louis Kronenberger, 'Sholom Asch's Great Trilogy', *The New York Times*, 22 October 1933, p. BR1.
2. For more on Bergelson and his literary career see in *David Bergelson: From Modernism to Socialist Realism*, ed. by Joseph Sherman and Gennady Estraikh (Oxford: Legenda, 2007).
3. For more on Der Nister and his literary career see *Uncovering the Hidden: The Works and Life of Der Nister*, ed. by Gennady Estraikh, Kerstin Hoge, and Mikhail Krutikov (Oxford: Legenda, 2014).

CHAPTER 1

Jewish Geography in Three Cities: St Petersburg, Moscow, and Warsaw in 1897

Jeffrey Veidlinger

Scholem Asch's epic trilogy *Farn mabl* (Before the Storm) sweeps across the three largest urban centres in the early twentieth-century Russian Empire: St Petersburg, Moscow, and Warsaw. For this reason, the novel, which was an American bestseller in Edwin and Willa Muir's 1933 translation, is more commonly known by the name the Muirs used — *Three Cities*. The work, originally published in three volumes — *Peterburg* (St Petersburg, 1929), *Varshe* (Warsaw, 1930), and *Moskve* (Moscow, 1931) — follows Zachary Mirkin, the son of a wealthy Jewish merchant, who seeks self-fulfilment during the turmoil of the pre-revolutionary era. The first volume is set among the Jewish elite of St Petersburg, and begins as an anti-Semitic senator seeks legal advice from the illustrious Jewish advocate Solomon Halperin. In Halperin's chambers, we meet the advocate's aide, Zachary Mirkin, heir to the vast fortune of his widowed father, the wealthy and assimilated Jewish merchant Gabriel Mirkin. Zachary becomes engaged to Nina Halperin, the daughter of the advocate, but falls instead for her mother Olga Stepanova. Nina, for her part, prefers Zachary's father. Thus, Asch sets up a generational conflict between the older generation of assimilated Jews, who have earned their respectable societal positions, and a younger generation, which has inherited monetary wealth, but yearns instead for a feeling of spiritual or national belonging. The next volume takes the reader to the squalid Jewish quarter of Warsaw, where Zachary imbibes the revolutionary fervour of the time, renounces his wealth and family patronage, and ekes out a living as a tutor. In the final volume, Zachary finds himself in Moscow, where he helps the revolutionary forces win the city.

Despite the novel's much-critiqued plot weaknesses, Asch was largely successful in depicting the socio-demography of the cities he featured. However, critics and admirers alike have repeatedly mischaracterized Asch's geography. Both Ben Siegel and Oscar Cargill, for instance — two of Asch's admiring critics — repeatedly refer to the Jewish quarter of Warsaw as depicted in Asch's opus as a 'ghetto', conflating the ghetto of the wartime period with the city's pre-war geography.[1] Yet elsewhere Ben Siegel correctly notes that *Three Cities* moves 'far beyond shtetl and ghetto'. Siegel also misplaces the entire trilogy, incorrectly writing 'Asch centers on the Russian Pale and its Russian and Polish Jews', even though none of the novel's action whatsoever is set within the Pale of Jewish Settlement.[2] This chapter attempts to provide a demographic analysis of the real world that Asch describes.

The primary source base for this chapter is the First General Census of the Population of the Russian Empire, taken in 1897. This census was organized by Petr P. Semenov-Tian'-Shan'skii and Aleksandr G. Troinitskii, through the Central Statistical Committee of the Ministry of Internal Affairs.[3] The co-organizers of the census celebrated its achievements for surveying the population of approximately one-sixth of the earth's surface and utilizing the latest data-processing equipment provided by the American inventor Herman Hollerith. One hundred and fifty thousand surveyors distributed a questionnaire, consisting in most cases of fifteen questions, to 129 million people. Contemporary statisticians, however, expressed frustration with the glacial rate of publishing the data — it took over ten years for the figures to be tabulated and published — and historians have often questioned the census's findings, pointing to confusion in the ways questions were asked and interpreted, as well as inconsistencies between the results of the census and other sources. Many historians and sociologists of Jewish life, in particular, have largely discounted the census, arguing that it probably undercounted Jews since fears of taxation and military conscription kept Jews from answering truthfully. Although there is no evidence to support these particular arguments, it is reasonable to believe that many Jews living illegally outside the Pale of Settlement would have avoided census-takers.[4]

Current scholarship on the census is divided between those who provide meta-analyses of the census, often pointing to the subtle conscious and unconscious ways in which the officials responsible for the census formed and manipulated national identities[5] and those who have utilized and tested the statistical data the census actually provided.[6] Among the latter, more recent scholarship has come to appreciate the consistency of the data and the methodologies used to collect it, and more advanced computational methodologies and comparative studies have upheld much of the census data over competing sources that had led earlier generations to question it.[7] In particular, the census data has been shown to be more accurate for large urban centres where literacy rates tended to be higher and competent census surveyors were easier to find.[8] That being said, any demographic data that purports to measure such large numbers with precision poses the risk of providing a false sense of certitude. It is ironic, though, that many of those most eager to dispose of the hard data are all too willing to write history on the basis of literary representations. At the same time, those who seek to debunk literary representations as mere mythology could benefit from testing the landscape of literature against hard data. Sholem Aleichem remains, to this day, a more commonly cited source for the historical study of fin-de-siècle Eastern European Jewish life than does the 1897 census.

Since the census of 1897 was never replicated — the empire it studied disintegrated before a new census could be conducted — the census is best at providing a snapshot of a moment in time. In fact, in contrast to other censuses of the period, the 1897 census was deliberately designed to document the population on a single day. Many of the problems scholars have encountered in utilizing it have stemmed from their efforts to correlate its data with other statistical sources, such as police reports or Soviet censuses. One needs to be careful in attempting to correlate data that was collected using different criteria. For instance, Benjamin Nathans has noted inconsistencies in the number of Jews residing in St Petersburg across police censuses, city censuses, and the 1897 General Census. He points out that these disparities can be explained by differing criteria for identifying Jews: the police censuses defined Jews as anybody whose passport was marked Jewish, whereas the city census and the 1897 General Census used native language as a signifier of national identity. Comparisons across time are made even more difficult by changing definitions of native language: in 1869 the city defined native tongue as one's first language, the 1890 city census defined native tongue as the language customarily used at home, and the General Census of 1897 defined native tongue simply as the language which each correspondent considers to be native.[9]

★ ★ ★ ★ ★

The census counted 5,110,587 Jews in European Russia and Poland, where they comprised 4.97 per cent of the region's total population, or 42 per cent of the total world Jewish population. As elsewhere where Jews resided, they were more urban than their neighbours. In 1897, 48.8 per cent of Jews in European Russia lived in cities, compared with 13 per cent of the general population. By 1910, about 35 per cent of Russia's Jews lived in metropolitan urban centres, cities with populations of over ten thousand.[10] Jacob Lestschinsky, who has conducted some of the most important demographic work on world Jewry, shows that Russian Jews, were, however, considerably less urban than Jews elsewhere in the world — in much of Western and Central Europe and the Americas well over 90 per cent of Jews were urban. Nevertheless, by 1897 the census shows that the Jewish population of the Russian Empire was gravitating toward the largest urban centres in the empire.

At the turn of the century, St Petersburg, Warsaw, and Moscow were the three largest cities in the Russian Empire. According to the 1897 census, St Petersburg had a population of 1,264,900, Moscow of 1,038,600, and Warsaw of 626,000. These were not, however, the largest Jewish cities in the empire — at least not yet. Only Warsaw, where the census counted 210,526 Jews, was a truly large Jewish centre. In fact, it was the world's second largest, falling only behind New York City. Warsaw's Jewish population constituted 34 per cent of the total population of the city.

Jews, who were still officially barred from living in the Russian interior, barely registered in the censuses for St Petersburg and Moscow. St Petersburg had an official Jewish population of only 16,340, constituting 1.5 per cent of the city's population, whereas the census listed Moscow's Jewish population at a paltry 7,813 individuals, constituting 0.7 per cent of the city's population.

Jewish Population of Three Largest Cities in Russian Empire, according to 1897 Census

	Total Population	Jewish Population	% Jewish
St Petersburg	1,264,900	16,340	1.5
Warsaw	626,000	210,526	34.0
Moscow	1,038,600	7,813	0.7

Note: On this and subsequent tables, percentages may not total 100 due to rounding.

In Warsaw, most Jews lived in the north-west of the city (Beliansky and Povonzkovsky), where the highest concentration of Jews in all of Europe resided. These rapidly growing districts had a distinctly Jewish character: Beliansky was 89 per cent Jewish and Povonzkovsky was 69 per cent Jewish. They were also squalid and overcrowded. By contrast, the Mokotovsky district, in the south-west, was only 6 per cent Jewish. Warsaw was also a rapidly expanding city, and by the early twentieth century was four times more densely populated than St Petersburg and three times more densely populated than Moscow.[11]

Distribution of Jewish Population in Warsaw, by district, according to 1897 census

	Total Population	Jewish Population	% of Jewish Pop. in District	% of District that is Jewish
Beliansky	48,321	42,779	20.3%	89%
Povonzkovsky	52,545	36,244	17.2%	69%
Yerusalimsky	51,766	27,397	13.0%	53%
Vol'sky	57,864	23,960	11.4%	41%
Mostovsky	60,400	23,467	11.1%	39%
Soborny	41,646	14,110	6.7%	34%
Pragsky	57,113	15,435	7.3%	27%
Tovarny	42,408	8210	3.9%	19%
Zamkovsky	55,208	7939	3.8%	14%
Lazenkovsky	57,887	4609	2.2%	8%
Novosvetsky	48,242	3388	1.6%	7%
Mokotowsky	50,789	2988	1.4%	6%

Source: *Pervaia vseobshchaia perepis' naseleniia Rossiiskoi imperii 1897 g.*, ed. by N. A. Troitskii (St Petersburg: N. L. Nyrkin, 1905), LI, 46–47.

The population of Warsaw had grown exponentially since its incorporation into Russia in 1815, and the growth of the Jewish population, in particular, had outpaced the growth of the non-Jewish population, owing primarily to lower infant mortality rates, higher life expectancy rates, and most importantly in-migration from the countryside. Between 1882 and 1897, the city's total population had grown by 62.9 per cent and its Jewish population by 71.3 per cent. Only a little over half the population (50.4 per cent) of the city had been born within the city environs according to the 1897 census, with 14 per cent having been born in the surrounding villages of Warsaw Province. Aside from Warsaw, the largest contingent of migrants came from the provinces of Grodno, Volhynia, Minsk, Vilna, and Kiev, all provinces within the Pale of Jewish Settlement. Asch's fictional Zachary Mirkin, who migrates from St Petersburg to Warsaw in *Farn mabl*, certainly took an unusual route of migration.

Warsaw was a family city. The census shows that it had a larger female than male population, with 102.7 females to every 100 males. This ratio contrasts starkly with the other major Russian cities, which tended to have more men than women, as men tended to find work in the city, leaving their families back home in the country. St Petersburg for instance had 83.7 women for every 100 men and Moscow had 76.5 women for every 100 men. Thus, whereas St Petersburg and Moscow were still largely migrant cities, where male workers and military personnel lived away from their families, Warsaw was a family city. As Stephen Corrsin shows, Jews, in particular, tended to migrate to Warsaw as family units, whereas Catholics — who were the majority in the city — were more likely to migrate as single women (the men, presumably, would either continue to work in the village or migrated out of the country altogether). As a result, the gender ratio between Jewish men and women in the city was more equalized than that of Catholics (in 1897 there were 92 Jewish men to every 100 Jewish women, whereas there were 86 Catholic men for every 100 Catholic women). Largely as a result of having more intact families, Jewish birth rates in the city were also higher and infant mortality rates lower.[12]

Later city censuses show us that the rate of Jewish growth continued. In 1908 the Jewish population of Warsaw had grown from 219,149 in 1897 to 277,787 in 1908 to 317,828 in 1913.[13] In 1913, the Jewish population was 37.6 per cent of the total population of the city. Exactly 100 years earlier, in 1813, there had only been 8,000 Jews in the city, constituting 12 per cent of the population. In other words, in one hundred years the population had risen by a factor of 40, compared with the overall population which had only risen by a factor of 12. The 1914 census of the city of Warsaw shows that it was continuing to grow at a rapid rate, particularly the suburbs. On the eve of the 1917 Revolution, about a fifth of all Jews in Congress Poland lived in Warsaw.[14]

The much smaller Jewish populations of St Petersburg and Moscow were also concentrated in select districts near the downtown core. Nearly a quarter of the Jewish population of St Petersburg (22 per cent) lived in the Spasskaya district, and another 18 per cent in the adjacent Moskovskaya district. These districts included the area surrounding the Ekaterininskii Canal (today *kanal Griboyedova*) in the south-west part of the urban core and the Podiacheskii district around Sadovaya and Voznesenskaya streets, where large numbers of artisans resided.[15] Although the Jewish population of the city was concentrated in these districts, its presence was still numerically marginal: Jews comprised only 3.2 per cent of the total official

Jewish Population of St Petersburg by District, according to 1897 census

	Total Population	Jewish Population	% of Jewish Pop. in District	% of District that is Jewish
Spasskaya	114,065	3608	22.1	3.2
Kolomenskaya	66,280	1446	8.8	2.2
Moskovskaya	143,162	2887	17.7	2.0
Kazanskaya	56,691	889	5.4	1.6
Liteinaya	110,892	1780	10.9	1.6
Narvskaya	109,598	1618	9.9	1.5
Admiralteiskaya	41,041	443	2.7	1.1
Rozhdestvenskaya	94,447	967	5.9	1.0
Vasilevskaya	113,958	863	5.3	0.8
Peterburgskaya	98,554	728	4.5	0.7
Vyborgskaya	77,542	574	3.5	0.7
Alexandro Nevskaya	104,146	537	3.3	0.5

Source: *Pervaia vseobshchaia perepis'*, XXXVII, 50–55.

population of the Spasskaya district and only 2.0 per cent of the total official population of the Moskovskaya district, which was also the largest district in the city as a whole. The fewest Jews lived both in the outer suburb of Alexandro-Nevskaya and in the downtown Admiralteiskaya district, the latter of which was largely inhabited by the city's most prosperous residents.

The 1897 census counted only 7,813 Jews in Moscow, of whom 62 per cent (4,813) were men. Jews as a whole constituted less than 0.7 per cent of the total population of the city, and were concentrated in the Myasnitskaya district — an area in the north-east of the downtown core roughly between today's Kitai Gorod and Chistye Prudy — where the 1,422 Jews constituted 18.2 per cent of the population. The Sretenskaya district, to the immediate north-west of Myasnitskaya also hosted some 833 Jews, or 10.7 per cent of the city's Jewish population. In total 56.3 per cent of the Jewish population lived in the six inner districts on the northern bank of the Moscow River.

Jewish Population of Moscow by District, according to 1897 census

	Total Population	Jewish Population	% of Jewish Pop. in District	% of District that is Jewish
Myasnitskaya	56,423	1422	18.2%	2.5%
Gorodskaya	21,039	488	6.2%	2.3%
Sretenskaya	48,904	833	10.7%	1.7%
Iauzskaya	31,759	519	6.6%	1.6%
Tverskaya	63,022	728	9.3%	1.2%
Arbatskaya	40,844	412	5.3%	1.0%
Serpukhovskaya	35,679	347	4.4%	1.0%
Prechistenskaya	42,499	275	3.5%	0.6%
Lefortovskaya	73,266	434	5.6%	0.6%
Khamovnicheskaya	57,650	316	4.0%	0.5%
Sushchevskaya	87,444	402	5.1%	0.5%
Meshchanskaya	102,974	516	6.6%	0.5%
Basmannaya	45,414	199	2.5%	0.4%
Rogozhskaya	82,962	327	4.2%	0.4%
Piatnitskaya	66,905	291	3.7%	0.4%
Presnenskaya	69,541	199	2.5%	0.3%
Iakimanskaya	52,212	105	1.3%	0.2%

Source: *Pervaia vseobshchaia perepis'*, XXIV, 66–97.

Language Usage

In Warsaw in 1897, nearly 177,000 residents (28.3 per cent of the city population) listed Yiddish as their mother tongue. Among Jews alone, 83.7 per cent listed Yiddish. These figures stand in stark contrast to the earlier census of 1882, which counted 127,917 Warsaw residents who professed Judaism (33.4 per cent of the total population), of whom only 10,031 gave Yiddish as their mother tongue (2.6 per cent of the total city population). By appearances, Yiddish had gone viral in the intervening decade. In reality, these figures are deceptive. The reason for this discrepancy has been studied by Shatzky and Corrsin,[16] both of whom show conclusively that the skewed results were the consequence of a deliberate campaign among the assimilated Jews of the city who controlled the *kehile* board to persuade Jews to identify their nationality as Polish in the 1882 census as a statement of support for the Polish national movement, and as a rebuke of the recent pogroms.

Mother Tongue of Jews in Warsaw, according to 1897 census

	Men	Men %	Women	Women %	Total	Total %
Yiddish	84,986	84	91,277	83.4	176,263	83.7
Polish	13,189	14.3	15,592	13	28,781	13.7
Russian	2,542	2.5	2,010	1.8	4,552	2.3
Other	426	0.4	504	0.5	930	0.5

Source: *Pervaia vseobshchaia perepis'*, LI, 48–51.

In general, linguistic differences correlated very closely with religious differences: 98.8 per cent of Catholics declared Polish as their native language; 94 per cent of Orthodox declared Russian, and 83.7 per cent of Jews declared Yiddish. Of those Jews who cited other languages, 13.7 per cent declared Polish, and 2.3 per cent declared Russian. In contrast to popular stereotypes of Yiddish as a women's language, men were slightly more likely to identify Yiddish as their mother tongue (84 per cent) than women (83.4 per cent). As Irish Parush has argued in a different context, it is possible that women were given greater freedom to explore non-Jewish languages.[17]

Native Language of Jews in Warsaw by District, according to 1897 census

District	Jews	Native Yiddish speakers	% of Jews listing Yiddish
Pragsky	15,435	15,383	99.7
Povonzkovsky	36,244	34,529	95.3
Tovarny	8210	7697	93.8
Beliansky	42,779	36,290	84.8
Soborny	14,110	11,575	82.0
Yerusalimsky	27,397	21,852	79.8
Lazenkovsky	4609	3655	79.3
Mokotovsky	2988	2267	75.9
Zamkovsky	7939	6000	75.6
Vol'sky	23,960	17,980	75.0
Mostovsky	23,467	17,478	74.5
Novosvetsky	3388	1833	54.1

Source: *Pervaia vseobshchaia perepis'*, LI, 52–73.

Language usage also differed sharply by district: in the Povonzkovsky district, 95 per cent of Jews listed Yiddish as their mother tongue, compared with 85 per cent in the Beliansky district, and 99.7 per cent in the Pragsky district. The varying character of Warsaw's districts is also reflected in memoir literature. With less precision, the memoirist Bernard Singer recalled:

> On Muranowska, Mila, Nalewki, the couples spoke exclusively in Yiddish. On Bielanska these same strollers mixed Polish with Yiddish, and in the Saxon

Gardens and on the Marszalkowska they spoke exclusively Polish. Towards evening they returned to their quarter. And again on Bielanska Polish was mixed with Yiddish, and on Nalewki Yiddish ruled.[18]

In Moscow, Jews were, of course, less likely to list Yiddish as their mother tongue, with fewer than 60 per cent choosing to do so. In the Myasnitskaya district, where the largest Jewish population resided, nearly 50 per cent listed Yiddish as their mother tongue. On the other hand, in the Serpukhovskaya district, in the southern part of the city, nearly all Jews identified Yiddish as their mother tongue. As a general rule, the closer to the downtown core Jews resided, the less likely they were to list Yiddish as their mother tongue: fewer than 40 per cent did so in the two most central districts: Tverskaya and Arbatskaya. Proximity to downtown usually translated into linguistic acculturation.

Native Language of Jews in Moscow by District, according to 1897 census

District	Jews	Native Yiddish speakers	% of Jews listing Yiddish
Serpukhovskaya	347	338	97.4%
Meshchanskaya	516	453	87.8%
Lefortovskaya	434	377	86.9%
Khamovnicheskaya	316	270	85.4%
Presnenskaya	199	155	77.9%
Gorodskaya	488	375	76.8%
Sretenskaya	833	636	76.4%
Rogozhskaya	327	245	74.9%
Sushchevskaya	402	258	64.2%
Basmannaya	199	125	62.8%
Iauzskaya	519	274	52.8%
Piatnitskaya	291	150	51.5%
Myasnitskaya	1422	699	49.2%
Prechistenskaya	275	129	46.9%
Iakimanskaya	105	40	38.1%
Arbatskaya	412	155	37.6%
Tverskaya	728	265	36.4%

Source: Pervaia vseobshchaia perepis', XXIV, 60–65.

The rate of Jews listing Yiddish as their mother tongue in St Petersburg fell between those of Warsaw and Moscow. In St Petersburg, 70.3 per cent of Jews legally residing in the city listed Yiddish as their native tongue. The pattern of residence by district was similar to that of Moscow. Those living in the outskirts of the city — in Rozhdestvenskaya and Vyborgskaya — were more likely to list Yiddish as their native tongue than those in the central core districts of Admiralteiskaya and Liteinaya. As a whole, though, Jews were more likely to list Yiddish as their mother tongue everywhere in the imperial capital than they were in Moscow. Even the most acculturated Jews of Admiralteiskaya listed Yiddish as their mother tongue more than 40 per cent of the time. If we take native language as a key component of assimilation, the Jews of St Petersburg were considerably less assimilated than those of Moscow.

Native Language of Jews in St Petersburg by District,
according to 1897 census

District	Jews	Native Yiddish speakers	% of Jews listing Yiddish
Rozhdestvenskaya	967	861	89.0%
Vyborgskaya	574	491	85.5%
Peterburgskaya	728	585	80.4%
Narvskay	1618	1272	78.6%
Alexandro Nevskaya	537	415	77.3%
Spasskaya	3608	2712	75.2%
Kolomenskaya	1446	1055	73.0%
Moskovskaya	2887	1836	63.6%
Vasilevskaya	863	540	62.6%
Kazanskaya	889	513	57.7%
Liteinaya	1780	1010	56.7%
Admiralteiskaya	443	191	43.1%

Source: *Pervaia vseobshchaia perepis'*, xxxvii, 54–83.

Literacy

The 1897 census revealed that 49.4 per cent of male Jews in the empire and 38.9 per cent of female Jews were literate. These findings have been staunchly criticized for decades by scholars who have refused to believe that the 'People of the Book' could have been so illiterate. When we remove children from the equation and focus on the ages of 10–39, literacy rates improve significantly, but as we will see in our detailed study of the three cities, Jewish literacy rates still compared unfavourably with those of other minority groups within the empire. Boris Brutzkus and Arthur Ruppin, two of the first scholars to address the census's findings on Jewish affairs, dismissed the literacy figures entirely. Without presenting any concrete evidence, they surmised that many Jews probably considered their literacy as too self-evident to merit mention or that they did not count literacy in Hebrew. Alternatively, they suggested that census workers were unwilling to admit literacy in Hebrew or Yiddish as true literacy, or were incapable of testing for these languages.[19] These suggestions, however, are problematic. For one, there were Jewish census surveyors, and it is reasonable to believe that they were employed in areas of high Jewish population concentration. Second, there was no literacy test; literacy was determined on the basis of self-reporting. Further, the census form that surveyors used asked about literacy in other languages. The form's instructions required the surveyor to pose the question 'can you read?'. The instructions continued,

> [H]ere, enter the word 'yes' for those who are able to read Russian and the word 'no' for those who are unable to read in any language. For those who are not able to read in Russian, but only in some other language, the name of the other language must be added to the word 'yes'. For example, 'yes, in Tatar'.

In other words, the census defined literacy as the ability to read, regardless of the ability to write. An additional question on some census sheets, particularly for large cities, asked whether the respondent had received any primary education. If the answer to this question was 'yes', the respondent was registered as literate even if the respondent had answered 'no' to the previous questions about being able to read. It is still possible, of course, that some census surveyors or respondents themselves did not consider Yiddish or Hebrew to be a language, and so still answered 'no' to all questions, but since Yiddish was recorded as a language of literacy in other cases and listed as such in the published census, this seems unlikely.[20]

More recent research on the topic of Jewish literacy has demonstrated that the literacy results of the 1897 census are consistent with results from the 1926 census, with American immigration data of eastern European Jews, and with marriage contracts and other documentary evidence.[21] Based on the available evidence, it seems that the type of universal literacy long assumed to have existed among male Jews has been vastly overstated. Certainly, as we shall see, in the large cities of the Russian interior — St Petersburg and Moscow — where legal residency was restricted to the Jewish elites, literacy rates were well above the norm, but Jewish literacy rates in Warsaw were about the same as the general rates for the empire as a whole. Contrary to common expectations, the census data shows that residency in a large metropolitan centre — with easy access to schools, newspapers, and libraries — did not, in and of itself, lead to significantly higher general rates of literacy, let alone universal literacy.

In Warsaw, only 43.5 per cent of the Jewish population by religion was listed as literate according to any of the three criteria. This figure contrasted unfavourably with Warsaw's Orthodox population (68.5 per cent) and Catholic population (59.4 per cent). Even highly acculturated Jews — those Jews who listed Polish as their mother tongue — still had a literacy rate of only 63.1 per cent.

Literacy Rates in Warsaw by Religion,
according to 1897 census (per cent)

	Men	Women	Total	Gender gap
Jewish	51.5	36.1	43.5	15.4
Orthodox	68.2	69.9	68.5	−1.7
Catholic	62.7	56.6	59.4	6.1

Source: *Pervaia vseobshchaia perepis'*, LI, 51–55.

Literacy Rates in Warsaw by Native Tongue,
according to 1897 census (per cent)

	Men	Women	Total	Gender gap
Yiddish	47.9	31.1	39.2	16.8
Russian	73.9	71.9	73.3	2.0
Polish	63.2	57.1	59.9	6.1

Source: *Pervaia vseobshchaia perepis'*, LI, 77.

The rate of Jewish literacy is similarly unimpressive if looked at from the perspective of native tongue. Using this metric, 39.2 per cent of Yiddish-speakers were listed as being literate according to any of the three criteria. The majority of those Yiddish-speakers who were listed as being literate (65 per cent) were identified as being literate in the Russian language. Put another way, 26 per cent of the total

Yiddish-speaking population (literate and non-literate) was identified as being literate in the Russian language. An additional 13 per cent of the total Yiddish-speaking population was identified as being literate in another language but not in Russian. Since the census surveyors stopped the literacy segment of the questionnaire as soon as they got their first indication of literacy, we cannot know how many of those who were literate in Russian were also literate in another language. It is reasonable to assume, though, that many Yiddish-speakers who were literate in Russian were also literate in either Hebrew or Yiddish. It is also not possible to know which other language they were literate in — those who answered that they were literate in another language could have been referring to Yiddish, Hebrew, or even Polish. The suggestion, though, that the low literacy rates are a result of confusion over whether Hebrew literacy would count seem unrealistic in the large cities, where respondents who were not literate in Russian were specifically asked if they were literate in another language.

Jewish literacy rates do look significantly better, though, when age is taken into account. Among respondents who were between the ages of 10 and 39, the overall literacy rate of Yiddish-speakers rises to 51.5 per cent, still a generally unimpressive figure. The literacy rate of Yiddish-speakers in this age group still falls below that of the general population of the city for the same age group, which was listed at 68.4 per cent.[22]

Literacy Rates among Yiddish-speakers in Warsaw by language of literacy, according to 1897 census (per cent)

	Men	Women	Total
Literate in Russian	32.1	19.5	25.6
Not literate in Russian, but literate in another language	14.7	10.7	12.6
Received primary education, but	1.1	0.9	1.0

Source: Pervaia vseobshchaia perepis, XXXVII, 88-115

Notably, the census figures also show a much larger gender gap in literacy rates among Warsaw Jews (measured both by religion and language) than other groups. There was a 16.9 per cent gap between male and female rates of literacy among Yiddish-speakers. Even in the district of Mokotovskaya, which was the most literate district in the city with a Jewish literacy rate of 52 per cent, there was still a 14 per cent gap between the genders.

In St Petersburg, as well, literacy rates among the Jewish minority (72.4 per cent) trailed in comparison to other ethnic minorities, but were slightly higher than the rate for the Orthodox majority (61.3 per cent), and also had a significantly larger gender gap than other minorities. Among those Jews who listed Russian as their native language — again the most acculturated segment of society — the literacy rate was higher at 84 per cent, but still below the figure for German-speakers. The gender gap also decreased among the more acculturated segments of the Jewish population: among Jews who listed Russian as their native language there was only a 5 per cent gap between male literacy (86 per cent) and female literacy (81 per cent). Whereas in Warsaw, Jews tended to be less literate in Russian than the rest of the population, the opposite was the case in St Petersburg, where 72 per cent of Jews were literate in the imperial language compared with 58 per cent of the total population. The only major ethnic group with a higher literacy rate than the Jews was the Germans, with an 89 per cent literacy rate. The gender gap was also smaller among Jews than among some other groups with a 12.1 per cent gap between women and men as a whole and a 5 per cent gap between Jewish women and men who listed their native tongue as Russian. By contrast the city as a whole had a 29 per cent gap between the genders. Nevertheless, only 66 per cent of Jewish women in St Petersburg were literate in Russian. Literacy rates among Jews were also considerably higher in the urban core than they were in the suburbs.

St Petersburg Literacy by Religion according to 1897 census (per cent)

	Men	Women	Total	Gender gap
Jewish	78.1	66.0	72.4	12.1
Orthodox	72.0	48.3	61.3	23.7
Catholic	76.5	72.8	75.1	3.7
Lutheran	85.8	86.5	86.2	−0.7

Source: *Pervaia vseobshchaia perepis'*, XXXVII, 56–59.

St Petersburg Literacy by National Language according to 1897 census (per cent)

	Men	Women	Total	Gender gap
Yiddish	74	60	68	14
Russian	72	49	62	23
German	89	89	89	0
Ukrainian	76	62	73	14

Source: *Pervaia vseobshchaia perepis'*, XXXVII, 56–59.

Jewish Literacy Rates in St Petersburg, by select census district, according to 1897 census (per cent)

	Men	Women	Total	Gender gap
Kazanskaya	85	77	81	8
Admiralteiskaya	83	72	79	11
Moskovskaya	79	71	75	8
Spasskaya	76	60	68	16

Jewish literacy rates were significantly higher in Moscow than in Warsaw, and compared favourably with the Orthodox majority, but lagged behind the Catholic minority, both in terms of raw numbers and gender gap. Again, if we look at the most acculturated segment of the Jewish population — Jews who identified Russian as their native tongue — the figures improve to 84.3 per cent for men and 74 per cent for women (79.7 per cent overall), but still fall behind the corollary figures for Catholics. Jewish literacy rates also improved in the central districts of the city with the rate in Tverskaya reaching 81.9 per cent, although gender gaps remained large. In total, 43.7 per cent of the population that declared Yiddish as their mother tongue

(46.7 per cent of men and 38.1 per cent of women) was listed as being literate in the Russian language.

Literacy Rates in Moscow by Religion,
according to 1897 census (per cent)

	Men	Women	Total	Gender gap
Jewish	78.4	66.3	73.8	12.1
Orthodox	67.3	38.5	54.8	28.8
Catholic	86.0	82.9	84.9	3.1

Jewish literacy rates in the downtown core of Moscow,
by census district, according to 1897 census (per cent)

	Men	Women	Total	Gender gap
Tverskaya	87.4	75	81.9	12.4
Myasnitskaya	86.9	70.2	79.9	16.7
Arbatskaya	81.5	71.6	77.4	9.9

Source: *Pervaia vseobshchaia perepis'*, XXIV, 66–69.

Occupational Distribution

In Warsaw, Jews were distinguished from non-Jews by their occupational structure as well as their language and religion. About 88 per cent of pedlars in Warsaw were Jewish, 66 per cent of textile and clothing traders, and 55 per cent of traders in agricultural products. Their representation in certain fields of manufacturing was also pronounced — 44 per cent of textile manufacturers were Jewish and 36 per cent of manufacturers of agricultural products were Jewish. Put another way, in Warsaw, Jews were 26 times more likely than non-Jews to be pedlars, 7 times more likely to be traders in textiles and clothing, 4 times more likely to be traders in agricultural products, 3 times more likely to be textile manufacturers, and twice as likely to be food product manufacturers. Incidentally, despite a widespread association between Jews and the criminal world, particularly prostitution, Jews were slightly less likely than non-Jews to be listed as prostitutes. At the other end of stereotypical Jewish occupations, Jews in Warsaw were also less likely than non-Jews to be in a private legal practice — only 3 per cent of private practice lawyers in the city were Jews.[23]

In general, there were fewer occupational distinctions between Jews and non-Jews in St Petersburg than in Warsaw. Since legal residency in the city was highly selective, St Petersburg was able to restrict residency to Jews who fulfilled needed economic niches and to refuse residency to those who were engaged in occupations deemed undesirable. Jews in the imperial capital, for instance, were only 1.2 times as likely to be listed as pedlars and slightly less likely than non-Jews to be textile manufacturers. Jews were still 3.5 times as likely to be engaged in the textile trade. Jews also gravitated toward the printing business, where the 361 Jewish printers (including 21 women), represented 2 per cent of the total printers in the city. Put differently, Jews were 3.2 times as likely as non-Jews to be in the printing industry.

There were only 17 Jews in private legal practice, but even this small number represented 2 per cent of the total number of lawyers in the city. Jews were 2.8 times as likely to be employed in private legal practice than non-Jews.

In Moscow, where Jewish residence was prohibited to most of the population, many of the Jews who were counted by the census were military recruits: a large plurality of Jews (45 per cent of the total working population) listed the military as their employer, at a rate of over fifteen times that of the non-Jewish population. Jews were also 9 times as likely as non-Jews to be listed as pedlars, 9 times as likely to be engaged in the textile trade, 2.8 times as likely to be engaged in the manufacture of textiles, 2.7 times as likely to be engaged in agricultural trade, and 2.7 times as likely to be in private legal practice.[24]

Cultural Institutions

The cultural life of the three cities reflected their socio-economic make-up. Despite its small size, St Petersburg served as the administrative centre of Jewish culture in the waning years of the Empire. It was here that most of the cultural and social organizations that sprang up in the wake of the March 1906 regulations on societies and unions were headquartered. By 1908, a relatively small group of community activists had established a Jewish Literary Society, a Jewish Historical and Ethnographic Society, a Society for Jewish Folk Music, a Jewish Society for Development and Education, and a Society for the Protection of the Health of the Jewish Population, to name but a few. Moscow's Jews got in the act, as well, establishing a Jewish Music Society and Jewish Society of Art and Literature, as well as a Jewish student union.

The St Petersburg and Moscow societies, though, did not — for the most part — view their mission primarily as serving the Jews of their own communities, but rather saw themselves as the vanguard for Russian Jewry as a whole. Both the Moscow and St Petersburg OPE (Obshchestvo dlia rasprostraneniia prosveshcheniia mezhdu evreiami: Society for the Spread of Enlightenment among the Jews of Russia), for instance, spent much of their budgets on subsidizing libraries in the provinces and encouraging the reform of primary education in the provinces. The Jewish Evening Courses established in St Petersburg also hoped to educate teachers, who could then spread their knowledge to the provinces. Similarly, the Society for the Protection of the Health of the Jewish Population saw itself as a resource for the provinces and conducted outreach activities to connect with provincial Jews.

In Warsaw, by contrast, cultural activities were directed more prominently inward, toward local audiences. Warsaw's Jews were less interested in (and less able to) establish the types of formal societies that were headquartered in St Petersburg, and instead directed their efforts toward Yiddish culture with mass appeal. The 1909 move of the Yiddish daily *Der fraynd* from St Petersburg to Warsaw most clearly represents this shift. The paper was cultivated by the elite of St Petersburg, but was relocated to the Jewish centre of Warsaw when the paper matured. Warsaw was also the home of the most popular Yiddish daily, *Haynt*, which began to appear in 1908. Soon thereafter, Noah Prylucki together with his father Zvi established the Yiddish daily, *Moment*. Binyomin Shimin's publishing house, to give another example, printed large editions of popular books on travel, popular science, and world classics directed to mass readerships. The major St Petersburg-based Jewish-oriented publications, on the other hand, tended to be more scholarly Russian-language periodicals, like *Evreiskaia starina* or *Perezhitoe* or, alternatively Yiddish papers with smaller runs like *Dos yidishe folksblat*. The Yiddish theatre of Warsaw, too, was tremendously popular — it was here that the famed Kaminska troupe was based, and in 1906 there were five major Yiddish theatrical performance spaces in the city, including the Muranover/Ermitazh. When the Kaminska Yiddish theatre troupe visited St Petersburg in 1909, on the other hand, critics noted that it was met with indifference. It was in Warsaw, too, with the support of Y. L. Peretz and other Yiddish literary luminaries, that some of the first organized efforts were made to establish a literary Yiddish theatre. By the early years of the twentieth century, many of these troupes began to introduce more highbrow material into their repertoires in order to counter accusations of *shund* (trash).[25]

Conclusion

By 1926 — the next time a full census was taken of Moscow — Yiddish, with 131,000 native speakers in the city, was the most common native language after Russian. There were more than four times as many native Yiddish-speakers as native Polish-speakers (the third most common native language in the city) in the Soviet capital. The Jews of Moscow were also listed as being 87 per cent literate: the most significant jump in literacy was among women, and there was now just over a 1 per cent differential between men's and women's rates of literacy. Jewish literacy rates in the city far exceeded the literacy rates of Russians, who were only 74 per cent literate with a 17 per cent differential between men and women. Yet, only 34.3 per cent of the city's Jewish residents declared Yiddish to be their mother tongue, and only 20.5 per cent of Jews in the city claimed to be able to read the language. By contrast, 64.5 per cent of Jews claimed Russian as their mother tongue. In Leningrad, too, the 84,000 Jews in the city in 1926 constituted the second largest nationality after Russians, and also tended to be significantly more literate than the majority group. As had been the case in Moscow, only a small percentage — 31 per cent — of Leningrad's Jews claimed Yiddish as their native tongue, with 68.4 per cent identifying Russian. Only 22.7 per cent claimed they could read in Yiddish. Thus, by 1926 in the two capitals with a total Jewish population of 215,724 there were only 46,141 individuals who reported being able to read Yiddish.

Sholem Asch had intentionally created a literary snapshot of the urban landscapes of Moscow, St Petersburg, and Warsaw at the moment of their transformation. As the data from the 1926 Soviet census suggests, during the first quarter of the twentieth century these cities would be altered beyond recognition, both politically and demographically.

Without much of the archival and governmental data that historians traditionally rely upon to study the sociological composition of common folk, students of Jewish history have often turned to literary portraits in pursuit of historical data. In many cases, such an approach only serves to accentuate embedded prejudices towards the elite. Much Yiddish literature, however, made its mark with a type of realism that sought to depict the lives of common folk. Sholem Asch, for instance, was famously unwilling to shy away from the depiction of urban prostitutes or ordinary small-town folk. Zachary Mirkin, the protagonist of *Farn mabl*, on the other hand, is clearly of the elite, but Asch's subtle portrayals of the urban milieus in which Mirkin finds himself shed light, as well, on Asch's perspective of how ordinary folk lived in the three largest cities in the Russian Empire. No doubt, Asch's extensive personal travels helped him paint his urban landscapes.

The differing cultural and moral values portrayed in Asch's trilogy were reflected as well in the stark demographic differences the 1897 census reveals between the cities. Whether it is the squalid block in which Madame Hurvitz of Warsaw resides, adjacent to the weaving factory, or the 'luxurious establishment in the most modern quarter of the city',[26] in which Gabriel Mirkin had set up his mistress, Asch's literary portraits of the cities are consistent with findings from the census data.

Notes to Chapter 1

1. See, for instance, Oscar Cargill, 'Sholem Asch: Still Immigrant and Alien', *College English* 12.2 (1950), p. 71.
2. Ben Siegel, *The Controversial Sholem Asch: An Introduction to his Fiction* (Bowling Green, OH: Bowling Green University Press, 1976), p. 88.
3. Juliette Cadiot, 'Le Recensement de 1897: Les limites du contrôle impérial et et la représentation des nationalités', *Cahiers du Monde Russe*, 45. 3/4 (2004), 441–63.
4. For the census see Thomas K. Edlund, 'The Russian National Census of 1897', *Avotaynu* 16, no. 3 (Fall 2000), pp. 29–39;
5. Cadiot, 'Le Recensement de 1897'.
6. Michael C. Hickey, 'Demographic Aspects of the Jewish Population in Smolensk Province, 1870s-1914', *Acta Slavica Iaponica*, 19 (2002), pp.; 84–116.
7. Jacques Silber, 'Some Demographic Characteristics of the Jewish Population in Russia at the End of the Nineteenth Century', *Jewish Social Studies*, 42. 3/4 (1980): pp. 269–80.
8. Rowney and Stockwell, 'The Russian Census of 1897', p. 226.
9. Benjamin Nathans, *Beyond the Pale: The Jewish Encounter with Late Imperial Russia* (Berkeley: University of California Press, 2004), p. 94.
10. Cadiot, 'Le Recensement de 1897', p. 441.
11. Stephen D. Corrsin, *Warsaw before the First World War: Poles and Jews in the Third City of the Russian Empire, 1880-1914* (Boulder: East European Monographs, 1989), p. 13.
12. Ibid., p. 26.
13. Lestschinsky, *Dos idishe folk in tsifern* (Berlin: Klal-Farlag, 1922), pp. 77–78.
14. Ibid., p. 24.
15. Nathans, *Beyond the Pale*, pp. 116–20.
16. Jacob Shatzky, *Geshikhṭe fun yidn in Varshe.*, III (New York: Yidisher Visinshafṭlekher Insṭiṭuṭ, hisṭorishe sektsye, 1947), p. 125; Corrsin, *Warsaw before the First World War*, pp. 28efor
17. Iris Parush, *Reading Jewish Women: Marginality and Modernization in Nineteenth-Century Eastern European Jewish Society* (Hanover, NH: Brandeis University Press, published by University Press of New England, 2004), pp. 71–96.
18. Corrsin, *Warsaw before the First World War*, p. 37.
19. Arthur Ruppin, 'Die russischen Juden nach der Volkszählung von 1897', *Zeitschrift für Demographie und Stastik der Juden*, 2.1 (1906), p. 5; Boris Brutzkus, *Stastika evreiskogo naseleniia* (St Petersburg: Siever, 1909), p. 47.
20. For more discussion on literacy as recorded in the 1897 census see A. I. Gozylov, *Perepisi*

naseleniia SSSR i kapitalisticheskikh stran (Moscow: Upravlenie TsUNKhU SSSR, 1936), p. 127; and Gregory Guroff and S. Frederick Starr, 'A Note on Urban Literacy in Russia, 1890–1914', *Jahrbücher für Geschichte Osteuropas*, 19. 4 (1971), 520–31.
21. Joel Perlman, 'Literacy among the Jews of Russia in 1897: A Reanalysis of Census Data', Working Paper No. 182 (December 1996); Shaul Stampfer, 'Literacy among Jews in Eastern Europe in the Modern Period', *Polin*, 7 (1992), 63–87.
22. *Pervaia vseobshchaia perepis'*, LI,, pp. 74–77.
23. *Pervaia vseobshchaia perepis'*, LI, 152–57.
24. Ibid., XXIV, 224–41.
25. For more on Jewish cultural life in the late Russian empire see, Jeffrey Veidlinger, *Jewish Public Culture in the Late Russian Empire* (Bloomington: Indiana University Press, 2009).
26. Sholem Asch, *Three Cities: A Trilogy*, trans. by Willa Muir and Edwin Muir (New York: G. P. Putnam's Sons, 1943), p. 73.

CHAPTER 2

Missionaries of the Jewish Nation: Meeting Points between Russian and Polish Jewry before the First World War

Joanna Nalewajko-Kulikov

Preliminary Remarks

Although until the end of July 1915 the Kingdom of Poland belonged to the Russian Empire, with which it shared the same ruler, legislation, and official language, historians tend to treat Polish and Russian Jewry separately. This division stems from the traditional narrative, which highlighted the distinctive character of the Kingdom of Poland (which lost its autonomy within the Empire in 1867) and which was favoured especially by Polish scholars. Similarly, historians who research the history of Jews in the tsarist Russia are rarely interested in the Jewry of Congress Poland and vice versa, as if these were two isolated worlds that never or hardly ever came into contact with each other.

Is it really the case? It is reasonable to assume that in a single country there must have been many opportunities for contact — people did business together, travelled to study in St Petersburg or Dorpat, and became involved in the same illegal political parties. But what was the scope of such activities? The writer Avrom Reisen, who came to Warsaw from Koidanava (which at that time belonged to the Minsk gubernia and today is known as Dzyarzhynsk, Belarus) around 1899, wrote in his memoirs: '*a journey to Warsaw was considered distant. Visiting Warsaw was nearly the same as visiting a foreign country. [Warsaw] belongs to the same emperor, but it is Poland, after all*'.[1]

In their memoirs, activists of the Jewish community in St Petersburg suggested that their counterparts in the Kingdom of Poland were not keen to maintain close ties. As the lawyer and political activist Genrikh Sliozberg wrote:

> The community in Warsaw in the early 1890s was managed by assimilationists, i.e. by Jews who considered themselves to be Poles of Mosaic faith. It was clear that they did not want to see their interests being associated with the interests of the Russian Jewry. If Warsaw maintained relationships with St Petersburg, it was limited to extraordinary cases, when it was necessary to obtain some favourable decision from the central authorities.[2]

Yakov Frumkin, a lawyer, a social activist, and historian of Russian Jewry, shared this view when he observed in 1904 that 'although Jewish activists in Warsaw gave me a warm welcome, [. . .] they evaded any joint action with Russian Jews, and in any case they could not bear to think that Russian Jews might want to meddle in their business'.[3]

So to what extent did these two communities feel they belonged to the greater community of east European Jewry — if we can speak about such a community at all?[4] Did the migration of the so-called Litvaks to Congress Poland change anything in this respect? As far as I know there is no extensive research into this topic, so this article will ask questions rather than answer them.[5]

★ ★ ★ ★ ★

Russian Jews — commonly known in the Polish lands as Litvaks[6] — started to migrate to the Kingdom of Poland in the 1860s, as the economic ties between the Kingdom and the rest of the Russian Empire grew tighter (although François Guesnet argues that isolated cases of migration occurred as early as in the 1850s).[7] When Russian became the official language of the Polish administration, speakers of Russian gained new work opportunities, including other professions than that of travelling salesman.[8] Moreover, from 1868 onwards, the Jews from Russia could travel freely across the Polish border.[9] The greatest number of Litvak immigrants came at the turn of the 1880s and 1890s, following a wave of pogroms in Russia and the expulsion of Jews from several cities, notably Kiev (1886) and Moscow (1891).

Unfortunately, there are no reliable estimates of the number of Litvaks who settled in Poland. According to the available calculations, between 1897 and 1913 c. 250,000 Litvaks lived in Congress Poland, which accounted for one-sixth of the entire Jewish population in the country.[10] Undoubtedly — the sources are unanimous on this matter — their presence was visible, also because they were different from the Polish Jews. Vital Zajka writes:

> Lithuanian Jewry was a separate entity in terms of ethnological features such as food, utensils, clothing, dwellings, folklore, patterns of behaviour and local ethos. There seems also to have been a separate physical type ascribed to Lithuanian Jewry, as reflected in the stereotype of the Litvak as black-haired, dark-eyed, and relatively tall.[11]

The Jewish culture and folklore perceived Litvaks as rational and cold opponents of Hasidism. But in the Kingdom they quickly became associated with the Russian culture, business skill, and, in general, a more secular nature and a greater political awareness.[12] The founder of the first Hebrew school for girls in Warsaw, Puah Rakovsky, herself born and raised in Białystok, noted that among Russian Jews who came to Poland after their expulsion from Moscow in 1891 there were many Zionists: 'Those Russian and Lithuanian Jews brought Zionism to Poland.'[13] They were also responsible for the development of the Jewish socialist movement in Poland: for example the leaders of the Warsaw social democratic group in 1894–95 came from Vilna and until 1897 operated only among other Litvaks. Similarly, the first Bund committee in Lodz was composed of Litvaks alone.[14]

Since Litvaks often spoke only Yiddish and Russian and maintained close professional and business ties with the Russian market, the Polish society tended to perceive them as an instrument in the hands of the tsarist authorities whose task was to Russify Poland. This is why Poles harboured aversion and fears because of their conspicuous presence; even the proponents of Jewish assimilation and acculturation were not free of such feelings. 'I am by no means an anti-Semite', wrote Eliza Orzeszkowa, a popular writer known for her sympathy for Jews, 'but I must admit the Russian kind of Jews is not the nicest kind, and that a party which is in three quarters composed of them is not the nicest party possible'.[15] Similar remarks (some of them even more critical) can be found in many documents of the era, private or public, made by leading Polish intellectuals.

Polish Jewry was not always keen to give their Russian brothers a warm welcome either. Genrikh Sliozberg describes the differences in mentality in his memoirs:

> The conflict between the Russian Jews of nationalist persuasion and the representatives of Polish assimilation started to grow only after the Moscow expulsion, when many Moscow factory owners moved to Warsaw. This conflict was deeply rooted in politics. Polish Jewry strove to maintain good relations with Poles [. . .] The influx of Russian-speaking Russian-Jewish groups to Warsaw and Lodz gave Poles a reason to disregard the concerns of Polish Jews, who wanted to express their solidarity with Polish national interests, and to blame Jewry for the betrayal of Polish culture [. . .][16]

The Warsaw-born journalist and writer A. Almi (Eliahu Chaim Sheps) confirms in his reminiscences that Jews in Warsaw did not trust the newcomers:

> For the Warsaw Jewry each Jew who spoke slightly differently from the Warsaw locals was a Litvak. So not only the Ukrainian or Courland Jews were dubbed Litvaks, but also Jews from Polish towns and shtetls, such as a Kalisz, Wloclawek, or Miedzyrzec.
>
> It must be said that Warsaw Jews were not very fond of Litvaks. The prejudice arose because a great number of Litvaks, the true ones, belonged to the *enlightened* and all of them wore short, German-style clothing, which religious Jews from Warsaw viewed as outrageous.
>
> The economic factor was also significant. The Litvaks were said to take the most profitable positions for themselves [. . .] The prejudice and the attitudes held by Warsaw Jewry towards the Litvaks were almost the same as the feelings held by Poles towards Jews in general.[17]

The Litvaks gave as good as they got: as early as 1866, Peretz Smolenskin admitted that Litvaks disliked Polish Jews, whom they thought to be ignorant and superstitious.[18] Puah Rakovsky confessed after many years: 'in the forty-six years I later lived there [in Warsaw — J.N-K.] I remained the Litvak — I was absolutely unable to assimilate with my Polish brothers and sisters'.[19] Rakovsky's memoirs clearly show that the majority of her Warsaw circle was composed of people who arrived from beyond the borders of Congress Poland. The Hebrew press published complaints from Litvaks who felt isolated in Warsaw, 'as if here were no Jews at all', and even considered establishing a community of their own, Agudat Bnei Lite.[20]

Volhynia-born Zvi Prylucki, who moved from St Petersburg to Warsaw to publish the first Warsaw daily in the Yiddish language, *Der Veg*, recorded in his memoirs a conversation he had with the journalist and Zionist leader Nahum Sokolov shortly after his arrival:

> I came to Warsaw in early 1905 with a licence to publish the *Der Veg* daily, and from the very beginning I felt a completely different atmosphere from that in St Petersburg.
>
> During my visits at [Nahum] Sokolov's we happened to talk about it — [he] said that I was bound to miss St Petersburg, because the internal and external conditions in Warsaw were radically different from those in St Petersburg. There, Jews had to heed only one side, and in Warsaw two: the tsarist administration and the Polish society. And each side would like the Jews to play obedient puppies.
>
> The internal differences [in Jewish society] are substantial, too. With respect to culture, the Jews who enjoy the right to reside in the Russian capital are more or less the same. But Warsaw is stratified in this respect. Sokolov said that at that time there were many conflicts between the Polish Jewry and the Litvaks. Polish Jews are spread across different Hasidic synagogues, which compete with one another. Often, the Hasidim of one rebbe pester the Hasidim of another. And finally there is an enormous gap between all of them and the so-called 'progressive' Jews.
>
> Sokolov added that one should also bear in mind that in St Petersburg Jews accounted for a mere 2 per cent of the society, and that there were streets where only a few Jewish families lived, and that this isolation led Jews to grow close to one another. It should be noted that in Warsaw, Jews did not experience the isolation and estrangement that might have united them. The explanation, however, did not change the essence, and Sokolov admitted that Russian Jewry had specific virtues.[21]

Sliozberg's and Prylucki's observations seem accurate. For the Jews the capital of the empire was 'a laboratory of selective integration'.[22] Under the reign of Alexander II, some Jews were allowed to live outside the Pale of Settlement. In this number were servicemen, rich merchants, university graduates, and artisans who had adequate skills. The largest Jewish community outside the Pale was located in St Petersburg. According to estimates, in the early 1880s the capital city hosted legally *c.* 16,000 Jews and just as many illegally. This group was well educated and represented mainly the rich bourgeoisie or liberal professions, and it was characterized by fast language acculturation: on the eve of the First World War half of Petersburg Jews used Russian as their vernacular language.[23]

Warsaw, in turn, the third biggest city in the Empire, in contrast to St Petersburg did not require Jews to have a residence permit or exercise a profession needed in the capital, which was an obvious advantage. At the same time, it could boast all the qualities of a big city of which ambitious and talented youth from smaller towns could only dream.[24] 'Why are you still stuck in the shtetl muds?', a friend from Warsaw wrote to Avrom Zak in Indur (Yiddish: Amdur) in the Grodno gubernia. 'Come to Warsaw. Life is interesting here. There are theatres, newspapers, writers.'[25]

Newcomers were surprised by two things in Warsaw: 'the noise around the station, rows of cabs which compared to cabs in Minsk [. . .] looked like aristocratic carriages, [. . .] a crowd of elegant ladies and gentlemen mingled with Polish Jews in their famous cabbie caps, a mixture of languages — Polish, Yiddish and Russian',[26] and first of all the dialect used by Warsaw Jewry, which was different from the Yiddish used in the Pale of Settlement and which at first sounded foreign and was hard to understand.[27]

A significant percentage of Yiddish writers and journalists who before 1914 laid the foundations for the development of modern Yiddish culture in Polish lands were actually Litvaks. Many of them decided to settle in Warsaw inspired by Yitskhok Leybush Peretz, who at the end of the nineteenth century established in his apartment at 1 Ceglana Street an informal literary salon, which was actually a centre of modern Jewish culture. One of the people under his influence was Avrom Reisen, who was already quoted above: 'I couldn't believe I was in Warsaw where Peretz lived, where all the great people and newspapers were...'[28]

Jewish newspapers and periodicals with their offices became one of the key meeting spots for Polish and Russian Jewries — or maybe between Polish Jews and Russia as such. But how about the Russian-Jewish press — was it read in Congress Poland? The *Voskhod* monthly, which in 1885–99 was the only Jewish periodical in Russian, attained in 1895 a maximum of 4,397 subscribers from five biggest cities of the Empire: Odessa (420), St Petersburg (168), Warsaw (144), Kiev (128), and Moscow (95).[29] In 1887, the publisher of *Voskhod*, Adolf Landau, looked for a correspondent in Warsaw who could provide information about Jewish life in Poland and about the so-called Jewish question in Poland.[30] According to Vladimir Levin, in 1890s the readership of *Voskhod* in Congress Poland grew substantially: in 1890, in Piotrkow gubernia there were only eight subscriptions, whereas five years later there were eighty-three.[31] In 1911, the *Rassvet* weekly had 440 subscribers in Congress Poland, although in subsequent years this number declined gradually.[32] Unfortunately, we do not know how popular *Fraynd* was in the Kingdom of Poland; it was the first Yiddish daily in the Russian Empire and started to appear in 1903 in St Petersburg. Apparently it did not dedicate much attention to news from Congress Poland, although it printed contributions by Polish Jewish authors such as Peretz.[33]

The situation changed when after the 1905 revolution a mass daily press emerged in Warsaw.[34] The majority of publishers, editors, and journalists from such periodicals were Litvaks. It is likely that their great contribution to the development of the Jewish press was closely linked to their intellectual background; since the early nineteenth century, Lithuania had been the centre of the Haskalah movement in the regions spreading to the east from the German-speaking lands and was quick to adopt modernity in its various aspects.[35] Lithuania was the birthplace of two major political movements in modern Jewish history — Zionism and Bundism. And the possibility to educate the masses in their vernacular language was definitely an expression of such modernity.

The flagship of the Litvak circles, at least in the eyes of the Polish public opinion, was *Haynt*, the most conspicuous, recognizable, and popular daily, established in 1908 by Shmuel Yankev Yatzkan.[36] Published in Warsaw and from the onset strongly connected to the city (a separate page of the newspaper was dedicated to local news already before the First World War), *Haynt* was at the same time distributed widely among readers abroad. A survey conducted in 1913 among

Jewish students in Moscow revealed that Jewish newspapers (Hebrew and Yiddish) were read by 16 per cent of students, including *Fraynd* (6 per cent), *Haynt* (7 per cent), *Ha-Tsefirah* (7 per cent), and *Ha-Zman* (3 per cent).[37] So it is noteworthy as an example of the presence of the Russian-Jewish or simply Russian context in the Jewish periodicals in Warsaw.

A selective comparison of different issues of *Haynt* published before 1914, which are available in the Jewish Historical Institute in Warsaw and in the online resources of the National Library of Jerusalem, suggests that *Haynt* had at least two mutations, Warsaw and provincial, but it seems the latter was addressed mainly to the residents of the Pale. It is confirmed by the statistics of correspondence submitted to the newspaper; undoubtedly a part of it came from self-styled amateur correspondents. For example, out of nineteen contributions of January 1919 that I found, ten were sent in from cities and towns located beyond the borders of the Kingdom of Poland (including Riga, Minsk, Pinsk, and shtetls from the Kiev and Volhynia gubernias), and in May 1913 there were nine such contributions out of ten (e.g. Vitebsk, Dvinsk, Slonim, and Bobruysk). The pieces that were printed the most often came from Białystok and Vilna, and — within the Kingdom — from Lodz.

The announcement column in *Haynt* also revealed strong links to Russia and the Pale of Settlement. Next to numerous advertisements of Russian-made products one could find there pieces advertising many Russian-Jewish press titles, such as *Rassvet, Novyi voskhod*, and *Evreiskaia starina*, and no Polish titles (with the exception of *Przeglad Codzienny*, which advertised in 1913–14).[38] These advertisements were in part or in full printed in the Cyrillic script, which in the Polish newspapers of the era happened only occasionally. Zvi Prylucki recalls that the leading Warsaw Polish-language daily *Kurier Warszawski* refused to print an announcement by *Der Veg* in Yiddish, arguing that if they agreed to publish announcements in Yiddish they would have to accept announcements in Russian, and they did not want to do that.[39] Even the Zionist *Zycie Zydowskie* weekly, which ideologically was close to *Haynt*, in the advertisements of the Russian-Jewish press printed the address of the periodical phonetically in Polish. The prevalence of the Cyrillic script in the advertisement columns of *Haynt* (individuals or schools also published announcements in Russian) confirmed the stereotype of Russified Litvaks.

This close connection with the Russian and Russian-Jewish milieux is, however, the most conspicuous in the articles published in the daily, both in the ideological pieces showing the editors' views and in the implied content, so to speak. For example the editorial of 9 (22) January 1909 complained that in contrast to the Russian newspapers that wrote about Sholem Aleichem's anniversary in Kiev, the Polish press mentioned Jewish matters only in the context of scandals and did not recognize Jewry as such, but perceived them as some 'yids' that were supposed to represent the entire community. When the popular St Petersburg activist and philanthropist baron Horace Günzburg died, *Haynt* dedicated almost the entire first page to his person, including a biographic feature, the tone of which was clearly laudatory. 'The death of baron Günzberg means the death of an entire era in the history of Russian Jewry', the article reads. 'For many years Jews in Russia looked up to Günzberg as the sole guardian of the community [*klal-farzorger*]'.[40] And yet, although the text stressed that kashrut was observed in the baron's household as strictly as in the house of 'the most pious Hasid', which supposedly aimed to appeal to the more conservative readers, the question remains to what extent this name was actually familiar to the readers from Radomsk, Pultusk, or Zdunska Wola.

Another meaningful example of such an attitude was the work of Hillel Zeitlin, who until November 1910 was one of the crucial contributors of *Haynt* (later he went over to the competitors from *Moment*). Zeitlin, one of the greatest moral pundits of the era, was responsible for answering the letters that readers sent in to the newspaper. When a reader asked him to recommend some reading suitable for Jewish students who did not know Hebrew, Zeitlin recommended first and foremost the works on Judaism and Jewish history published in Russian and German, including the works of Simon Dubnow, Russian translations of Haskalah texts, articles from *Voskhod* or the Russian–Jewish encyclopaedia. He clearly thought that proficiency in Russian was obvious and natural, in contrast to proficiency in German.[41] He failed, however, to mention any achievements of the Polish-speaking and assimilated Polish Jewry, such as the translation of the Tanakh by Izaak Cylkow.

Zeitlin's silence speaks for itself; it was an example of the strong anti-assimilation movement present in the Yiddish media. It was directed against the acculturated elites of Polish Jewry, belonging to the circle of the *Izraelita* weekly and presiding over the Warsaw Jewish community. The Yiddish newspapers accused them of having become Poles and avoiding contacts with the Jewish masses, not allowing for their emancipation and disregarding Yiddish as a 'jargon'. The pro-assimilation circles reacted with a strong anti-Litvak discourse (which actually was perfectly in line with Polish public opinion),[42] and in turn blamed the Yiddish newspapers and Litvaks in general for artificial divisions between the Polish Jews and the rest of Polish society, and accused them of stirring up revolt among the uneducated masses. Litvaks were commonly perceived as agents of Russification who served the interests of Russia, or at least of the Russian Jewry. The journalist, poet, and political leader Samuel Hirschhorn asked rhetorically: 'Interestingly, assimilationists who recommended disinterested assimilation could not stand the Russian-speaking Jews who had just arrived from inland gubernias. Maybe perchance they saw in them, like a monkey in the mirror, their own caricatures?'[43] The conflict between Litvaks and Assimilationists was present not only in the press, but also within the Warsaw community. In 1909 *Haynt* sued Jakub Loewenberg, member of a rich merchant Warsaw family and former member of the Jewish community council. What is worthy of note is that Loewenberg hired a Polish attorney Julian Krzycki, who had gained recognition as a defence counsel in political cases, and *Haynt* as their counsel hired S. O. Gruzenberg from Petersburg[44] and Aba Olshvanger from Warsaw.[45]

Anti-Litvak sentiment in Congress Poland reached a peak twice: in 1909,[46] with a strong outbreak of anti-Litvak panic in the Polish newspapers, and then in 1912, during the Fourth Duma elections.[47] The Jewish newspapers were openly accused of serving the interests of the Russian Jewry in the Polish territory (especially that *Haynt* interviewed Maxim Vinaver asking for his opinion on the elections).

Assimilationists in one of their open letters warned Jewish voters:

> Do not be deceived. You need to understand that the offices of nationalist papers can be easily moved from St Petersburg to Warsaw, and from Warsaw back to St Petersburg; your agitators will go away, but you will be left behind; their fate is not bound to this land while you have strong ties with it; the fights and social hatred will reach you and not them. Understand that these people are not your friends.[48]

After the election, a leading Warsaw daily published in Polish, *Kurier Warszawski*, wrote:

> Jews who live here, in our lands, who live off us, who benefit from our hospitality, chose to ignore us and to say it openly, so we need to reveal to the Polish nation that the only factor they hold reliable are the Russian Jews or Petersburg nationalists, who can and may make decisions about ideas, people, and tactics in our country.[49]

The outbreak of the First World War sidelined the debate about Litvaks in Congress Poland, and with time they 'polonized' themselves, i.e. they started to think of themselves as Polish Jews. However, as late as 1919, an official Polish report on the 'Jewish question', presented at the peace conference in Paris, mentioned Litvaks as those who

> have taken the attitude of entire strangers, and created in Poland a Jewish press, [and who] were at first the chief representatives of the Jewish national movement. Thanks to their brutal, aggressive ways, they won for their cause, by and by, the masses of local Jews.[50]

★ ★ ★ ★ ★

The influence Litvaks had on Polish–Jewish relations in the twentieth century seems underestimated.[51] These relations before the First World War would surely take a different turn if it hadn't been for the Yiddish daily press edited by Litvaks. The high number of copies they published proves that their vision of the world appealed to contemporary readers, which means that these newspapers could address the readers in a language they understood. And it was the language of a new Jewish politics with Jews in its centre — not as a religious community anymore, but as a nation — with all the advantages and drawbacks of such definition. Maybe the cultural heritage of Litvaks was of some importance too, because in that culture the printed word was even more significant than in other Jewish communities.[52] It might have been related to the experience of the mechanisms of Russian politics, albeit on its margins, in St Petersburg (for example Prylucki and Yatzkan lived for some time in the capital of the Empire). There can be no doubt that many different factors coincided, with Litvaks playing the main role, and significantly changed the face of the Polish Jewry.

Translated from Polish by Weronika Mincer

Notes to Chapter 2

1. Avrom Reisen, *Epizodn fun mayn lebn*, I (Vilne: Farlag fun Boris Kletskin, 1929), p. 191; emphasis added.
2. Genrikh B. Sliozberg, 'Dela minuvshikh dnei', in *Evrei v Rossii: XIX vek*, ed. by Victor E. Kelner (Moscow: Novoe literaturnoe obozrenie, 2000), pp. 247–496 (p. 485). See also Brian Horowitz, 'Henrik Sliozberg: A Mirror of Petersburg Jewry in Late Tsarist Days', in Horowitz, *Empire Jews. Jewish Nationalism and Acculturation in 19th- and Early 20th Century Russia* (Bloomington: Slavica Publishers, 2009), pp. 139–52.
3. Yakov G. Frumkin, 'Iz istorii russkogo evreistva (vospominaniia, materialy, dokumenty)', in *Kniga o russkom evreistve ot 1860-kh godov do revolutsii 1917 g.*, I (Jerusalem: Gesharim; Moscow: Mosty kul'tury; Minsk: MET, 2002), p. 91. Both Sliozberg and Frumkin write about their experience with the part of Jewry that was the most acculturated to the Polish society. It is possible that the relationships between particular Hasidic courts differed.
4. The relevance of the term 'East European Jewry' is discussed by Mordechai Zalkin in his inspiring article 'Lithuanian Jewry and the Concept of "East European Jewry"', *Polin*, 25 (2013), 57–70. I would like to thank Goda Volbikaite who pointed me to this text.
5. Gennady Estraikh pointed to the 'still relatively unexplored Polish–Litvak cultural clash' in his article 'The Kultur-Lige in Warsaw: A Stopover in the Yiddishists' Journey between Kiev and Paris', in *Warsaw. The Jewish Metropolis. Essays in Honor of the 75th Birthday of Professor Antony Polonsky*, ed. by Glenn Dynner and François Guesnet (Leiden: Brill, 2015), pp. 323–46 (p. 324; see especially n. 3).
6. In Yiddish, the term 'Litvaks' (*litvakes*) describes Jews from the historical Lithuania; apart from contemporary Lithuania these lands include also Belarus, Latvia, and north-eastern Poland. In Polish this term was used extensively to designate all Jews who arrived in the Kingdom of Poland from Russia, mainly from the western gubernias of the Pale of Settlement (i.e. the actual Litvaks), but also those from Moscow (after the expulsion of Jews in 1891) or Volhynia. Here I use the word 'Litvak' in its broader, Polish sense, because it was in that context that it was used in the contemporary political discourse. There can be no doubt, however, that among such defined 'Litvaks' there must have been other internal divisions related to their place of origin or the dialect of Yiddish they spoke.
7. François Guesnet, 'Migration et stéréotype: le cas des Juifs russes au Royaume de Pologne à la fin du XIXe siècle', *Cahiers du Monde Russe*, 41.4 (2000), 505–18 (p. 508).
8. Ibid., p. 509.
9. Piotr Wrobel, 'Jewish Warsaw before the First World War', *Polin*, 3 (1988), 156–87 (p. 162).
10. Guesnet, 'Migration et stéréotype', p. 513.
11. Vital Zajka, 'The Self-Perception of Belarusian-Lithuanian Jewry in the Eighteenth and Nineteenth Centuries', *Polin*, 14 (2001), 19–30 (p. 23).
12. François Guesnet, 'Litwaken', in *Enzyklopädie jüdischer Geschichte und Kultur*, ed. by Dan Diner, 5 vols (Stuttgart: Verlag J. B. Metzler, 2011–14), III (2012), 551.
13. Puah Rakovsky, *My Life as a Radical Jewish Woman: Memoirs of a Zionist Feminist in Poland*, ed. by Paula E. Hyman (Bloomington and Indianapolis: Indiana University Press, 2002), p. 59.
14. Moshe Mishkinski, 'Regional Factors in the Formation of the Jewish Labor Movement *in* Czarist Russia', *YIVO Annual of Jewish Social Science*, 14 (1969), 27–52 (p. 30).
15. Lesław Sadowski, *Polska inteligencja prowincjonalna i jej ideowe dylematy na przełomie XIX i XX wieku (na przykładzie guberni łomżyńskiej, suwalskiej i Białegostoku)* (Warsaw: PWN, 1988), p. 234.
16. Sliozberg, 'Dela minuvshikh dnei', p. 486.
17. A. Almi, *Momentn fun a lebn* (Buenos Aires: Tsentral farband fun poylishe yidn in Argentine, 1948), pp. 181–82. The same was confirmed by columnist Samuel Hirschhorn: 'on average the relationships between Polish and Lithuanian Jews were very similar to the relationships between the "natives" — the Christians — and the "newcomers" — the Jews' (S. Hirszhorn (Hirschhorn), 'Litwaki', *Głos Żydowski*, 29 April 1906, p. 178).
18. Max Weinreich, 'A polemik tsvishn Tsederboymen un Peretz Smolenskinen vegn yidishe dialektn', *YIVO Bleter*, 5 (1933), 401–03.

19. Rakovsky, *My Life as a Radical Jewish Woman*, p. 47. Zalkin, 'Lithuanian Jewry and the Concept of "East European Jewry"', pp. 65–67, lists many examples of aversion or even enmity towards Litvaks.
20. Jacob Shatzky, *Geshikhte fun yidn in Varshe*, III (New York: YIVO, 1953), p. 184.
21. *Archiwum Ringelbluma: Konspiracyjne Archiwum Getta Warszawy*, XXVIII: Cwi [Zvi] Pryłucki, *Wspomnienia (1905–1939)*, ed. by Joanna Nalewajko-Kulikov, trans. from Yiddish by Agata Kondrat (Warsaw: Wyd. Uniwersytetu Warszawskiego; Żydowski Instytut Historyczny, 2015), pp. 18–19.
22. Benjamin Nathans, *Beyond the Pale: The Jewish Encounter with Late Imperial Russia* (Berkeley: University of California Press, 2002), p. 83.
23. Benjamin Nathans, 'Saint Petersburg', in *The YIVO Encyclopedia of Jews in Eastern Europe* <http://www.yivoencyclopedia.org/article.aspx/Saint_Petersburg> [accessed 5 September 2015].
24. On the fin-de-siècle Jewish Warsaw see Wrobel, 'Jewish Warsaw Before the First World War'.
25. Avrom Zak, *In onheyb fun a friling* (Buenos Aires: Tsentral farband fun poylishe yidn in Argentine, 1962), p. 62.
26. Reisen, *Epizodn fun mayn lebn*, p. 192. See also Stephen D. Corrsin, 'Aspects of Population Change and of Acculturation of Jewish Warsaw at the end of the Nineteenth Century: The Censuses of 1882 and 1897', *Polin*, 3 (1988), 128–32. According to the 1897 census only 2.2 per cent Jews in Warsaw declared their mother tongue to be Russian.
27. Reisen, *Epizodn fun mayn lebn*, p. 193. Alexander Mukdoni (born in Liakhovichi in Belarus, since 1906 in Warsaw) wrote along the same lines: 'The Polish Yiddish was still unfamiliar to me and I couldn't fully understand their [Warsaw Jews' — J.N.-K.] hysterical cries'. See A. Mukdoni, *In Varshe un in Lodzh*, I (Buenos Aires: Tsentral farband fun poylishe yidn in Argentine, 1955), p. 37. More about the Warsaw Yiddish see Ewa Geller, *Warschauer Jiddisch* (Tübingen: M. Niemeyer, 2001).
28. Reisen, *Epizodn fun mayn lebn*, p. 194.
29. Victor E. Kelner, *Ocherki po istorii russko-evreiskogo knizhnogo dela vo vtoroi polovine XIX–nachale XX w.* (St Petersburg: Rossiiskaia natsionalnaia biblioteka, 2003), pp. 65–66.
30. Ibid., p. 67.
31. Vladimir Levin, 'Zur Verbreitung jüdischer Zeitschriften in Rußland: Sprache versus Geographie', in *Die jüdische Presse im europäischen Kontext 1686–1990*, ed. by Susanne Marten-Finnis und Markus Winkler (Bremen: Edition Lumière, 2006), pp. 107–09, see especially table 4.
32. Levin, 'Zur Verbreitung jüdischer Zeitschriften in Rußland', p. 113, table 6.
33. Sarah Abrevaya Stein, *Making Jews Modern: The Yiddish and Ladino Press in the Russian and Ottoman Empires* (Bloomington: Indiana University Press, 2004), pp. 36, 51. Good analysis of *Fraynd* is to be found in Alexander Frenkel, 'Voskhozhdenie i zakat "Der Fraind" — pervoi v Rossii ezhednevnoi gazety na idishe (1903–1914)', *Arkhiv evreiskoi istorii*, 6 (2011), 104–22.
34. Joanna Nalewajko-Kulikov, '"Who Has Not Wanted to Be an Editor?": The Yiddish Press in the Kingdom of Poland, 1905–1914', *Polin*, 27 (2014), 273–304.
35. Zalkin, 'Lithuanian Jewry and the Concept of "East European Jewry"', p. 62.
36. For more information about *Haynt* see Nalewajko-Kulikov, '"Who Has Not Wanted to Be an Editor?"; Chaim Finkelstein, *Haynt — a tsaytung bay yidn* (Tel Aviv: Farlag Y. L. Perets, 1978). On Yatzkan see Nathan Cohen, '"An Ugly and Repulsive Idler" or a Talented and Seasoned Editor: S. Y. Yatzkan and the Beginnings of the Popular Yiddish Press in Warsaw', *Jews in Russia and Eastern Europe*, 1–2 [54–55] (2005), 28–53.
37. A. E. Ivanov, *Evreiskoe studenchestvo v vysshei shkole Rossiiskoi imperii nachala XX veka: kakim ono bylo?* (Moscow: Novyi khronograf, 2007), p. 375.
38. *Przegląd Codzienny*, published in Warsaw between 1913 and 1914 and edited by Stanislaw Mendelsohn, was probably the only periodical that defended Jewish rights during the economic boycott.
39. *Archiwum Ringelbluma*, p. 26.
40. 'Baron Horats (Naftoli Herts) Gintsburg z'l', *Haynt*, 3 March 1909, p. 1.
41. Hillel Tsaytlin (Zeitlin), 'Brivelekh fun lezer un tsum lezer (III)', *Haynt*, 6 May 1910, p. 3.
42. For more extensive information see G. Krzywiec, 'Prasa żydowska w zwierciadle polskiej

opinii publicznej (1905–1914)', *Studia z dziejów trójjęzycznej prasy żydowskiej na ziemiach polskich (XIX–XX w.)*, ed. by Joanna Nalewajko-Kulikov in collaboration with G. P. Bąbiak and A. J. Cieślikowa (Warsaw: Neriton; Instytut Historii PAN, 2012), pp. 267–98.
43. Hirszhorn (Hirschhorn), 'Litwaki', 179.
44. The initials most probably stand for Oskar O. Gruzenberg, renowned for the Beilis trial. His brother, Semyon O. Gruzenberg, was a philosopher, academic teacher, and editor in the Russian-Jewish press.
45. 'Der "Haynt"-Loewenberg protses', *Haynt*, 17 November 1909, p. 1.
46. For more information see Nalewajko-Kulikov, ' "Who Has Not Wanted to Be an Editor?" '.
47. For information about the elections see Stephen D. Corrsin, *Warsaw before the First World War: Poles and Jews in the Third City of the Russian Empire (1880–1914)* (Boulder: East European Monographs, 1989), pp. 89–106.
48. 'Nowa odezwa', *Nowa Gazeta*, 3 November 1912, p. 4.
49. 'Wczorajszy wybór', *Kurier Warszawski* (morning supplement), 9 November 1912, p. 1.
50. Franciszek Bujak, 'The Jewish Question in Poland', in *Ekspertyzy i materiały delegacji polskiej na konferencję wersalską 1919 roku* (Warsaw: Polski Instytut Spraw Międzynarodowych, 2009), p. 403.
51. The fact that in the recently opened Museum of the History of Polish Jews the core exhibition does not take into account the problem of Litvaks at all is meaningful, although this issue is essential to understand Polish–Jewish relationships in the Second Polish Republic; the word 'Litvak' is used only in the description of the interwar Vilna.
52. Zajka, 'The Self-Perception of Belarusian-Lithuanian Jewry in the Eighteenth and Nineteenth Centuries', pp. 26–27.

CHAPTER 3

What the Readers Think: Two Reader Surveys in the *Literarishe bleter*

Sima Beeri

The proclaimed goal of *Literarishe bleter* (Literary Pages),[1] a weekly journal published in Warsaw between 1925 and 1939, was the maintenance of a high professional and intellectual standard while concomitantly providing a publication accessible and attractive to all social and political strata. Ideologically, it advocated non-partisan Yiddishism, in the spirit of the defunct Kiev Kultur-Lige.[2] Nakhman Mayzel, its main and later sole editor, stressed that *Literarishe bleter* was a journal for the masses and not solely for the intelligentsia. Because the target readership was so broad, the task of consistently achieving this goal required the constant monitoring of the readership base as well as a good understanding of their preferences. This consideration provided us with a unique insight into readers' preferences and opinions in the form of two reader surveys carried out by the editorship of the journal and then, more extraordinarily, printed within the pages of *Literarishe bleter* for the readers to consider.

Finding out readership preferences was clearly linked to readers' feedback on the then new publication, but even more so it arose out of an economic concern to increase the number of readers, particularly that of subscribers, in order to guarantee the journal a working budget. To obtain a response from its most committed readers, the joint editors in 1925, and subsequently Mayzel alone from 1928 to 1929, created two surveys. Questions for the first survey were published on the front page of the journal, and in both cases questionnaires in the form of flyers were inserted into *Literarishe bleter*. The results of those surveys were published in later copies of the journal. Although the data is partial and subjective, it nevertheless provides an overview both of the opinions and cultural preferences of the readership in its responses and of the editorship in the posing of its direct and, on occasion, even bold questions, especially with regard to *Literarishe bleter*'s open political stance (see question 6 in the 1925 survey). Such a glimpse into the interaction between reader and editor is particularly illuminating and fortunate in a publication where an original, founding statement of intent was not provided with the first issue and the journal was, in Mayzel's words, 'left to speak for itself'. The programmatic statement of intent mentioned in previous discussions was published only later, inserted on the final page of the fourth issue in 1924 and sharing space with a variety of advertisements and other announcements. This statement and the two surveys provide the main source of information available about the relationship between readers of *Literarishe bleter* and its editor. It could also be applied to readers' opinions in a more general context.

The first questionnaire, then, was added to issue no. 59 in 1925 as a flyer and consisted of fifteen questions printed on one half of the sheet, with blank spaces on the other half opposite each question in which answers were to be written. Evidently, this large piece of paper was inserted into the middle of the publication, folded in half.[3] The flyer questionnaires themselves did not survive; however, the questions were printed on the front page of the issue. Moreover, a list of the questions was repeated, along with some responses, in issues 65–72 as well as in Mayzel's later autobiography, *Geven amol a lebn* (There Once Was a Life). More than 600 completed questionnaires were returned within the first couple of weeks from 184 towns and villages in Poland as well as from abroad. Subsequently more forms arrived, with the final total reaching 617.

The following are the questions as they were posed in the 1925 questionnaire:

1. Are you a regular or an occasional reader of *Literarishe bleter*?
2. Are you generally satisfied with the journal?
3. What issues and problems interest you most in *Literarishe bleter*?
4. Which contributors of *Literarishe bleter* do you prefer? (List no more than ten names)
5. Which additional writers, in your opinion, should be featured in *Literarishe bleter*?
6. Are you satisfied with the unaffiliated, non-political policy adopted by *Literarishe bleter*?
7. Are you satisfied with our position with regard to the language question?
8(a). Do we need to enlarge or diminish our fiction section?
8(b). Would you like to see serialized novels in the journal?
9. Should we publish more articles on world literature, or should we concentrate more on Yiddish literature?
10. Would you like to see longer serious discourse, or short informative articles?
11. Are you satisfied with the large-newspaper format of *Literarishe bleter*? Should we convert it into a smaller journal format?
12. Do you think we need to extend our illustrated section?
13. Do you think that we should enlarge *Literarishe bleter* and increase the price proportionally?
14. How do you like the style of presentation of *Literarishe bleter*?
15. What tactics should be employed for expanding the number of subscriptions, purchases, readers, and friends?

The answers for the first 1925 questionnaire given here are based on the 617 questionnaires returned. Because the data arrived over a period of time, *Literarishe bleter* published amended versions of the survey; therefore, discrepancies in numbers for various questions occur in the collective data. In addition, the problem of evaluation is a significant one. Mayzel points out that only one reader of a single copy of the paper was able to respond, because there was only one copy of the survey inserted within its pages, this despite the fact that the survey itself testifies to multiple readership per copy. Moreover, the survey was not constructed in a scientific manner: some questions required short answers; some, yes/no answers; some, graded answers; and the like. Some questions have no recorded response, either in the pages of the journal or in Mayzel's memoir. I have therefore separated the answers according to the type of response that they called for.

The following questions required the reader to provide short answers:

Question	Question (1925)	Replies	Comments
1	Are you a regular or an occasional reader of *Literarishe bleter*?	602	Responses published included the following: 'Because of high unemployment, I am only an occasional buyer but I am a constant reader of *Literarishe bleter*'; 'Not only am I a constant reader but a very loyal one'; 'I have switched from *Wiadomosci Literackie* and became a loyal and regular reader'; 'I am a regular reader. I will go hungry in order to purchase *Literarishe bleter.*'
3	What issues and problems interest you most in *Literarishe bleter*?	610	literature: 240, Yiddish literature: 79, ORDER? theatre: 161, art: 128, criticism: 134, modern Yiddish literature: 39, science (*visnshaft*): 68, Yiddish culture: 40, Yiddish language: 27, philosophy: 23, music: 18, education: 9, library organization: 8, cinema: 7, cultural — in general: 3.
4	Which contributors of *Literarishe bleter* do you prefer? (Name no more than ten names)	Impossible to assess from the data presented	Nakhman Mayzel: 365 Alter Katsizne: 349 Melekh Ravitch: 324 Peretz Markish: 252 Dr Avrom Gliksman: 247 Dr Mikhl Vaykhert: 218 Israel Joshua Singer: 211 A. Litvak (Khayim Yankl Helfand): 160 Arn Zeitlin: 131 Max Erik: 129

Question	Question (1925)	Replies	Comments
5	Which additional writers in your opinion should feature in *Literarishe bleter*?	Impossible to assess from the data presented	Sholem Asch: 241 Hersh David Nomberg: 221 Shmuel Niger: 133 Dr Khaim Zhitlovsky: 115 Zelig Segalovich: 110 H. Leyvik: 96 David Bergelson: 79 Joseph Opatoshu: 77 David Einhorn: 67 Itshe Meyer Vaysenberg: 56

The following questions required responses in a variety of forms:

Question	Question (1925)	Replies	Responses
2	Are you generally satisfied with the journal?	602	Positive feedback: 558 (93%) Negative feedback: 30 (5%) No response: 14 (2%)
6	Are you satisfied with the unaffiliated, non political policy adopted by *Literarishe bleter*?	615	Positive feedback: 486 (79%) Negative feedback: 48 (8%) No response: 83 (13%)
7	Are you satisfied with our attitude with regard to the language question?	554	Yes: 330 (60%) Not entirely: 69 (12.5%) No: 94 (17%) Did not understand question: 61 (11%)
8(a)	Do we need to enlarge or diminish our fiction section?	528	Enlarge: 213 (40%) No change: 157 (30%) Diminish: 158 (30%)
8(b)	Would you like to see serialized novels in the journal?	528	Yes: 91 (17%) No: 420 (80%) No response: 17 (3%)

The following questions required the respondent to give preferences:

Question	Question (1925)	Replies	Responses
9	Should we publish more articles on world literature, or should we concentrate more on Yiddish literature?	591	World literature: 151 (25.5%) Yiddish literature: 222 (37.5%) Both: 218 (37%)
10	Would you like to see longer serious discourse, or short informative articles?	610	Serious: 403 (66%) Short informative: 81 (13%) Both: 63 (10%) No response: 61 (11%)

The remaining questions have no reported responses: 11 ('Are you satisfied with the large-newspaper format?'), 12 ('Do you think we should extend our illustrated section?'), 13 ('Do you think we should expand and increase price?'), 14 ('How do you like the style of presentation?'), 15 ('What tactics should be employed for expanding the number of subscriptions?').

This survey is singular in the annals of the Yiddish press of the time: on the one hand, the inquiry into readership preference is extraordinary, and in addition, the fact that even partial results were published for the enlightenment of that same readership is without precedent. Mayzel himself provides some commentary and further information about this 1925 survey in his later memoir. In order to substantiate the accuracy of the survey, Mayzel lists all of the 200 places, 184 in Poland and 16 outside, from which responses were sent.[4] His first concern is the satisfaction of his readership, and he comments that most of those who were partially dissatisfied with the journal (in question 2: 105 out of 602, i.e. 17.4%) mentioned their dissatisfaction with the treatment of the language question in *Literarishe bleter*. Mayzel attributed this response in particular to the extremist supporters of Hebrew and the 'leftists'.[5] His interpretation of this particular question about readership appreciation is very telling: it highlights the problematic of covering Yiddish in the *Literarishe bleter*, given the nationalist controversies on the left over the use of Yiddish. It also supports Nathan Cohen's contention that political boycotting might have had an impact upon the journal's circulation. Mayzel states elsewhere that the only party with which the journal is affiliated is 'the party of literature'.[6]

It is significant in this regard that publisher Boris Kletzkin, known for his leftist political affiliations, had taken over publication of the journal in the previous issue, and Mayzel had already received a complaint voicing the fear that the paper might degenerate.[7] However, he had included question 6 ('Are you satisfied with the unaffiliated, non-political policy adopted by *Literarishe bleter*?') purposefully in order to address the question of political neutrality. In effect, it was a signal to the readership that the editorial policy of the journal meant to accentuate its unaffiliated stance. Out of 617 questionnaires, 486 (79%) were satisfied with this approach. Only 48 were totally dissatisfied. These figures constitute both an endorsement of Mayzel's political openness and demonstrate the readership's interest in a non-political cultural journal. The fact that question 4 confirmed Mayzel's popularity with the readership ('Which contributors of *Literarishe bleter* do you prefer?') can be seen as further appreciation of his general editorial policy and professionalism, and he admits to being encouraged by it.[8] At this stage, by the time the responses were published in 1925, the editorship consisted only of Mayzel and Melekh Ravitch.

The second survey was conducted three and a half years later, in 1928–29. The results of this survey were published in three instalments in issues dated 8 March 1929, 22 March 1929 and 12 April 1929. According to Mayzel, approximately 400 forms were returned, but many of them had been filled in by more than one person. This practice is within keeping with the fact that each copy purchased would be shared by multiple readers. Interestingly, in comparison with the previous survey, this one contained approximately 200 responses fewer. Mayzel offered a clarification, claiming that although the number of forms returned had diminished, many of them were signed by several people, and therefore the general response to this survey encompassed thousands of readers.[9] The three articles in *Literarishe bleter* are the only information available for this 1928–29 survey. Moreover, not all of the questions were answered or even referred to in those articles. Therefore, some of the questions and answers are missing in this section. These are the questions from the 1928–29 survey as they can be reconstructed:

1. Are you a subscriber of *Literarishe bleter*? Do you buy your copies or do you read them elsewhere?
2. Are you a regular or an occasional reader?
3. What issues and problems interest you most in *Literarishe bleter*?
4. Do you always read the poetry and short stories in *Literarishe bleter*?
5. Are you more interested in Yiddish literature or in world literature?
7. Should the theatre section be enlarged?
8. What sections of the journal should be expanded? (The number of this question is not indicated in this article. It is my assumption that it follows from the previous question.)
9. Are there enough illustrations in the *Literarishe bleter*?
10. Would you like to see a novel serialized in *Literarishe bleter*?
13. With how many readers, approximately, do you share your copy of *Literarishe bleter*?
14. Does your local library carry copies of *Literarishe bleter*? If not, why?
15. Can the number of subscriptions and reader be increased, according to you?
(?) Would you like to see longer, serious discourse, or short informative articles?
(?) Are you satisfied with the price per issue of *Literarishe bleter*?
(?) Which additional writers, in your opinion, should be featured in *Literarishe bleter*?

Question	Question (1928/29)	Replies	Responses
1	Are you a subscriber of *Literarishe bleter*? Do you buy your copies or do you read them elsewhere?	403	Subscribers and regular buyers: 350 (87%) Reading in libraries or renting from newsagents: 33 (8%) No response: 20 (5%)
2	Are you a regular or an occasional reader?	591	Responses include: 'I was a subscriber but had to stop for lack of funds'; 'I would subscribe but the yearly subscription fee is too high for me'; 'Send me the journal, but at a lower price'; 'When a journal arrives a day late, it spoils my Shabes'.
3	What issues and problems most interest you in the *Literarishe bleter*?	610	Everything: 169 (42%) Criticism of Yiddish and world literature: 127 (13%) Yiddish theatre: 33 (8%); some would like to see articles on cinema Yiddish cultural issues (schools, YIVO, philology): 30 (7%), with 7 of the 30 interested in the Yiddish-Hebrew question Yiddish literature: 21 (5%); for world literature, they read non-Jewish periodicals World literature: 14 (3.5%) Modern Yiddish literature: 13 (3.5%)

WHAT THE READERS THINK 39

Question	Question (1928/29)	Replies	Responses
4	Do you always read the poetry and short stories in *Literarishe bleter*?		Short stories and poetry: 253 (64%) Short stories: 60 (15%) Poetry: 17 (4%) Occasional fiction reader: 54 (14%) Against any fictional section: 12 (3%) (because they consider it a publication about literature, not consisting of it)
5	Are you more interested in Yiddish literature or world literature?	392	Yiddish: 185 (47%) World: 65 (17%) Both: 142 (36%)
8?	What sections of the journal should be expanded?	381	Many respondents said that all sections should be expanded. 'Expand it all, but don't raise the price'. 113 want the literary criticism and art criticism expanded with emphasis on contemporary Yiddish literature. 74 — theatre, music and sculpture, 64- literature, 39 — Bikher-velt (World of Books) section, 31 — popular culture, 29 — world literature, 18 — news, 28 — science, 12 — essays on art and philosophy, 11 — Hebrew literature translated into Yiddish.
9	Are there enough illustrations in *Literarishe bleter*?	360	No: 180 (50%) Yes: 180 (50%)
10	Would you like to see a novel serialized in *Literarishe bleter*?	400	No: 302 (75%) Yes: 98 (25%)
13	With how many readers, approximately, do you share your copy of *Literarishe bleter*?	335	1 58 responses 2 68 3 88 4 39 5 25 6 8 7 4 8 3 10 13 The remaining respondents shared their copies among 20 to 60 readers each, for example due to public library usage
?	Would you like to see longer, serious discourse, or short informative articles?	375	Longer serious discourse: 308 (82%) Short informative articles: 68 (18%)

What is significant about this second survey of 1928–29 is that Mayzel does not mention it at all in his memoir. Our only source of information, and of his analysis and interpretation of the results, lies in the pages of *Literarishe bleter*. There are several observations to be made based on this information, which suggest that changes occurred in the interval between the two surveys. First of all, Mayzel, who has by

Fig. 3.1. Nakhman Mayzel, Peretz Markish, Joseph Opatoshu, Israel Joshua Singer and Melekh Ravich, around 1922

that time become the sole editor of *Literarishe bleter*, has designed what he terms a 'general' survey, whose questions pertain to literary issues alone; other questions of a more social, political, or linguistic nature are to be postponed for a later survey.[10] This later survey never takes place. Secondly, in introducing the subject of the second survey, Mayzel makes a point of indicating the great significance of the first survey for the publishing policies of the journal. During its first year of publication, he emphasizes the fact that the journal contained no fiction but concerned itself solely with questions of literary criticism and problems of publication. With issue no. 44 in 1925, the editors decided to include a fiction section, and the first survey was designed, at least in part, to ascertain reader response to this addition.[11] The second survey was intended to focus on the literary questions that occurred as a result of converting the journal into a more belletristic one.

It begins with a question, which did not occur in the earlier survey, asking the reader to indicate where and how (s)he obtained a copy of the journal. There are several questions on the topic of issue acquisition, the most significant being question 13 ('With how many readers, approximately, do you share your copy of *Literarishe bleter*?'). Only 58 of 335 readers who responded did not share their copy. Therefore, circulation figures for *Literarishe bleter* are not indicative of the circulation of the journal, since the readership far exceeds the number of copies published. On the one hand, this response clearly substantiates Mayzel's claims of a readership greater than circulation figures would indicate, exonerating him of the charge of exaggeration of his readership, which was later often levied against him.[12] On the other hand, it is possible to see the influence of the great economic world crisis under way at that point and its effects on what constituted a microcosm, Yiddish readership of a literary journal. The number of shared copies is a notable indication of lack of purchasing power as well as of the resourceful cohesion of a tight Yiddish literary audience. In Questions 1 and 2, whose results are combined in the article reporting them[13] ('Are you a subscriber of *Literarishe bleter*? Do you buy your copies or do you read them elsewhere?' and 'Are you a regular or an occasional reader?'), whereas 350 of 403 indicated they were subscribers or permanent readers, 33 added that they always read someone else's copy, went to the library, or rented a copy from the newsstand. This last practice is an indication of the widespread nature of the economic depression, touching purchaser and seller alike. Moreover, when readers were asked which, if any, sections of the journal should be expanded (Question 8), the response was overwhelmingly in favour of expanding at least one, if not all, sections. But, in response, *Literarishe bleter* printed a comment, which must have been disappointing:

> In the last year, without raising the price, we have augmented the journal from 16 to 20 pages, and occasionally to 24. We are the only publishers in Poland not to raise the price of our publication, despite the higher cost of printing and paper. More than that we cannot do.[14]

Mayzel consistently attempted to accommodate his readership, but the economics of publishing such a complex journal increasingly threatened to defeat him, and the subject of funding became a recurrent theme in the years to come.

Question 14 ('Does your local library carry copies of *Literarishe bleter*? If not, why?') is interesting also in this regard, especially since it was not a question posed in the first survey of 1925. In the first survey, the journal had only been in circulation for a year, and it can be assumed that libraries had not yet begun to subscribe and were waiting to gauge the paper's success. Equally important is the fact that the economic situation was not so grave, and there was hope that readers could afford to purchase a copy, even at an increased price for an enlarged journal, as the survey indicated in its question directed to this topic. By the second survey, the fact that the readers were sharing copies was well known, and the question of where the sharing took place became the salient one. In 1929, according to the survey, a significant number of libraries now stocked copies of *Literarishe bleter*. Of those that did not, we see two types of short answer. Either the library was non-existent or lacked funds at this point, or there was opposition to carrying the journal. One library's lack of copies is a censorship issue, according to a reader who writes from Bessarabia. The other reasons for opposition are not elaborated in reader response, although one reader suggests that Yiddish is not welcome in his assimilated Jewish library.

Mayzel included a curious item in his reporting of the results of the second survey: a list of every respondent, including his or her place of residence. The list was partial, dependent upon his receiving the responses in time to publish them in the current number. The entire list encompasses 391 names out of a total of 407 respondents, and is published in no. 51 (1928), no. 52 (1928), no. 2 (1929), no. 4 (1929), and no. 6 (1929). He gave no indication of his motive for the inclusion of such a list in the pages of the journal. We can only surmise that either he wanted to substantiate the verity of the survey, or that he was appealing to the reader's vanity in seeing his name in print, and in this way he hoped to encourage more responses as well as purchases.

Despite the fact that the questions in each survey are not entirely identical and that the number of reader responses is different, some attempt at comparison is possible.

(a) The questions regarding subscribers and regular or occasional readership (1925, question 1; 1928–29, questions 1 and 2) have a similar general response in both surveys, but the 1928–29 variant indicating a worsening economic situation.

(b) The questions on reader preferences (1925 and 1928–29, question 3) also do not indicate real change, with the addition of the subject of YIVO, which had been included in the journal after the first survey had taken place. The breadth of interest remains remarkable.

(c) The questions regarding a preference for Yiddish versus world literature (1925, question 9, 1928–29, question 5) indicate a significant change. Interestingly, readers in 1928–29 indicated that, if they were to read world literature in translation, they could read it in Polish periodicals, and that therefore they preferred to see only Yiddish literature in the publication. As a result, the percentage of those who prefer Yiddish literature rises from 37.5% in 1925 to 47% in 1928–29. *Literarishe bleter* readers are thus less interested in seeing world literature in its pages, although those who desire it cite the need to embrace world literature and culture as part of the quest to become part of a world community.

(d) The questions regarding the readers' wish for serialized literature in the journal (1925, question 8(b); 1928–29, question 10) touched upon an issue that was crucially important to many literary and non-literary papers. If a novel were serialized, it would encourage, if not guarantee, the sale of future issues in which its continuation occurred. What is curious about *Literarishe bleter* is that the readership was not in favour of such content. In 1925, 80% of readers answering the question were against the inclusion of a serialized text, and in 1928–29, 75% shared that opinion. This was a live issue in 1929 in part because a prose work published in instalments the previous year, Maxim Gorky's autobiographical novel *My Universities*, had elicited a myriad of letters from readers. Some claimed that there was no need to occupy in each issue two pages, which could be allocated to something else, because the whole book could be purchased and read. Others held the opposing view and requested more of the same.

e. The questions regarding a choice between lengthy complex articles versus short informative articles (1925, question 10; 1928–29, no number) indicate the journal's commitment to the education of its readership while at the same time voicing a concern about the accessibility and readability of such articles. In fact, both surveys indicate a preference for longer more educative articles, and the percentage of those approving such content actually increases, from 66% in 1925 to 82% in 1928–29. This fact highlights the calibre of readership of Literarishe bleter. It does not indicate the level of formal education but rather, the level of openness and the thirst for information.

f. On the subject of illustrations, (1925, question 12; 1928–29, question 9), an insertion which often appealed to readers and encouraged purchase, Literarishe bleter's readers were divided, insofar far as we know from the second survey (the first survey has no data). Some readers thought that illustrations occupied important space needed for articles, whereas others appreciated it, in particular, fine art illustrations. The nature of this preference indicates the public for whom *Literarishe bleter* was published.

All in all, these surveys taken together give a picture not only of the readership, but also of the editorial policies and dilemmas, which arose in the publication of such a unique journal. Mayzel is seen here as an editor immersed in the question of his readership's interests, but also as someone who would refrain from fulfilling their desires if he considered them deleterious for the journal's well-being. For example, he could not conceive of a way of enlarging the journal further without raising the price, despite his readers' wishes, nor would he dispense with serialized fiction, in part because of his commitment to literature but also because of the economic advantage, although a significant percentage of readers felt it occupied too much space. In addition, his commitment to Yiddish and language studies kept the subject well represented in *Literarishe bleter*, despite the fact that only 60% approved of his language policies in 1925 as well as the fact that he did not repeat the question in the second survey. The initial intention was to carry out similar periodic surveys, but no further surveys were compiled during the next ten years of publication. From an historical point of view, this data clearly provides an insight into the Yiddish reader's reality, preferences, and practices during this crucial period in Poland. Economic pressures have an admitted effect, but what is remarkable is the continuing commitment to and passionate interest in a Yiddish literary and cultural journal by an increasingly impoverished Yiddish-speaking public.

Notes to Chapter 3

1. For further information on *Literarishe bleter*, see Sima Beeri, 'Language in Its Place: Yiddish as Seen through the Historical Prism of *Literarishe bleter* 1924–1939', PhD thesis, University College London, 2013.
2. See Gennady Estraikh, 'The Kultur-Lige in Warsaw: A Stopover between Kiev and Paris', in *Warsaw: The Jewish Metropolis: Essays in Honor of the 75th Birthday of Professor Antony Polonsky*, ed. by Glenn Dynner and François Guesnet (Boston: Brill, 2015), pp. 323–46.
3. Nakhman Mayzel, *Geven amol a lebn: dos yidishe kultur-lebn in Poyln tsvishn beyde velt-milkhomes* (Buenos Aires: Tsentral-farband fun Poylishe Yidn in Argentine, 1951), p. 217. This is the only description available for the format of the first survey, and it is somewhat sketchy.
4. Ibid., pp. 219–21.
5. 'Di redaktsiye git tsu: "Tsvishn di *teylvayz* tsufridene zenen dos rov nisht tsufridn mit undzer shtelung tsu der shprakhn-frage. Fun ekstrem-hebreyistishe krayzn iz men nisht tsufridn, ober oykh fun links vern mir oft falsh oyfgefast un men iz nisht tsufridn...".' ('The editors add: "Among the *partly* satisfied [readers] the majority are not satisfied with our attitude to the language problem. People from the extreme Hebraist circles are unhappy, whereas also leftwingers wrongly interpret our stand and that makes them unhappy . . ."') -- Mayzel, *Geven amol a lebn*, pp. 221–22.
6. *Literarishe bleter*, 7 August 1925, p. 15.
7. Ibid.
8. Mayzel, *Geven amol a lebn*, pp. 224–25.
9. 'Vos undzere lezer hobn tsu zogn (sakh-haklen fun undzer ankete)', *Literarishe bleter*, 8 March 1929.
10. *Literarishe bleter*, 8 March, 1929, p. 185 (front page).

11. Ibid., p. 186.
12. Mayzel, *Geven amol a lebn*, p. 218. Mayzel states there that the initial number of copies printed was 2,000 and that it rose later to between 7,000 and 9,000. He claims that this figure indicated a readership of 25,000. It was this figure that incurred criticism, but from the practice of shared copies indicated in the survey of 1928–29, it is clear that readership and printed copies are not the same.
13. *Literarishe bleter*, 8 March 1929, p. 185 (front page).
14. *Literarishe bleter*, 22 March 1929, p. 230.

CHAPTER 4

Moscow Threefold: Olgin, Bergelson, Benjamin

Harriet Murav

The distinction between Moscow and St Petersburg is a well-established topos in canonical Russian literature. Pushkin, Gogol, and Dostoevsky construe St Petersburg as a place of fantasy, dream, nightmare, and abstraction. Life in St Petersburg is an imitation of an imitation of something in Tolstoy's *Anna Karenina*, while Moscow, in contrast, is a space of traditional values and historic Russian identity.[1] When Chekhov's three sisters long for change, the target and projection of all their hopes is Moscow, and not St Petersburg; Moscow is the site of their unattainable future. The three twentieth-century Jewish writers who are the subject of this chapter seem to have taken a page from Chekhov's book. For Moyshe Olgin, David Bergelson, and Walter Benjamin, Moscow is a space of aspiration. Moscow belongs to the future. Moscow is in the process of construction; it is the new city par excellence, having excised organic forms and concepts from its new cityscape. For Olgin and Bergelson, Moscow has severed all connection to the historic Russian past; Moscow is no more a Russian city than any other nationality, because it has transcended mere national identity. Benjamin is less certain on this point.

Olgin, writing on May Day 1924, represents Moscow as a time machine, hurtling us into the future, where all contradiction and ambiguity are resolved. The conflicting aspirations of millions join in one relentless march forward. For Bergelson, visiting Moscow in August–September 1926, the time machine of the new city moves us so quickly and so far that we become more creative, more energetic, and even younger. Both Olgin and Bergelson ventriloquize what Vladimir Papernyi calls 'kul'tura 1' (culture 1).[2] This term refers to the emphasis in revolutionary culture of the 1910s to the 1920s on shedding the burden of the past — in contrast to 'kul'tura 2' (culture 2). 'Culture 2' recuperates the past, but only in the service of the bright future, so that prior events point forward to the triumph of socialism. Nonetheless, the past still lingers in the Moscow cityscapes of the three authors.

Bergelson reveals a proclivity toward the time of the past, reproducing in his description of Moscow the belatedness and delay characteristic of the timescape of the shtetl. Benjamin (who also visited Moscow in December 1926–January 1927) represents Moscow's timescape as a time warp, where no two paths intersect, where all meetings are missed, and the city's inhabitants and visitors are perpetually in a state of frustrated waiting. Benjamin's Moscow is Bergelsonian. Benjamin's subsequent theorization of time, particularly in his 1940 essay on history, can be fruitfully used to think about the problem of time in Bergelson's essay and beyond. This chapter is about the image of Moscow, but also about encounters that we could imagine taking place in the realm of ideas and art, confluences in thought, without the necessity of empirical evidence of influences exerted by one author on another. Dan Miron uses the term 'contiguity' to characterize these parallels and intersections; the spatial metaphor is appropriate for an examination of Moscow as a highly charged space in the mid-1920s.[3]

Moyshe Olgin (1878–1939), a leading socialist of his time, emigrated from Russia to New York in 1914.[4] He wrote studies of Yiddish and Russian literature, and a biography of Gorky, in addition to other works. He was the founder and chief editor of *Frayhayt* (Freedom), the American communist newspaper. His vignette (in Russian the term is 'ocherk') on Moscow, 'Der ershter may in Moskve' ('The First of May in Moscow'), was published in his *Fun mayn togbukh* (From My Dairy) in 1926.[5] Olgin describes the massive motion that has overtaken the entire city: 'battalion after battalion, fifteen to twenty people abreast' stream past the viewing platform, on which Olgin is privileged to stand. The streets of Moscow are transformed into 'living streams of bodies', all in unison. Workers from a steel factor march past 'lock step as if they were welded together' ('geyen geshlosn, vi tsunoyfgehamert').[6] Women workers, 'drunk with youthful joy', pass by. Voices from the marchers call out greetings and slogans to the dignitaries on the platforms; the pioneers proclaim their constant readiness for action; 'all the oppressed peoples' of the world are acknowledged, and everyone is united in joy ('un freylekh, freylekh! Ale eyns!').[7] On 1 May, the workers' holiday, Moscow is at the centre of the world, and Red Square is the epicentre: 'like exotic colourful snakes the rows of people were drawn from all over to one point — to the Kremlin, to Red Square' ('Vi dike kolirndike shleyng, hobn zikh de mentshn-rayen getsoygn fun umetum tsu eyn punkt — tsum kreml, tsu der krasnaya ploshtshad').[8] The spatial metaphor of the centre and the periphery will be of importance to Bergelson's representation of Moscow as well.

The triumph of Bolshevism is evident from the unity of the marchers. In the May Day celebrations individuals are no longer separate beings; they have been transformed into a mass body. Olgin writes: 'if you looked at a street, it seemed to you to be a river of heads, a living, seething stream of bodies' (a kuk gegebn af a gas, hot zikh oysgedakht, az dos iz a taykh fun kep, a lebediker, kokhiker shtrom fun kerper').[9] The disaggregation of individuals into bodies and parts of bodies, both in this line and elsewhere ('red laughing faces', 'white teeth in laughing mouths'), reminiscent of Eisenshtein's montage, creates the effect of a mass subject, a new type of human being and a new form of collective identity. The exploitative conditions of capitalist labour alienate individuals from the products of their labour, their own bodies, and the surrounding social and natural world. Moscow creates a new communal and collective socialism that restores what capitalism destroyed: the capacity of individuals to find their embodiment in the human world. Moscow thus appears as a place of gargantuan transformation. A glimpse of the enormous scale of social and physical change can be seen in the metaphor of the seething stream of bodies. This is not a street-level view, but rather, from the perspective of the heights above. Although Olgin does not explicitly say so, the narrative focus from which bodies merge into a single stream cannot be anything else than an aerial view. Moscow creates a new way of seeing on a mass scale. Bystanders on the viewing stand are elevated to new heights.

Mass phenomena are in evidence in Moscow not only on May Day, however. In his essay 'In the Shadow of Monuments: Notes on Iconoclasm and Time', Mikhail Yampolsky notes that Benjamin was struck by the monolithic quality of the movement of its automobile and sleigh traffic: 'Thus, even the traffic in Moscow is, to a large extent, a mass phenomenon.'[10] Yampolsky concludes that Soviet civilization as a whole sought to replace chronological time with the illusion of stasis and stability. Yampolsky's perspective can deepen our understanding of the differences and continuities between the three authors who are the subject of this chapter. Yampolsky points out that Moscow's architecture was designed to distinguish between the ceaseless movement on the streets and the stillness of the squares with their monuments. The stillness of Soviet monuments, according to Yampolsky, has to do with their timelessness; the monument escapes historicity because it symbolizes the perfection of the future in the present; it is eternal and not human, solid and fixed. The viewing platform on which Olgin finds himself in 1924 is just such a space of stillness. It is also the centre of the concentration of power. Power is untouched by the frenzied movement that surrounds it and from which it marks itself off.

At the very epicentre of this space, however, something is missing. Lenin had died three months earlier, leaving 'a black spot in the joy of the red holiday' ('s'iz do a shvarts posikl in der royter yontevdiker freyd'). The contrast between mass movement and the reverent stillness that marks the central point cannot conceal the illusory nature of the spectacle of power. At its core, it is empty: Lenin is not there. His work, of course, continues. He is responsible for the stream of bodies that flows past the viewing stand.

Olgin's portrait of Moscow on May Day 1924 conveys the message that the monumental effort of an incalculable mass of people has achieved its ultimate goal and celebrates its own perfection. We could conclude from this that utopia, which occupies no space, similarly takes no time. Everything is already attained; there is nothing more to do, no possibility of action and no differentiation from sameness. Henri Bergson's characterization of time as retardation usefully unpacks the underlying temporal premise of Olgin's characterization of May Day in Moscow. The French philosopher Bergson reasoned that if time were not the process of holding things back, if everything could be given all at once and once and for all, there would be no time.[11] Olgin's snapshot of May Day Moscow creates a similar image: a space in which everything has already happened, where there is no distinction between past, present, and future. Hence, paradoxically, Moscow represents a moment out of time.

There is one exception to this rule. In a passage I have not yet quoted, Olgin introduces a discordant element into the youthful joy of Moscow. The churches on

Red Square are confused by the holiday:

> Klingt oybn in an altn tserkve-turem der zeyger mit a heylikn tsiterndikn klang. Vundern zikh di alte kloysters, vos iz do geshen. Tut ergets a klap dos toyte harts inem filhundertyorikn hoyfn binyonim. Hey, vakht af! A naye tsayt iz gekumen![12]

> [From above in an old church tower the clock lets out a holy quivering sound. The old churches wonder what is happening here. Somewhere the dead heart of a building hundreds of years old tries to beat. Hey, wake up! A new time has come!]

The dead past flares up in the tremulous chiming of the tower clock. Olgin's use of personification is reminiscent of Bergelson. In *Opgang* (*Descent*) two churches in the shtetl are startled in their sleep and wake up for a moment, 'nisht derkont nisht zikh aleyn un nisht di gegnt' ('recognizing neither themselves nor the district around them').[13] They have found themselves in an alien surrounding, namely, in an area predominantly inhabited by Jews, as Joseph Sherman points out.[14] Both Bergelson's and Olgin's churches are asleep; Bergelson's churches are lost in space, while Olgin's are lost in time. Bergelson returns to the image of churches in his novel *Mideshadin* (Judgment), the first chapters of which were published in his journal *In shpan* (In harness) in 1926. In the fictitious place known as Kamino-Balke, a former monastery houses the terrifying prison and execution centre. The monks are long gone, but the uncanny, Esher-like architecture of the place generates all kinds of ghosts: '[i]t was strange: the church was dead, absolutely dead, but then suddenly, its bells would chime' ('es vert dokh modne: er iz toyt, toyt der kloyster, plutsim klingt er').[15] In Moscow of 1926, there is no grey zone where the past lingers. Olgin uses the distress of the churches to emphasize the obsolescence of Russian Orthodoxy, in contrast to the workers' holiday being celebrated in Red Square.

In his miniature of Moscow in 1926 Bergelson, like Olgin in 1924, also emphasizes the future that has already been achieved. Bergelson's article came out in *Frayhayt* on 5 September 1926.[16] The year 1926 was momentous for Bergelson, who publically shifted his allegiance toward the Soviet Union at this time. Cutting his ties to the anti-communist New York daily *Forverts* (Forward) and joining the staff of the communist newspaper, together with other steps he took in the same year, including a penitential letter to the Moscow Yiddish newspaper *Der emes* and his critical essay 'Dray tsentrn' ('Three Centres') — signalled his new commitment to the Soviet Union.[17] In 'Three Centres', Bergelson designated Moscow, and not Warsaw or New York, as the wellspring of Yiddish literature.[18] Jewish culture in America was the product of assimilationist 'allrightniks', who were abandoning Yiddish (their native language) and replacing it with English. In so doing, they were converting both their bodies and their souls. Bergelson explicitly uses the language of religious conversion, including the terms 'optsushmadn' and 'toyfn', to critique American Jews, who attempt to assimilate by means of language. The propertied classes feel that 'if baptismal water (shmad-vaser) converts only the body, language converts also the soul (di nishome)'. The loss of Yiddish meant nothing less than the loss of Jews. Bergelson dismissed Yiddish literature in Poland as merely 'sentimental Yiddishism'. The 'conscious Jewish worker' has no desire to lose Yiddish, Bergelson writes elsewhere in this essay, because to do so would be to risk transforming oneself into an 'impotent and sterile stammerer' (in a shafungslozn impotentn kvatpe).[19] Only Yiddish literature in Soviet Russia could avail itself of the fresh perspective made possible by the union of the intelligentsia with the workers.

Bergelson opens his essay 'Moskve' by comparing the Moscow of 1921 with the Moscow of 1926.[20] In 1921 Moscow resembled a ghost town; former shopkeepers had become 'shadows without their property'. Even the weather conspired to return Moscow to a state before civilization had taken hold; geography changed, shifting Moscow and Siberia into closer proximity. The cold that froze Moscow's broad streets and inhabitants was like 'a greeting from Siberian storms' ('a grus fun Siberer zaverukhes'). The city seemed to have been thrust back to a time when there were no buildings, no city, and no land, but only water; Moscow's numerous structures had regressed to 'frozen waves on the sea' ('hayzer — farfroyrene khvalyes af a yam'). People lacked heart and feeling. Time itself regressed: 'higher than all the rooftops, higher than all the sharpest spires of the churches, the large invisible clock turned its hand backwards'.[21] Moscow in 1921 was 'the world of chaos' ('oylem-hatoye'). The term 'oylem-hatoye' also means a kind of purgatory, a way station in which atonement was made for prior sins; Bergelson also hints at this meaning in his reference to the bourgeoisie deprived of their livelihood. Bergelson's link between Moscow of 1921 and the remote past can be contextualized in light of other authors working at the same time who used similar tropes of the archaic and the primitive to describe what was utterly new.[22]

In 1926, in contrast, the 'world clock' that hangs over Moscow is modern, 'reliable, precise, its solid steel hands turn from ten to eleven and from eleven to twelve indicating the time of tomorrow and the day after — the time of the future'.[23] The focus on the future eliminates the present; there is no timepiece that indicates 'now'. Bergelson's portrait of Moscow in 1926 thus resembles Olgin's in that both situate Moscow temporally as beyond time; the Moscow of 'today', that is, 1926, has no present. Instead of ghosts from the past, Bergelson finds in Moscow in 1926 'joyful youngsters'.[24] Moscow is a place that 'heals by making people younger'.[25] Bergelson's emphasis on Moscow as the city of the future is consistent with the emerging templates of what was to become socialist realism. Although, as Katerina Clark shows, most socialist realist novels were not set in Moscow, the 'myth' of Moscow 'as capital of a highly centralized society, was to be an enhanced space, ahead of its time physically as the leaders were politically'.[26] Socialist realism did not become an officially promulgated aesthetic until 1932; Bergelson's essay is from 1926; he was, like the city he described, ahead of his time.

Bergelson's 1926 portrait of Moscow's clock contrasts sharply with his depiction of the shtetl clock in 'Tsvishn emigrantn' ('Among Refugees'), published a year later in 1927. The protagonist of this work, the self-styled 'Jewish terrorist' — describes his grandfather's peculiar habit of buying a clock on the occasion of a death in the family, so that every clock in the house remembered and marked death ('yeder zeyger a keyver, a yortsayt').[27] Moscow's clock looks forward and transports the inhabitants of the city to their joyful future, but the shtetl clock can only look back in mourning. In remarks made in Warsaw in 1930, Bergelson would emphasize this distinction between forward- and backward-looking Yiddish literature. He used the image of the clock to make his point. Yiddish literature from America and Poland could be compared to a clock that had a beautiful face and played beautiful melodies, but could not give the correct time. Yiddish literature from the Soviet Union, in contrast, was like a symphony orchestra playing on an express train.[28] Those left behind on the platform strain to catch its melodies as it rushes by.

These distinctions and Bergelson's own new commitments to the Soviet Union, however, do not mean that Bergelson definitively shed his interest in the past, or that he was unequivocal about the future of Jewish literature and his own future as an artist allied with the new country of the Bolsheviks. As an artist he could not transform himself into a new person, a person of the future. Even in his 1926 essay 'Moskve', he uses the language of the past to describe his delight in the city of the future. One of the leitmotifs of the essay is the new construction that is taking place in Moscow; Bergelson notes that ninety-two new buildings are underway, and this despite economic hardship. Bergelson takes particular interest in 'a big building under a glass roof' from which 'letters rush out to the whole world'.[29]

Ivan Retburg's design for the Central Telegraph Office began construction in 1926 and had a revolving glass globe in its entrance way. The constructivist style of the building, which refrained from decoration and referentiality, and emphasized instead clean abstract lines, demonstrated concretely (in all senses of the word) the definitive break with the past. Bergelson's construction of the link between the Moscow Central Telegraph Office and the entire globe built on the centre/periphery model long associated with Moscow. In the timeframe of the 1920s, Moscow was the supercharged core of socialism which radiated its force field to the entirety of Russia and beyond.[30]

It is significant, however, that the language Bergelson uses to describe the city that was being constructed right in front of him looks back to the biblical past. As he contemplates the building that 'sends letters out to the whole world' a quotation comes to mind: 'If not for its strength, I would rule over her and with an outstretched hand!' This is an adaptation of Ezekiel 20:33 'As I live, saith the Lord GOD, surely with a mighty hand, and with a stretched out arm, and with fury poured out, will I rule over you' (King James Version). Bergelson cites the biblical quotation, ironically, to enhance the force and power of the new Soviet regime, which utterly rejected religion. It is hard to imagine that the irony is anything less than deliberate. It is conceivable that by introducing Ezekiel's language about God's power in his paean to Moscow Bergelson subtly alludes to the doctrine of Moscow the third Rome, but in twentieth-century form and in a socialist guise. This was a sixteenth-century idea described by the monk Filofei in successionist terms: after the fall of Byzantium, Moscow was the last bastion of Orthodoxy and would survive until the end of time.[31] To evoke Moscow's God-like might in 1926 was to suggest that Moscow, the capital of the new Soviet Union, would outlast and prevail over all the other new political entities that had emerged after the chaos and upheaval of the Great War.

It is nonetheless also ironic that the love Muscovites feel for their future compels them to fall behind. Bergelson observes that the people around him are so interested in the new construction that they stop on their way to work in the morning to watch how things are coming along, and even though they look as if they will never forgive themselves for arriving late at work, they will commit the same sin on the following day, which will set in motion the same cycle of delay and regret. The same three components of anticipation, delay, and regret dog the lives of Bergelson's shtetl characters, who are perpetually late. The doomed engagement between Velvl Burnes and Mirl Hurvits drags on for four years before it finally ends; even though Meylekh's funeral is late in the afternoon — and the word 'late' is the opening word of *Opgang* — his friend Khaym-Moyshe arrives too late for it, and too late to have seen Meylekh alive. The condition of being late and having been left behind is the distinctive feature of Bergelson's characters, even when they turn out to be inhabitants of Moscow, the city of the future. Bergelson sets in motion a strange tension between futurity and the past. On the way to the future, Muscovites are always late. The question arises as to whether they will ever arrive.

Time in Bergelson's Moscow is not free from remnants of the past, and even the possibility of starting the clock over again. Bergelson writes that there are shadows in Moscow, 'shadows that are tied to the hardships, that come from not being afraid to, if necessary, start history from a brand-new beginning'.[32] The tortured prose reflects the strain of avoiding a direct discussion of the harsh consequences of the revolution and civil war, the massive number of deaths, and other forms of violence that form the core of many of Bergelson's Berlin stories, including, for example, 'Among Refugees' ('Tsvishn emigrantn') and 'Geburt' (Birth). The gangs of children begging on the streets of Moscow in 1926 — Bergelson describes them as begging for a puff from his cigarette — represent just one of the after-effects of the violence and dislocation that come from resetting the clock. The revolution may not be the decisive once and for all event that utterly destroys the past. There may well be another revolution, another turning of the clock back to the beginning, and another repetition of the 'world of chaos'. The cyclical and apocalyptic timescape on which Bergelson locates Moscow in 1926 in some ways anticipates the Moscow timescape found in post-Soviet fiction.[33]

Of the three authors under consideration, it is Benjamin who attributes the most irrationality to the quality of time in Moscow. In both his *Moscow Diary* and his essay 'Moscow' Benjamin emphasizes the extraordinary, contradictory timescape of Moscow in the mid-1920s. Benjamin spent December 1926 and January 1927 in Moscow, in large part to pursue an unsuccessful relationship with Asja Lacis. He arrives anticipating that the very first meeting he has planned will not come off: 'In the train I had made a mental note of the name and address of a hotel in case there should be nobody waiting for me at the station.'[34] Like a character in a Bergelson story, Benjamin finds himself left behind; Lacis suddenly jumps on a trolley without him. He goes to Red Square, expecting to meet Lacis, but she has already left. On another occasion, he 'wait[s] interminably at the Gos cinema'.[35] Even when he and Lacis arrive at the same place at the same time, Benjamin ends up waiting an hour for her. It would seem that in Moscow time and space have lives of their own, hostile to Benjamin's intentions.

There is no rationality, order, or predictability in the Moscow timescape. The qualities that characterize Benjamin's personal relationship with Lacis also appear in the lives of Moscow's inhabitants generally. Benjamin observes:

> I don't think there's another city with as many watchmakers as Moscow. This is all the more peculiar since people here do not get particularly worried about time. But there must be historical reasons for this. When you watch people on the street, you rarely see anybody rushing [. . .] It is quite significant that in some club or other [. . .] there is a poster on the wall with the exhortation: Lenin said, 'Time is money'. Just to express this banality, the highest authority had to be invoked.[36]

Moscow's economic life has not yet attained capitalist time; as this passage reveals, no one knows yet that 'time is money'. No particular value is placed on the next unit of time and how it is to be spent.

This gap proves extraordinarily frustrating for Benjamin when he tries to get a wake-up call in his hotel, which, the author says, 'elicited a Shakespearan monologue' from the hotel staff. Benjamin uses the scene both in his *Moscow Diary* and in his essay 'Moscow'. I quote from the latter:

> If we think of it we shall wake you, but if we do not think of it we shall not wake you. Actually we usually do think of it.[37]

The monologue continues in the same vein, with each successive statement cancelling the previous one. Any attempt to pin down a specific time in any sort of transaction in Moscow results in the answer 'seichas' ('right away', or, 'at once'), but 'seichas' can mean that you wait 'hours, days, or weeks until the promise is carried out'. The result, paradoxically, is a rich experience of time: 'Time catastrophes, time collisions are therefore as much the order of the day as the *remonte*. They make each hour superabundant, each day exhausting, each life a moment.'[38] Each hour has the capacity to be 'superabundant' because it has the potential to fulfil the expectation and waiting that began long before; it is in this sense that Moscow heightens the otherwise unremarkable quality of time in ordinary daily life. In the essay, Benjamin transforms the exasperating qualities of Moscow into a somewhat ironic triumph over what he will later characterize as 'homogeneous, empty time'. In his 1940 essay 'On the Concept of History' Benjamin theorizes a notion of history which replaces uniform and blank units of time with the messianic breakthrough of the radical transformation of the social character of the present. The superabundance of each moment in Moscow, of course, does not necessarily mean that the city is a space of messianic transformation.

The question whether Moscow had achieved radical change also remains open for Bergelson. He, like Benjamin, hesitates about the certainty of Moscow's leap into utter novelty. I touched on this earlier. Bergelson talks about 'shadows' in Moscow — 'shadows that are tied to the hardships, that come from not being afraid to, if necessary, start history from the beginning'.[39] Pressing the 'reset' button risks entering the realm of eternal return, as opposed to the straight arrow of a Marxist notion of historical teleology. In a letter from 1927, written after he had already returned to Berlin, Benjamin said that Moscow shows 'a range of possibilities' regarding the success of the revolution, which might yet fail or succeed. In another letter of 1927, to Hofmannsthal, Benjamin characterized what I have called the irrationality of time in Moscow as the incommensurability of two tempi: 'an archaic Russian tempo' and 'the new rhythms of the Revolution'.[40] For Bergelson the archaic tempo is not specifically Russian, but instead universal and even cosmic (the biblical 'world of chaos' is not meant to apply only to Jews). In Bergelson's portrait of Moscow in 1926 Benjamin's two tempi cannot be extricated from one another; the archaic necessarily underlines the newness of the revolution, which might have to take place all over again.

Juxtaposing the three images of Moscow by Olgin, Bergelson, and Benjamin reveals a degree of open-endedness with regard to time. For Olgin, Moscow has already achieved its future; a black spot, however, is found at its very core. This is the absence created by Lenin's death. For Bergelson and Benjamin, the issue is not so clear: the swift reliable hands of Moscow's clock, to use Bergelson's language, might have to be set back to the beginning again. Revolutionary redemption from the shadows of the past may yet be deferred, and the 'world of chaos' may reappear. Bergelson will revisit this question in fiction written in the same time period, namely, 'Birger-krig' ('Civil War') and *Mides-hadin*. At the end of 'Three Centres', he hints at this work, and his own predicament. Bergelson warns that 'the new Jewish artist will see unavoidable destruction crying to the heavens — the full severity of the law'.[41] The Hebrew term that appears in the original Yiddish text for 'the full severity of the law' is 'mides-hadin', the same phrase he uses for the title of his novel, set in 1920 during the civil war. The hero, the non-Jewish Bolshevik leader Filipov, hands down severe punishments for smuggling, speculation, espionage, and counterrevolutionary activities. Many of those who receive death sentences are Jews, but not because of Bolshevik anti-Semitism. The representation of the shtetl in the novel clearly indicates that this most typical Jewish space, with its social hierarchy, exploitative economic activities, religious practices, and interethnic conflicts, is on its way to extinction. In 'Three Centres', Bergelson warns that the renewal that will follow this period of destruction will be slow, 'perhaps very slow'. It is difficult to imagine that the type of 'new Jewish artist' he refers to in 'Three Centres' does not include the author himself. In 'Moskve' he names himself in precisely these terms: 'All told, I am a Jewish writer' ('ikh bin dokh sof kol sof a yidisher shrayber').[42] In both his fiction and non-fiction prose Bergelson circles back to the same issue. He — as an artist — is bystander to a new page of history, and as bystander, he staggers under the weight of the destruction each new page brings with it.

Notes to Chapter 4

1. V. N. Toporov and Iurii Lotman are considered the foundational figures in the development of a theory of the so-called St Petersburg text. Their work and articles by other authors on this theme can be found in *Semiotika goroda i gorodskoi kul'tury. Peterburg (Trudy po znakovym sistemam, XVIII)* (Tartu: Tartu University, 1984). For discussions of the Moscow/St Petersburg polarity, see for example, E. N. Ertner, 'Simvolika Moskvy i Peterburga: Konflikt dvukh "teskstov" russkoi literatury', in *Gorod kak kul'turnaia prostranstvo*, ed. by N. P. Dovotsova (Tiumen: Ekspress, 2003), pp. 201–07. For a discussion of Moscow as a 'global city', see Sarah Hudspith, 'Introduction', *Slavic Review*, 72.3 (2013), 453–57.

2. Vladimir Papernyi, *Kul'tura dva* (Moscow: Novoe literaturnoe obozrenie, 2006).
3. Dan Miron, *From Continuity to Contiguity: Toward a New Jewish Literary Thinking* (Stanford: Stanford University Press, 2010).
4. For more on Olgin, see Gennady Estraikh, *In Harness: Yiddish Writers' Romance with Communism* (Syracuse: Syracuse University Press, 2005), pp. 71, 92–94.
5. Moissaye J. Olgin, *Fun mayn tog-bukh* (New York: Frayhayt, 1926), p. 399.
6. Ibid., p. 275
7. Ibid., p. 277.
8. Ibid., p. 275.
9. Ibid.
10. Mikhail Yampolsky, 'In the Shadow of Monuments: Notes on Iconoclasm and Time', in *Soviet Hieroglyphics: Visual Culture in Late Twentieth-Century Russia*, ed. by Nancy Condee, trans. by John Kachur (Bloomington: Indiana University Press, 1995), pp. 93–112; Walter Benjamin, *Reflections: Essays, Aphorisms, Autobiographical Writings*, trans. by Edmund Jephcott (New York: Harcourt Brace Jovanovich, 1978); Gennady Estraikh, 'David Bergelson in and on America (1929–1949)', in *David Bergelson: From Modernism to Socialist Realism*, ed. by Joseph Sherman and Gennady Estraikh (Oxford: Legenda, 2007), pp. 205–21.
11. Henri Bergson, *Time and Free Will: An Essay on the Immediate Data of Consciousness*, trans. by Frank Lubecki Pogson (London and New York: G. Allen & Unwin; Humanities Press, 1971).
12. Olgin, *Fun mayn tog-bukh*, p. 276.
13. David Bergelson, *Descent*, trans. by Joseph Sherman (New York: Modern Language Association of America, 1999), p. 6.
14. See Sherman's discussion of this passage ibid., p. xxxvii.
15. David Bergelson, *Mides-hadin* (Vilna: B. Kletskin, 1929), p. 17. All translations from this text are by Harriet Murav and Sasha Senderovich.
16. Estraikh, 'David Bergelson in and on America (1929–1949)'.
17. See ibid., pp. 205–10.
18. The essay was first published in *In shpan* (April, 1926), 84–96. For the English translation, see David Bergelson, 'Three Centres (Characteristics)', in *David Bergelson: From Modernism to Socialist Realism*, ed. by Joseph Sherman and Gennady Estraikh (Oxford: Legenda, 2007), pp. 347–54.
19. David Bergelson, 'Dray tsentren', *In shpan*, 1 (1926), 84–96.
20. For a discussion of 'Moskve' and the English translation, see Gennady Estraikh, 'The Old and the New Together: David Bergelson's and Israel Joshua Singer's Portraits of Moscow Circa 1926–1927', *Prooftexts*, 26 (2006), 53–78. For the Yiddish, see David Bergelson, 'Moskve', *Frayhayt*, 5 September 1926.
21. Estraikh, 'The Old and the New Together', p. 65.
22. For a discussion of this metaphor in the work of Boris Pilnyak, see Michael Kunichika, '"The Scythians Were Here . . .": On Nomadic Archaeology, Modernist Form, and Early Soviet Modernity', *Ab Imperio*, 2 (2012), 229–55.
23. Estraikh, 'The Old and the New Together', p. 63.
24. Ibid., p. 62.
25. Ibid., p. 65.
26. Katerina Clark, 'Socialist Realism in Soviet Literature', in *Routledge Companion to Russian Literature*, ed. by Neil Cornwell (London and New York: Taylor and Francis, 2001), pp. 174–83.
27. David Bergelson, *Geklibene verk* (Vilno: B. Kletskin, 1928–30).
28. David Bergelson, 'Problemen fun der yidisher literatur', *Literarishe bleter*, 24 (1930), 437–39.
29. Estraikh, 'The Old and the New Together', pp. 53–78.
30. A recent discussion of this structure can be found in Mark Griffiths, 'Moscow after the Apocalypse', *Slavic Review*, 72.3 (2013), 481–504.
31. For a discussion of the political significance of this notion, see Daniel B. Rowland, 'Moscow — The Third Rome or the New Israel?', *Russian Review*, 55.4 (1996), 591–614.
32. Estraikh, 'The Old and the New Together', p. 67.
33. For a discussion, see Griffiths, 'Moscow after the Apocalypse', pp. 481–504.
34. Walter Benjamin, *Moscow Diary*, trans. by Richard Sieburth (Cambridge, MA: Harvard University Press, 1986), p. 9.

35. Ibid., p. 103.
36. Ibid., p. 47.
37. Walter Benjamin, *Reflections: Essays, Aphorisms, Autobiographical Writings*, ed. by Peter Demetz, trans. by Edmund Jephcott (New York: Harcourt Brace Jovanovich, 1978), p. 111.
38. Ibid.
39. Estraikh, 'The Old and the New Together', p. 67.
40. Benjamin, *Reflections*, p. 134.
41. Ellipsis added. Bergelson, 'Three Centres (Characteristics)'.
42. Estraikh, 'The Old and the New Together', p. 68.

CHAPTER 5

Sholem Asch's Moscow Sojourn, 1928

Gennady Estraikh

On 9 May 1928, Moscow saw the arrival of Sholem Asch, by then the most successful Yiddish writer, whose works appeared in print and on stage in many countries, both in the original and in translations.[1] Kornei Chukovskii, a close friend of Vladimir Jabotinsky in their Odessa youth and later an influential Soviet man of letters, wrote before the First World War: 'Sholem Asch is best known to us. To me he seems a magician, an enchanted person. I am happy to re-read a thousand times his "poem of Jewish life in Poland", *The Shtetl*.'[2] An avid globe-trotter, Asch became an American citizen in 1920, but he frequented Poland, where he was born in 1880, and spent long periods of time in France. Not long before his trip to the Soviet Union, the Association of Yiddish Writers and Journalists in Warsaw elected him as their honorary president. A distinguished and pretty affluent writer, he derived income from various sources, notably as a salaried contributor to the highest-circulating Yiddish daily *Forverts*, based in New York. In his civic activity, Asch played a visible role in the American Jewish Joint Distribution Committee, which sponsored, through its Agro-Joint affiliate, numerous projects in the Soviet Union, most notably the large-scale projects aimed at building and developing Jewish agricultural settlements in Crimea, Ukraine, and Belorussia.[3] While *Forverts* was a socialist newspaper, Asch essentially did not belong to any political movement, though ideals of social justice always remained dear to him. According to Shloyme Rosenfeld, his long-time literary secretary, Asch was a man of moods and 'could be a Bundist in the morning and a Zionist in the evening'.[4] As this chapter will show, at the time of his 1928 journey and in retrospect, his political oscillations coloured his attitude to the Soviet Union and, vice versa, Soviet ideologists' attitude to him.

The Russian writer Vladimir Lidin (Gomberg) later recalled that when he met Asch in Moscow, the foreign guest 'was a fairly handsome, if portly, self-assured middle-aged man, well-known in many countries and even famous in some of them. Although he made his first steps in literature in Poland, a real recognition came to him in Russia [. . .]'. Lidin was a young man when he read, in a Russian translation,

> the prose-poem *The Shtetl* by Sholem Asch, which came out in the [St Petersburg] Shipovnik Publishing House [. . .] His play *God of Vengeance* entered the repertoire of many theatres in Russia, and one of Sholem Asch's plays was staged at the [St Petersburg] Komissarzhevskaya Theatre.[5]

FIG. 5.1. Sholem Asch

Fig. 5.2. Sholem Asch and Maxim Gorky in Red Square, 10 June 1928

Max Reinhardt's staging of *God of Vengeance* in Berlin, in 1910, with Rudolph Schildkraut starring as the owner of the brothel Yekl Shapshovitsh, whose family is central in the play, enjoyed a particular success. In 1923, Schildkraut directed *God of Vengeance* as a Broadway production, which caused a widely publicized scandal following the indictment of the troupe for showing a play 'which would tend to the corruption of the morals of youth or others'.[6] Rather different was the evaluation of the play by socialists and even communists. Thus, when Schildkraut once again put on the play, this time in Yiddish, the literary critic Shakhno Epshteyn, then the co-editor of the American communists' Yiddish daily *Frayhayt* (Freedom), wrote that the play had clearly demonstrated that Asch's creativity had achieved a new level, characterized by renouncing 'the idealization of the moss-covered past'.[7]

A bond of long-standing friendship or, better yet, mutual respect linked Asch and Maxim Gorky. In 1922 *Forverts* published an interview, which Gorky, who sojourned in Berlin at that time, gave to Asch. Gorky accused Jewish Bolsheviks of being 'tactless'; he argued that 'irresponsible striplings, rather than all of them, participate[d] in defiling sacred places of the Russian people'. Gorky's words elicited a mixed reaction: Zionists agreed with him, while Jewish communists charged him with harbouring anti-Semitic prejudices.[8] The stir caused by the interview did not affect the relationship between Asch and Gorky. Significantly, Asch came to Moscow as an official guest rather than as a client of the Soviet state-run Intourist Agency. This happened thanks to the recommendation of Gorky, who himself returned to the Soviet Union in May 1928, thus responding to Stalin's invitation and bringing to an end the period of his life in emigration. A photo of Gorky and Asch standing in Red Square in Moscow appeared in print scores of times, confirming the words of the American Yiddish poet Aron Glantz-Leyeles that Asch 'always knew, where and with whom to be photographed'.[9]

Asch's colleagues on *Forverts* usually did not get a red-carpet treatment and had to be satisfied with purchasing a tourist package through one of the agencies linked with Intourist — the travel bureau of the New York-based Amalgamated Bank. The bureau's advertisements published in the newspaper (for instance, on 1 May 1928) hailed the trips as inexpensive, 'affordable to everyone', opportunities to see Soviet Russia. In 1927, when the *Forverts* editor Abraham Cahan took one of the 'affordable' tours, he, judging by his travelogue, shunned contacts with Soviet Yiddish writers. Instead, he looked closely at the Jewish agricultural colonies, the general social and political situation in the country, and the competition between Stalin, considered by Cahan a 'reasonable man' at that time, and Trotsky, whom Cahan had loathed since 1917, when Trotsky lived for a short time in New York and published several articles in *Forverts*.[10]

Encounters with Soviet colleagues left little trace also in Hersh David Nomberg's and Israel Joshua Singer's travel notes, serialized in *Forverts* in 1927 and later published in book form.[11] Singer even did not mention if he had a chance to see his erstwhile bosom friend Peretz Markish, who moved from Poland to the Soviet Union not long before. Neither Cahan, nor Nomberg, nor Singer experienced an official welcome of any sort. Even private contacts with them — representatives of the newspaper featuring articles by Mensheviks, Bundists, and other socialists, sceptical or critical of the Soviet regime — were low-key, almost furtive, meetings. Characteristically, *Tribuna evreiskoi sovetskoi obshchestvennosti* (Tribune of the Jewish Soviet Public), the periodical of the Society for Settling Toiling Jews on the Land, OZET in the Russian abbreviation, described Cahan as one of the 'most inveterate opponents of the USSR'.[12]

Soviet Jewish communists had serious grievances against Asch, too. For instance, they could not forgive him for writing an open letter to Marshal Józef Piłsudski, whose coming to power in Poland, in May 1926, had earned Moscow's opprobrium for being a reactionary coup d'état. Asch, on the contrary, characterized Piłsudski as 'the only contemporary Polish hero, who personifies the honorary aspirations and typical traits of the Polish nation'.[13] At the same time, Moyshe Litvakov, editor of the central Soviet Yiddish daily *Der emes* (Truth) and other communist functionaries working in the relatively narrow domain of Jewish cultural, propagandist, and administrative activities, realized that they had to take into consideration the opinion of more influential circles in the Soviet apparatus as well as of cultural figures in favour with the Kremlin. In 1928, *Tribuna evreiskoi sovetskoi obshchestvennosti* (no. 11, p. 25) published a note entitled 'Sholem Asch's oeuvre in Russian' reporting that the combined state and joint-stock publishing house Zemlia i Fabrika (Land and Factory), which was supervised by Gorky, had signed a contract with Asch to produce eight volumes of his writings.[14] Although initially it was planned that Isaac Babel would edit this multi-volume edition, Semen Gekht, a writer close to Babel, would do the bulk of the work. Ultimately only four volumes came out, which, however, still contrasted strikingly with the lack of Soviet book editions of Asch's works in Yiddish.[15]

Forverts featured a report describing episodes of Asch's Moscow sojourn. The report appeared as an anonymous 'letter from Moscow' and was almost undoubtedly authored by *Forverts*'s Moscow correspondent Zalman Wendroff, a Soviet citizen who in the pre-First World War years of his life enjoyed a minor success as a feuilleton writer on various Yiddish newspapers.[16] According to this report, local Jewish communist ideologists initially were not sure how to treat the guest:

> on the one hand, Sholem Asch is the great or even the greatest contemporary Yiddish writer; on the other hand, he is a conspicuous nationalist [. . .]
>
> As a result, none of the Yiddish litterateurs came to meet Asch at the railway station. He was welcomed there by a representative of VOKS, or All-Union Society for Cultural Relations with Foreign Countries. There was also a representative of the All-Russian Writers' Association, and some of Asch's friends and acquaintances came, but not even one of the *Yiddish* writers showed up.

Strikingly different was the welcome with which Moscow's Jewish officialdom met writers affiliated with the communist movement. For instance, in six months after the lukewarm reception of Asch, a commission was established to take care of welcoming the American Yiddish writer Abraham Reisen, who at that time collaborated with the communist daily *Frayhayt*. This commission included representatives from the Moscow City Council; Moscow Department of People's Education; central bureaus of the Jewish Sections of Communist Party and the Young Communist League; People's Commissariat of Education; Jewish sectors at the Communist University of the Peoples of the West and the Pedagogical Faculty of the Second Moscow State University; Jewish Scientific Society; societies of Friends of Jewish Theatre and Friends of Jewish Music; Moscow Jewish club Communist; OZET; ORT (Association for the Promotion of Skilled Trades); newspaper *Der emes*; bureau of Moscow worker correspondents; Moscow and Russian associations of proletarian writers; Federation of Soviet writers' associations (including All-Russian Writers' Association); Yiddish schools in Marina Roshcha (Moscow neighbourhood) and Malakhovka (Moscow outskirt); Young Pioneers Club No. 2; Central Jewish Library; and two predominantly Jewish artisanal cooperatives.[17] This list, which conspicuously excludes religious bodies, illustrates the organizational structure of contemporaneous Jewish life in Moscow.

Wendroff wrote that, in spite of the coolness of

> the 'official' reception, Asch was well received even by the 'extreme left' writers. Right on the next day following his arrival, Yiddish writers of all hues and tendencies, from the most left ones to the most traditional ones, began to stream to his hotel. The meetings were very cordial. Notwithstanding their extreme leftiness, the young writers still regard Asch as their teacher in literature. Each of them considered it their duty — and honour — to bring him their works [. . .]

The governing body of OZET found a way of putting the guest to good use, by inviting him to take part in the drawing ceremony of OZET's first lottery, which took place on 12 and 13 May in the building of Moscow Yiddish Theatre (2 Malaia Bronnaia St.). This troupe, which at that time was on a tour in Germany, performed Asch's plays in its early period, when it was based in Petrograd. Soon after moving to Moscow, the young theatre marked the III Congress of the Communist International (June 1921) with staging *God of Vengeance* for its delegates. The much-talked-of play remained in the troupe's repertoire for several years. Thus, in March 1924 it was shown to members of the Moscow Jewish club Communist.[18]

On the eve of his Soviet trip, Asch met with Solomon Mikhoels and Benjamin Zuskin, the two leading actors of the theatre. (Soon, following the decision of Alexander Granovsky, the troupe's founding director, to stay abroad, Mikhoels would become the head of the theatre. The role of Yekl Shapshovitsh was Mikhoels's first significant piece of work in his acting career.[19]) They met during a dinner at the flat of David Bergelson, who lived in Berlin in 1921–33. Zuskin described this meeting:

> We met, got into conversation with him. Asch said literally the following: '[. . .] No, I don't like your theatre. It's not a Jewish theatre. You make fun, mock at everything Jewish, everything that is dear to me', and so on in the same vein. We parted very coldly.[20]

In Moscow, in the foyer of the Jewish theatre, filled by workers and OZET activists from Moscow and other towns, the ceremonial part of the drawing began with a speech delivered by Nikolai Semashko, the People's Commissar of Public Health, who 'emphasized the role played by the Soviet public in providing aid to Jewish toilers'.[21] Asch, who also addressed the audience, said inter alia:

> Abroad, people hear tall stories that the Soviet regime is infected with anti-Semitism. It is for the first time in my life that I face a Jewish event whose participants are both Jews and non-Jews. In noble travails of toil, Jews have formed bonds with other peoples, and this is the best safeguard for work and peace among all peoples.[22]

Asch's words made a strong impression on Wendroff, who informed his *Forverts* readers that numerous invited guests from various corners of the Soviet Union, including a representative of a military garrison stationed in the town of Bryansk, cheered the Yiddish writer

> with loud applause, which pleasantly affected him. In contrast with many foreign visitors, he did not make a declaration of love to Communism or the Soviet Union. At the same time, he spoke very enthusiastically about Jewish colonization [in the Soviet Union].

On that intense day, the main winning tickets were drawn: a three-room 'house/flat in any area of the USSR'; forty-five Soviet bonds of the 1926 issue; two trips to the United States; two full equipment sets for an artisanal workshop; a new farmstead in a Jewish agricultural settlement. Other prizes included typewriters, volumes of the *Great Soviet Encyclopedia*, holidays in Crimea and Caucasus, and trips to Jewish agricultural colonies in Ukraine and Crimea. Pupils of the Marina Roshcha Yiddish schools were pulling winning numbers from the lottery drum. Some days later it became known that, while the winning ticket for a three-room house/flat remained unsold, both American trips had winners: a person called Rabinovich who worked at the Moscow office of the shipping agency Sovtorgflot and a twelve-year-old Russian girl from the Ukrainian town of Kremenchug; one of artisanal workshop sets went to a resident of the town of Ganja in Azerbaijan.[23]

Wendroff wrote in his report about other events of Asch's Moscow sojourn:

> The next day, Russian writers gave a reception in honour of Asch.
> Well-known Russian writers, such as Leonid Leonov, Boris Pilnyak, Efim Zozulya, Aleksei Svirskii, Abram Efros and Alexander Iakovlev, warmly welcomed him in the Herzen House [on Tverskoi Boulevard], where the club of the All-Russian Writers' Association is situated. [. . .] Everything went wonderfully — the dinner and the speeches. I think that Asch made a mistake deciding to speak 'in Russian'. Let alone that this had a rather tangential relation to the Russian language. In reality, he spoke a mixture of Russian, Polish, and Yiddish, inserting words from English and French. It was Asch's Esperanto, with his peculiar accent and one-of-a-kind grammar.
> If I were him, I would rather speak in Yiddish, with an interpreter.
> Yet it was a minor thing. After all, this kind of 'Russian', spoken by a 'foreign' writer, had its charm. Not to mention that everyone could understand what he wanted to say.

Lidin also mentioned the idiosyncrasy of Asch's Russian, but he hurried to stress that 'it was a speech of a deeply moved and excited person, so no one paid attention where he placed the stress or whether he used syntactic rules correctly'. According to Lidin, the guest became particularly emotional when the prominent Soviet journalist Mikhail Koltsov (Fridlyand) presented him with copies of the recently published Russian editions of Asch's books.[24]

★ ★ ★ ★ ★

In the 1920s, David Einhorn, characterized by the Soviet critical pundit Isaac Nusinov as 'the Bundist nationalist poet [. . .] singing of the decaying national life',[25] resided predominantly in Paris, but paid occasional visits to Berlin. There he heard Bergelson talking to Asch not long before the latter went to Russia. Conceivably, this could be the same dinner with Mikhoels and Zuskin among the guests. Asch asked Bergelson, who had already visited the Soviet Union, what he should anticipate from meeting Litvakov and other pundits of Soviet Yiddish culture. Bergelson, Asch's old friend or rather a rival, told him a coarse parable about a ritual allegedly practised at the Persian shah's court: a person accused of committing an offence would be brought to a room full of various gifts of nature and asked to choose any fruit available. The poor devil did not know that the selected fruit would be forced into his body through the anus. Bergelson argued that he was relatively lucky, because his choice had fallen on a pomegranate, but he had preordered a pumpkin for Asch.[26]

In fact, Bergelson described his experience of being subjected to a peculiar act of affable welcoming, which came combined with public humiliation.[27] No doubt, this mixed hospitality reflected the inferiority complex widespread among Soviet Yiddish writers and critics, who insisted time and again that they, rather their foreign counterparts, had achieved success in creating literature of high quality. Litvakov insisted that the Soviet literary circle ought to impose its hegemony upon the entire domain of Yiddish literature. The number of literary works or even their 'formally assessed quality' did not play, according to him, a crucial role in order to fulfil this task. Instead, Litvakov believed that 'a new manner, new style, new direction' were the factors that would 'ultimately bring the quantity and the quality'.[28]

On the occasion of Asch's visit, the ritual act of hospitality-cum-opprobrium took place on 15 May in the foyer of the Yiddish theatre. OZET sponsored a tea party reception to honour the unwanted guest, thrust upon them by Gorky and other Russian writers. On the surface everything appeared fine, at least in the beginning. The opening welcome came from the veteran Bolshevik Shimen Dimanshtein, who led the Jewish Commissariat and Jewish Sections of the Communist Party in the early Soviet years; now he chaired OZET's central board and, most importantly, headed the Nationalities Sector at the Department of Agitation, Propaganda and Press of the Central Committee of the Communist Party. The poets Aron Kushnirov and Izi Kharik, the prose writer Shmuel Godiner, and the critics Issac Nusinov and Yekhezkel Dobrushin spoke about Asch's literary work. *Der emes*, in its report on the event, noted that Asch rebuked those who did not support the Soviet Jewish colonization and that the audience thunderously applauded his story of visiting the Moscow Jewish pioneer club. The newspaper wrote that the foreign guest praised the club for training the teenagers how to deal with guns, seeing in it a sign that 'the Soviet state will never expire'. Yet, Asch later indicated that his words had been wrongly interpreted: he admired the readiness of the young people to defend the Jewish population.[29]

In reality, the reception ended with a scandal, which had nothing to do with the real or alleged misquoting of Asch's words about Jewish pioneers. In the middle of the event, Asch lost his temper, though (according to Boris Smolar, the Moscow correspondent of Jewish Telegraphic Agency) he tried to put himself in the mood of 'listening, watching and being silent'. Initially he really did not show any reaction to the speeches of Soviet functionaries, though Dimanshtein's words that writers should use Yiddish as 'a means rather than an aim in itself' might faze him. When the turn came for Yiddish writers and critics to make their contribution to the speeches part of the reception, those who knew Asch well enough realized, seeing the crooked smile spreading across his face, that every speech added fuel to his growing anger and that he was getting less and less able to contain himself.[30]

Among the roughly two hundred people who came to the tea party in Asch's honour there was also the author of the 'anonymous letter', describing the event for the newspaper *Forverts*:

> Certainly no other Yiddish writer received such a reception. Among those present at the banquet were all who happened to be in Moscow at the time — Yiddish litterateurs and journalists, Jewish scholars and, generally, the crème de la crème among Soviet Jewish activists, from people profoundly steeped in [Jewish] tradition to the most prominent Jewish communists, who were somehow associated with the Jewish colonization or Yiddish literature.
>
> It already has become an established tradition that an important guest must be first of all somewhat 'put in order'. An honour of this kind is in store only

for those who are deemed friendly to the Soviet Union and the work conducted among its Jewish population. As for enemies, there is no communication with them at all. Welcome guests receive great homage, but also a dressing down for actions incompatible with communist views.

This happened also to Sholem Asch. People listed his high creative accomplishments, hailed to heaven his great talent. *Dobrushin himself* [emphasis in text — G.E.] described him as a 'classic Yiddish writer'. At the same time, the speakers voiced their grievances about his nationalist 'deviations' and his statements made in the capacity of a civic activist, and so on.

I have to say that the bitter pills were wrapped in gold leaves: everything was said in a friendly manner and exceedingly politely, without attacking him personally. Some of the speeches, for instance Kushnirov's one, were truly hearty and moving, though a couple of times Kushnirov also did not miss the opportunity to 'throw the truth' into Asch's face — in the way he understood it.

Asch was not in the habit of listening to such speeches of welcome. It was clear that he took much to heart the critical remarks that sounded particularly harsh. Still, everything went peacefully until Litvakov took the floor. By the way, Litvakov was scheduled to be the last speaker before Asch's responding speech.

Litvakov is able to have a dig at someone regardless of whether the person deserves it or not. Yet his criticism, I think, was no sharper than what had been said by the previous speakers.

Nonetheless, according to Boris Smolar, Litvakov's words were sharp enough to make Asch angry. For instance, he said: 'Asch is really a talented writer, but his problem is that he rates his talent even higher than other people do'. The guest of honour's anger turned into rage when Litvakov mentioned Asch's open letter to Piłsudski. Wendroff chronicled this moment in his 'anonymous letter':

> [W]hen Litvakov touched on Asch's letter to Piłsudski and added that in Poland it apparently did not make such a strong impression as it did here, in Soviet Russia, Asch jumped up from his seat, banged his fist on the table and shouted out: 'Either Litvakov stops talking immediately, or I am going to leave this hall!' [. . .]
> I am skipping the details of this unpleasant incident. I'll mention only the following: this could develop into a huge public scandal if the chair [of the reception], Rachmiel Weinstein, and — astonishingly — Litvakov, known for his biting character, did not show restraint.

Boris Smolar also praised Aaron Weinstein, formerly a prominent Bundist (aka Rachmiel) and now one of the leading figures in OZET, who managed to lower the temperature of the conflict. Litvakov decided to discontinue his talk, arguing that he did not want to aggravate further his clash with the guest, but promised that he would use his newspaper to explain his attitude to Asch's writings.

In his concluding remarks, Asch emphasized that he had nothing to do with Communism and did not see any validity in the theory of class struggle. He considered the unity of the Jewish nation as the theoretical foundation for his creative work. He also explained the aim of his Soviet trip:

> Russia did not interest me before the emergence of Jewish colonies. Now,

when you are building a new life on the land, I want to have a look at what is happening here. But, mind you, I am interested in the Jewish life that is being constructed here, and not in the issues of class transformation.

Significantly, colonization was the focus of attention of all *Forverts* writers, including the editor Abraham Cahan.[31]

Hersh Smolar (no relation to Boris Smolar), who soon would be sent to Poland as a Comintern agent, also remembered and described the Asch–Litvakov conflict. In the late 1920s, Smolar periodically took part in meetings of the Central Bureau of the Party's Jewish Sections, headed by Alexander Chemerisky. Among the bureau's members was Maria Frumkin, widely known as 'Comrade Esther', rector of the Comintern's Communist University for the Peoples of the West (Smolar was at that time a student in this university's Yiddish department).

> The Central Bureau had discussed the issue of Sholem Asch twice. First — how to welcome him. Chemerisky and Esther emphasized the semi-official nature of Sholem Asch's visit (Maxim Gorky initiated his invitation) and the imperative of showing tact and even friendship to him, notwithstanding all the ideological problems associated with his writings and our disagreements with his political views. [. . .]
>
> Litvakov got the assignment to treat Sholem Asch in a delicate manner, though the bureau members knew very well that Litvakov felt himself in his element when he had a chance to get even with his ideological opponent or a writer whose work and views were not to his liking. [. . .]
>
> The second meeting of the Central Bureau left an imprint in my memory as the stormiest one. Chemerisky, who was hard of hearing, generally spoke loudly. During that meeting, his attitude to the scandal and possible repercussions found its expression in such a shouting stream of words that everyone prepared to hear him putting a motion to expel Litvakov from the bureau. However, this did not happen. Then Esther spoke and, while she was doing it, Litvakov was a sorry sight.[32]

On 20 May, *Der emes* reported that Asch had left Moscow for a trip to Jewish colonies. The trip lasted a fortnight, during which he visited colonies in Crimea as well as in the Kherson and Krivoy Rog districts of Ukraine. Although it happened to be a bad harvest year in the European south of the Soviet Union, he came back to Moscow carrying a positive impression from what he had seen. The colonists with whom he spoke expressed their satisfaction with their conditions of life under the Soviet government and thanked the state and the foreign sponsors for the help they had provided. Asch promised to inform American Jews that every cent, invested by them into the Soviet projects, had been used for good causes. He expressed the hope that the Jewish colonization would impede assimilation and facilitate the preservation of Yiddish. He also visited several shtetls, where he found Jews who vegetated in misery, unable to find a place for themselves in the new order.[33]

Upon his return to Moscow, Asch spoke about his skirmish with Litvakov:

> I have to make a statement. I am truly very sorry about the incident during the evening reception given by OZET before I left for the colonies [. . .] Partly it had to do with my spirited temper, but in some measure the other part of the conflict precipitated it.[34]

* * * * *

By the end of 10 June Asch departed from Moscow.[35] The first half of the day, which was Sunday, he spent with Gorky. They went together to Red Square (where the memorable photograph was taken) to see a sports parade. The Moscow evening newspaper, *Vecherniaia Moskva*, wrote that Asch was overwhelmed by the event and, yielding to the emotion he felt, said that by the end of his Soviet sojourn he had turned into an 'almost 100-percent communist'.[36]

On his way to Paris Asch made a stop in Warsaw, where he shared his impressions with Israel Joshua Singer. Asch did not forget his conflict with Litvakov and spoke about the Moscow editor as the only person who treated him badly during his Soviet trip. In general, however, he was happy to see the success of Jewish settlements, established and developed with the help of the Joint. The settlers' life remained difficult, but they had roofs above their heads and, though it did not appear as a land of plenty, they did not suffer hunger. At the same time, Asch spotted things that did not sit well with him. He found it disheartening to see the breakdown of the Jewish cultural environment, though many elements of it — most notably the shtetl and synagogues — endured under the new regime. At the same time, he did not believe that hundreds of Yiddish-medium Soviet schools could pose a serious obstacle for assimilation.[37]

In Paris, Asch once again saw Mikhoels and Zuskin — their theatre came to perform in the French capital. In Zuskin's words, he

> declared his love for us, told us that he benefited a lot from his trip to the USSR, that it turned him into our friend, and so on. At his villa outside Paris he arranged a tea party in honour of his 'dear Moscow guests'. [. . .] Apart from us, there were present [Isaac] Babel, [the artist Yisakhar Ber] Rybak, [the sculptor] Naum Aronson [. . .][38]

Both opponents of the Soviet regime and its advocates scoffed at Asch's observations of and comments on Jewish life in the Soviet Union. The communist *Frayhayt* wrote that Asch was a person with two tongues; he used one of them in the Soviet Union and another one when he left the country.[39] Commentators of the opposing camp dismissed his bifurcated vision of the Soviet Jewish establishment as a combination of dogmatic communists, notably Litvakov, and essentially reasonable state functionaries and intellectuals.[40] Still, in the 1920s, many foreign observers believed in the existence of such a dreamed-of Soviet country. In particular, this understanding of Soviet society remained characteristic partly of the coverage by *Forverts*.

Two years after his trip, Asch encountered Lidin, who came to Paris, and invited him to his house in Bellevue, near Paris. To all appearances, this old aristocratic house was the same venue where Asch entertained Mikhoels and Zuskin. Lidin recalled Asch words: 'Oh, Moscow was always hospitable to me [. . .] after Moscow, I feel bored everywhere else.' And by the end of their encounter he told his guest that he hoped to see him 'again, most probably in Moscow [. . .], where he left a part of his heart'.[41] Nonetheless, it did not mean (even if Asch really said these words) that he gravitated to Communism. In 1929, he wrote addressing communists, that:

> [W]e, [western] Jewish writers and artists, form an undisciplined element. The best way to deal with us is to expel us from your ranks, as Moscow has already done. You can see yourselves that this untamed milieu does not produce anything good for you. You will only maim our souls. (Have a look, for instance, at Moscow, at what has happened there with Yiddish literature.)[42]

The year 1929, or — in Stalin's words — 'the year of the great break with the past', introduced radical changes into the relations between Soviet and non-Soviet intellectuals. The new political and ideological picture of the world increasingly lacked half-tints, and rather turned to primary colours or even tended to be only black and white. Against this backdrop, Litvakov revisited the scandal that played out at the tea party on 15 May 1928. In his retrospective description of the event, the Moscow Yiddish literary elite 'tried and condemned Sholem Asch. They unmasked this literary prince of the middle and petite bourgeoisie and declared him a literary bankrupt.'[43] Litvakov's outspoken article ran on 3 July 1929, whereas in the September issue of the Kharkiv-based literary Yiddish journal *Di royte velt* (Red World) the poet Leyb Kvitko categorized Asch as an 'enemy of the working class'.[44] Earlier, at the end of 1928, Itsik Fefer wrote that the time came when, given the 'right-wing danger' posed to the state and the party, it became necessary to re-examine the attitude of Yiddish cultural circles to foreign guests. Thus, he could not understand why a book by the '*Forverts*-nik' Sholem Asch featured in the plans of the Kiev Yiddish publishing house Kultur-Lige.[45] Fefer's criticism took effect and this book disappeared from the plan.

Still, for a couple of years the inertia of the 1920s continued to play some role in Soviet cultural life. In 1930, the Leningrad publishing house Kniga (Book) brought out a Russian translation of the novel *The Rise of David Levinsky* by Abraham Cahan. In the same year, the Moscow publishing house Puchina (Sea's Abyss) issued a Russian translation of Israel Joshua Singer's novel *Shtol un ayzn* (Steel and Iron; in Russian its title was *Iosif Lerner*). In this year, again, the first volume of *Literary Encyclopedia* carried Isaac Nusinov's rather mild article on Asch (Litvakov mentioned that he felt Nusinov's 'mildness' also during the notorious May tea party). According to Nusinov, Asch was 'an artistic ideologist of the nationalist petty bourgeoisie' and therefore he

> for a long time showed a hostile attitude to the October revolution, because its consistent materialism appeared to him dangerous to [. . .] the nationalist and religious foundations of Jewish petty bourgeoisie, and its economic policy he considered detrimental to the well-being of the merchant elements.

However, seeing 'attention of the Soviet government to laborization of the Jewish masses and their settlement on the land', Asch changed his attitude to the Soviet Union and demonstrated it during his 1928 visit.[46]

Meanwhile, various events in Asch's life continued to irritate Soviet ideologists. Thus, in 1930, PEN clubs of France, Great Britain, and Austria celebrated his 50th birthday jubilee, the British and Argentinean PEN clubs elected him an honorary member, while the Yiddish PEN club made him its honorary president in 1932.[47] In an interview to the Viennese newspaper *Neue Freie Presse* Asch spoke about his dream that the International PEN Club would unite 'equal literatures, without any divisions into "big" and "little" cultures'.[48] By contrast, the International Conference of Revolutionary Writers, convened in Kharkiv in November 1930, characterized the International PEN Club as an 'association of prosperous bourgeois writers'.[49] It was particularly hard to make allowances for Asch after his 1931 novel *Moscow*. In the words of Isaac Deutscher, then a Polish communist, this piece of prose attacked 'the revolutionary ideology on behalf of petty bourgeois humanism, which reduced revolution to terror'.[50] The Yiddish literary scholar Max Erik (Zalman Merkin), who moved from Poland to the Soviet Union in the autumn of 1929, considered Asch an exponent of interests of the 'middle bourgeoisie in the period of imperialism and proletarian revolutions', who 'pours out his entire bitterness, his entire toothless fury on the labour movement, on the revolution, on the Bolshevism'.[51] In the Soviet Union, Asch's name became particularly odious in 1932, when the Polish government decorated him with the order of Polonia Restituta. (Elias Tobenkin, an American writer and journalist with a good knowledge of the Soviet Union, wrote in 1933: 'Although the Soviet Union and Poland have been at peace since 1920, it is Poland that, after France, is considered by Russia as the principal enemy'.)[52]

In 1934, during the First Congress of Soviet Writers, Itsik Fefer admitted that Soviet authors 'sometimes produce boring and shallow writings', although — he emphasized — even 'great masters, working in capitalist countries, are unable to surpass us [in quality]. Sholem Asch had relegated himself into the genre of boulevard novels.'[53] Fefer also ridiculed Asch in one of his poetic caricatures, describing him as a lackey of Adolf Hitler.[54] Shmuel Klitenik, who headed *Der emes*'s department of culture, further developed this trope by calling Asch a 'poet of fascism and clericalism'.[55]

* * * * *

Soviet ideologists' attitude to Asch began to improve when Abraham Cahan rejected Asch's 1939 'Christian' novel *The Nazarene* and *Forverts* launched a relentless smear campaign against the writer, accusing him of all mortal literary and ideological sins, including proselytizing. As a result, Asch's writings had disappeared from the *Forverts* pages, though until the summer of 1943 he received his contractual pay. Ultimately, Asch appeared as a 'friend of the Soviet Union' when he agreed to be the president of the Committee of Jewish Writers, Artists and Scientists, which welcomed Solomon Mikhoels and Itsik Fefer as the delegates of the Jewish Antifascist Committee.

In 1942, Asch explained his understanding of Jewish life in the Soviet Union:

> The fact that, despite all the zigzags which the history and world experienced in the recent twenty-four years, the Soviet regime has treated the Jews in such an open and honorable manner, that the Soviet government has showed this attitude to the Jews is, no doubt, a result of the manifested, visible participation of Jews in the Russian revolution. Freedom was not *conferred* on Jews in the Soviet Union, the Jews did not receive it as a *gift*. Rather, they gained it thanks to *their unyielding struggle during and for the sake of the revolution* [emphasis in original — G.E.]. This made anti-Semitism impossible [. . .] It disappeared as a reflection of the new attitude of Soviet peoples [. . .].[56]

Although Asch was unhappy to see Fefer as one of the Soviet delegates, he restrained himself from trying to settle old scores with the author of spiteful pronouncements and poetic lies. Moreover, he even invited the two delegates to his house in Stamford, where Fefer wrote warm lines dedicated to his hospitable colleague.[57] It seems that Asch was able to pass over a grudge. Thus, in the 1940s he actively contributed to *Morgn-Frayhayt* (the new name of *Frayhayt*), although its editor, Paul (Peysekh) Novick, had written many times about Asch's ideological sins.

In 1947, Leyb Kvitko, then chairman of the Moscow Yiddish section at the Soviet Writers' Union, said that 'prominent writer Sholem Asch turned into the most ardent friend of our country and our literature; he also reveals in his own creative works a tendency to give a new meaning to the world'.[58] Soviet ideologists' relatively warm attitude to Asch survived despite his decision to cut all the links with pro-Soviet circles. He did it when he learned about the repressions of Yiddish writers and other intellectuals. Soviet ideologists' warmth towards Asch can be attributed to the fact that he jumped off the pro-Soviet bandwagon at a forgivable juncture (at the end of the day, the Communist Party had officially condemned Stalinist 'excesses') and, significantly, remained even after his death in 1957 a black sheep in many western Yiddish circles. In any case, some decision-makers approved the 1966 publication of a volume of Asch's selected stories, translated into Russian. The book was produced by the Moscow publishing house Khudozhestvennaia literatura (Artistic Literature) with a respectable print run of 50,000. The story, which gave the title to the book, *People and Gods*, portrays two old poor widows, the Jewish one, Golda, and the Polish one, Antoniia, who live together in a little hovel, where 'two gods are flimmering — little Sabbath candles on the table and a little icon-lamp'.[59]

The initiative to publish this book came from Moisei (Moyshe) Belenki, the former director of the Moscow Yiddish publishing house Der emes, which was closed down in 1949, during the full liquidation of the Jewish Antifascist Committee and all remaining Soviet Jewish cultural institutions. In the mid-1950s, Belenki, who returned to Moscow after serving several years in the Gulag, prepared a never-realized programme for publishing over 100 volumes of Russian translations of Jewish literature.[60] In 1962, Belenki submitted a proposal to publish a two-volume edition of Asch's works, but one of the volumes — the long story *America* — finally came out as late as 2008, when the Moscow publishing house Tekst (Text) used the manuscript of a translation made in the 1960s.

Belenki's proposal found the support of two veterans of the Soviet Yiddish cultural world: the philologist and one-time editor-in-chief of the publishing house Der emes Eli Falkovich and the prose writer Joseph Rabin. Falkovich maintained that it would be gainful for Soviet readers to be introduced to the 'solid writer on social themes (*bytopisatel'*), master of [portraying] landscapes, still-lives and genre scenes; realist writer in a romantic wrapping (*oprava*), who fought for the right of people, including those at the bottom of the social scale, to live happily'. Rabin characterized Asch as a person who 'was not always stable in his views, and in politics, too, he was a man of moods'. Rabin also stressed that his literary legacy contained 'many progressive works, which educated ordinary, working people and portrayed their strength, their humanity and their protest against god in heaven and the wealthy on earth'. Rabin recalled that during the 1905 Russian revolution Asch 'was radically disposed' and even 'took the liberty of speaking against circumcision, which invited the rage of reactionaries and philistines'.[61] Thus, Asch's writings, at least some of them, had been qualified for access to the Soviet reader.

Notes to Chapter 5

1. 'Gekumen keyn Moskve Sholem Ash', *Der emes*, 10 May 1928.
2. Evgeniia A. Ivanova, *Chukovskii i Zhabotinskii: istoriia vzaimootnoshenii v tekstakh i kommentariiakh* (Moscow: Mosty kul'tury, 2005), p. 115.
3. These projects are analysed, for instance, in Jonathan L. Dekel-Chen, *Farming the Red Land: Jewish Agricultural Colonization and Local Soviet Power, 1924–1941* (New Haven: Yale University Press, 2005).
4. Shloyme Rosenfeld, *Sholem Ash fun der noent* (Miami: Shoulzon, 1958), p. 75.
5. Vladimir G. Lidin, *Sobranie sochinenii*, III (Moscow: Khudozhestvennaia literatura, 1974), p. 489.
6. Ben Siegel, *The Controversial Sholem Asch: An Introduction to His Fiction* (Bowling Green: Bowling Green University Popular Press, 1976), p. 38–40; Harley Erdman, 'Jewish Anxiety in "Days of Judgement": Community Conflict, Antisemitism, and the *God of Vengeance* Obscenity Case', *Theatre Survey*, 40.1 (1999), 51–74.
7. Shakhno Epshteyn, '"Gots nekome" un undzere naye gots straptshes', *Frayhayt*, 13 January 1925.
8. For a detailed analysis of this interview and its associated events, see Mikhail Agursky and Margarita Shklovskaia, *Iz literaturnogo naslediia: Gorkii i evreiskii vopros* (Jerusalem: Hebrew University, 1986).
9. Aaron Glanz-Leyeles, 'Maksim Gorki un Sholem Ash', *Inzikh*, 5.2 (1936), 61–62 (p. 61).
10. 'Soviet Government Condemned by Cahan', *The New York Times*, 19 November 1927; Gennady Estraikh, 'The *Forverts* Man in Moscow', *Leket: Yiddish Studies Today*, 1 (2012), 509–28 (p. 513).
11. Israel Joshua Singer, *Nay-Rusland* (Vilna: Boris Kletskin, 1928); Hersh David Nomberg, *Mayn rayze iber Rusland* (Warsaw: Kultur-Lige, 1928).
12. *Tribuna evreiskoi sovetskoi obshchestvennosti*, no. 1 (1927), p. 25.
13. Sholem Asch, 'An ofener briv tsu marshal Pilsudski', *Haynt*, 22 October 1926.
14. Viktor E. Kel'ner, *Ocherki po istorii russko-evreiskogo knizhnogo dela vo vtoroi polovine XIX–nachale XX v.* (St Petersburg: National Library of Russia, 2003), p. 225.
15. The volumes that came out: vol. II, *Mot'ka vor* (*Motke the Thief*, 1929); vol. 2, *Diadia Mozes* (*Uncle Moses*, 1929); vol. V, *Put' k sebe* (*The Way to Oneself*, 1930); vol. VII, *Mat'* (*The Mother*, 1929 and 1930) — see *Literatura o evreiakh na russkom iazyke, 1890–1947*, ed. by Viktor E. Kelner and Dmitry A. Elyashevich (St Petersburg: Akademicheskii proekt, 1995), p. 448.
16. 'Vos es hot pasirt mit Sholem Ashn in Moskve', *Forverts*, 5 June 1928. See also Estraikh, 'The *Forverts* Man in Moscow', pp. 509–28.
17. 'Tsu der bagegenish fun Avrom Reyzen', *Der emes*, 30 November 1928; 'Avrom Reyzen gekumen keyn Moskve: di bagegenish afn vokzal', *Der emes*, 8 December 1928.
18. 'Meldung', *Der emes*, 20 March 1924.
19. Moisei Belenki, 'Zhizn' i tvorchestvo Sholoma Asha', in Sholom Ash [Sholem Asch], *Liudi i bogi: izbrannye proizvedeniia* (Moscow: Khudozhestvennaia literatura, 1966), p. 6.
20. Vladislav V. Ivanov, *GOSET: politika i iskusstvo, 1919–1928* (Moscow: GOSET, 2007), pp. 104–06, 149, 376.
21. 'Pervyi den'' tirazha loterei OZET', *Izvestiia*, 13 May 1928; 'Rozygrysh OZET-loterei', *Izvestiia*, 15 May 1928.
22. Y. S-m, 'Der tirazh fun der gezerd-loterey', *Der emes*, 13 May 1928.
23. 'Ver hot gevunen a rayze keyn Amerike', *Der emes*, 18 May 1928; 'A rayze keyn Amerike', *Der emes*, 20 May 1928; 'Di groyse gevinsn in der "gezerd-loterey"', *Der emes*, 6 June 1928.
24. Lidin, *Sobranie sochinenii*, pp. 490–91.
25. Isaac Nusinov, 'Evreiskaia literatura', in *Literaturnaia entsiklopediia*, IV (Moscow: Communist Acedemy, 1930), p. 33.

26. 'Dovid Eynhorn vegn der geshikhte mit Sholem Ash in Moskve', *Forverts*, 23 June 1928.
27. For the welcome received by David Bergelson, see e.g. Gennady Estraikh, *In Harness: Yiddish Writers' Romance with Communism* (Syracuse: Syracuse University Press, 2005), pp. 82–83.
28. Moyshe Litvakov, *In umru* (Moscow: Emes, 1926), p. 27.
29. 'A glezl tey lekoved Sholem Ashn', *Der emes*, 17 May 1928; 'Tsum intsident Litvakov-Sholem Ash', *Haynt*, 27 May 1928.
30. Boris Smolar, 'Der skandal oyfn banket fun Sholem Ashn in Moskve', *Haynt*, 22 May 1928.
31. See e.g. Abraham Cahan, 'Jewish Colonization in Soviet Russia a Success', *Forverts*, 6 November 1927. 'From the mid-1920s on, a visit to the Jewish agricultural colonies in Ukraine and Crimea was practically mandatory for politically conscious Jewish tourists' (Daniel Soyer, 'Back to the Future: American Jews visit the Soviet Union in the 1920s and 1930s', *Jewish Social Studies*, 6.3 (2000), 124–59 (p. 141).
32. Hersh Smolyar, *Fun ineveynik* (Tel Aviv: Y. L. Peretz, 1978), pp. 288–90.
33. 'A shmues mit Sholem Ashn vegn zayn rayze ibern ratnfarband', *Der emes*, 12 June 1928.
34. 'Sholom Ash o evreiskikh koloniiakh v Krymu i na Ukraine', *Tribuna sovetskoi evreiskoi obshchestvennosti*, 11 (1928), 9–12.
35. 'Sholem Ash opgeforn', *Der emes*, 12 May 1928.
36. A. Rubinshteyn, 'Gorki un Sholem Ash', *Sovetish heymland*, 3 (1962), 114; Mikhail Vostryshev, *Moskva stalinskaia: bol'shaia illiustrirovannaia letopis'* (Moscow: Algoritm, 2008), p. 253.
37. G. Kuper [I. J. Singer], 'Vos Sholem Ash dertseylt vegn Sovet-Rusland', *Forverts*, 5 July 1928.
38. Ivanov, *GOSET*, pp. 376–77.
39. 'Ashs tsvey tsinger', *Frayhayt*, 11 July 1928.
40. See e.g. Bentsiyon Katz, 'Sholem Ashs ayndrukn fun Sovet-Rusland', *Haynt*, 1 July 1928.
41. Lidin, *Sobranie sochinenii*, pp. 492–93.
42. Nakhmen Mayzel, 'Der oyfshtand funem kinstler', *Haynt*, 8 November 1929.
43. Moyshe Litvakov, 'A klap in tish un a lek dem shtivl', *Der emes*, 3 July 1929.
44. Leyb Kvitko, 'Derklerung', *Di royte velt*, 9 (1929), 195.
45. Itsik Fefer, 'In atake', *Prolit*, 8–9 (1928), 62–65.
46. Isaa Isaac Nusinov, 'Sholom Ash', in *Literaturnaia entsiklopediia*, 1 (Moscow: Communist Acedemy, 1930), p. 289.
47. John L. De Forest, *My Hours with Sholem Asch* (Stamford: s.n., 1995), p. 106; Roman Roček, *Glanz und Elend des P.E.N.: Biographie eines literarischen Clubs* (Vienna: Böhlau, 2000), p. 89; Rachel Potter, 'Modernist Rights: International PEN 1921–1936', *Critical Quarterly*, 55.2 (2013), 66–80 (p. 74).
48. Sholem Asch, 'Ein Völkerbund des Geistes', *Neue Freie Presse*, 25 June 1928.
49. *Iz istorii mezhdunarodnogo ob"edineniia revoliutsionnykh pisatelei*, ed. by A. N. Dubovikov and others (Moscow: Nauka, 1969), p. 52.
50. Isaac Deutscher, 'Fashizm v evreiskoi literature (tvorchestvo Sholoma Asha)', *Literatura mirovoi revoliutsii*, 7 (1931), 99–1-2 (p. 100); see also Alexander Wat, *My Century: The Odyssey of a Polish Intellectual*, ed. and trans. from the Polish by Richard Lourie (New York: New York Review Books, 1977), 57–58.
51. Max Erik, *Sholem Ash, 1900–1930* (Minsk: Belorussian Acedemy of Sciences, 1931), p. 100.
52. Elias Tobenkin, *Stalin's Ladder: War and Peace in the Soviet Union* (New York: Minton, Balch, & Co., 1933), p. 47.
53. 'Preniia po dokladu A. M. Gor'kogo i sodokladam', *Literaturnaia gazeta*, 22 August 1934.
54. Itsik Fefer, *Fayln af mayln* (Kiev: State Publishing House of the National Minorities of Ukraine, 1935), pp. 165–68.
55. Shmuel Klitenik, *Verk un shrayber: zamlung fun kritishe artiklen* (Moscow: Emes, 1935), pp. 34–61.
56. Nakhmen Mayzel, 'A bagegenish un a shmues mit Sholem Ashn', *Yidishe kultur*, 6 (1942), 11–12.
57. 'Itsik Fefers a lid', in *Pinkes far der forshung fun der yidisher literatur un prese*, ed. by Shlomo Bickel and Hyman B. Bass (New York: Congress for Jewish Culture, 1965), pp. 359–60.
58. 'Dnevnik plenuma', *Literaturnaia gazeta*, 8 July 1947.
59. Sholom Ash [Sholem Asch], *Liudi i bogi: izbrannye proizvedeniia* (Moscow: Khudozhestvennaia literatura, 1966), p. 66.

60. Gennady Estraikh, *Yiddish in the Cold War* (Oxford: Legenda, 2008), p 53.
61. Gennady Estraikh, *Evreiskaia literaturnaia zhizn' Moskvy, 1917–1991* (St Petersburg: European University Publishing House, 2015), pp. 134–35. In fact, Asch wrote about circumcision in 1908 — see e.g. 'Undzer nayer farzorger', *Haynt*, 15 October 1908.

CHAPTER 6

Der Nister's 'Leningrad': A Phantom *fartseykhenung*

Sabine Koller

Zey ruen nit, ot di shotns. Zey lebn umvandlerish und me ken zey, dakht zikh, oft af di dekher zen, fun eyn dakh afn andern umshpatsirn, fun eyn moyer-arayngang tsum andern, un fun di karnizn, frizn, maskes, dakh-vazes, trep un ganikes aropkukn.

[They don't rest, the shadows. They live restlessly, and one can often see them, it seems, on the roofs, strolling from one roof to another, from one entryway to another, and looking down from cornices, friezes, masks, urn finials, stairs, and balconies.]

DER NISTER, *Hoyptshtet* (Leningrad), p. 55

Becoming Capital, Becoming Soviet: Der Nister's *Hoyptshtet* (Capitals)

In 1934, the Kharkiv publishing house Literatur un kunst (Literature and Art), published a collection of literary portraits of Kharkiv, Leningrad, and Moscow under the title *Hoyptshtet* (Capitals) by the Yiddish writer Der Nister (The Hidden One; pen name of Pinkhes Kahanovitsh; 1884–1950).[1] *Moskve* and *Leningrad* were written in 1932; *Kharkov*, the first sketch of the cycle, in 1933, about a year before the capital of the Ukrainian Soviet Socialist Republic was transferred to Kiev. At that time, the former Symbolist author Der Nister earned his living as a journalist, a translator, and an author of books for children.[2] In his reportage *Moskve* (Moscow), he describes an imaginary meeting between the first-person narrator and the German poet Heinrich Heine in the sedulously reconstructed Soviet capital. The narrator promptly apologizes for his audacious account, which might be appropriate in a fantastic tale by Borges, but not in a socialist documentary narrative: 'ikh antshuldik zikh do in klamern far ale yene, vos zeynen kegn yeder fantastik un oystrakhtung-elementn in yeder un bifrat in der fartseykhenung-kunst: kh'hob do af zeyern a gebot oyver geven' (I apologize in parentheses to all those, who are opposed to any fantastic and imaginary elements in every art and especially in the reportage: I have violated here one of their commandments).[3] Nevertheless, the stupefying meeting between two Jewish authors, a living and a dead one, remains part of Der Nister's sketch.[4]

Dead men haunting the streets are not an uncommon appearance in the literature of St Petersburg, the former capital of the Russian Empire, renamed Leningrad in

1924 after Lenin's death. Nikolai Gogol's St Petersburg tale 'Shinel' (The Overcoat, 1842) is a story of a lonely petty bureaucrat Akaki Akakievitch. When his precious overcoat, the only thing in his life he has ever loved, gets stolen, he dies of sorrow only to reappear as a ghost at night. Living dead are a recurring feature in the puzzling and grotesque fiction of the famous city, be it Pushkin's countess in *Pikovaya dama* (The Queen of Spades, 1833), Odoyevsky's carcasses in his Hoffmanian prose cycle *Russkie nochi* (Russian Nights, 1844), or Anna Akhmatova's bohemian revenants in *Poema bez geroia* (Poem without Hero, 1940–62/65). St Petersburg ghosts make occasional appearances in Yiddish literature as well. In *Petersburg* (1929), the first part of Sholem Asch's novel trilogy *Farn mabl* (Before the Flood, translated into English as *Three Cities*, 1929–31), we encounter the following picture:

> Vi sheydim voltn arumgegangen iber di gasn: sheydim-mentshn, sheydim-ferd, mit oysterlishe, yene-veltike oyszeens, mit penemer vi fun khaloymes aroys, mit shotn farshpinte gufim, vi kranke iluzyes [. . .] un men veyst nisht mer, vos es iz a mentsh un vos es iz a shotn. . .[5]

> [Ghosts walked the streets: ghostly horses, ghostly human beings, strange creations of an underworld, with faces such as those seen in dreams, with phantasmal bodies out of some feverish nightmare [. . .] actual body and shadow could no longer be distinguished from one another . . .][6]

What Asch tells us about bourgeois St Petersburg at the turn of the twentieth century re-emerges in Der Nister's *Leningrad*. Ghosts, occasionally of very famous people, walk the streets of the city. Whereas in *Moscow* the ghost of Jewish Heinrich Heine makes a surprising appearance, the narrator of *Leningrad* meets another dead, but rather anti-Jewish, literary celebrity, Fyodor Dostoyevsky.

Der Nister's primary task in *Hoyptshtet* is to give a vivid picture of the three growing socialist cities: the former Imperial Russian capital Petersburg–Petrograd–Leningrad, the present Soviet capital Moscow, and the Ukrainian capital Kharkiv.[7] But there is a secondary, less obvious task he has set for himself: reshaping his literary identity after 1929, the year of the *Great Break*.[8] The publication of the story 'Unter a ployt' (Under a Fence), which became his Symbolist 'swan song', 'caused an ideological upheaval which prevented Der Nister's fiction from being published for the next five years'.[9] *Hoyptshtet*, his first book publication after these five years, became a pivotal moment in Der Nister's struggle for survival. The former Symbolist poet and prose writer tried to transform himself into a Socialist author.

According to the editorial preface to *Hoyptshtet*, Der Nister's three sketches of Kharkiv, Leningrad, and Moscow were among the first Yiddish texts in the genre of *fartseykhenung*.[10] The ambivalent nature of this classic socialist genre in Nister's interpretation is striking. Der Nister invents the Yiddish sketch while subverting its established literary norms. He creates a documentary narrative and carnevalizes it at the same time. He appropriates the officially approved genre using creative devices that were officially stigmatized. Documentary narratives played an important role in the Soviet ideological and literary system. The key feature of the *ocherk* is its artistic ambition of 'writing from nature' (*pisanie s natury*).[11] It aims to give a precise description of typical and characteristic features of a culture or society. Imagination plays here a minor role, giving way to journalistic reflections and scientific insights.

To create a true picture of a social situation, it prefers statistical accuracy to stylistic mastery. The Russian *ocherk* started its career in literature as a journalistic genre in the first half of the nineteenth century as the so-called 'physiological sketch'. The prominent Russian positivist critic Belinsky praised the genre for its ability to reproduce reality in its entire truth. In the Soviet period, Lenin himself chose the *ocherk* genre to educate the masses through 'life-like examples and specimen from all spheres of life'. Since it aims at showing the 'fruitful practice of remodelling reality', the *ocherk* documentary narrative has an enormous 'cognitive-organisational power'. In 1929, Maxim Gorky inaugurated the journal *Nashi dostizhenia* (Our achievements), which entirely consisted of *ocherks*.[12]

Der Nister's triple portrait of the past and present Soviet capitals is a surprising product of literary transformation and Sovietizing self-education. *Hoyptshtet* is a laboratory between facts and fiction in a transition period of a symbolist author trying to become a socialist one. In *Kharkov*, the narrator describes the enthusiastic construction of the new Ukrainian capital as a model for the modern socialist city. In *Leningrad* and *Moscow*, the dark tsarist past interferes with the bright socialist present of the all-embracing proletarian brotherhood. Der Nister's literary portrait of Moscow at the time of the competition of projects for the Palace of the Soviets that was never built dwells primarily on the successful rebuilding of the 'country's heart' and its inhabitants.[13] Be it Moscow under the early tsars, haunted by the rude punishing methods of the Boyars, or the more recent Moscow of 1920, a year of hunger or a 'naked year' as the writer Boris Pilnyak called it, the historical past presents an ideal frame for the dynamic present. After the Great Revolution, Moscow's evolution is so breathtaking that even Pushkin or Gogol (whose monuments Der Nister mentions with derision), themselves victims of the backward spirit of old Russia's cultural order, fail to understand the new Soviet spirit.[14] Western capitalism and its 'ideishe khaos' (spiritual chaos, p. 189) cannot compete with the elevating feelings of the new socialist order based on education of the masses. Der Nister fits the exigencies of a conformist depiction of socialism.[15]

Still, there are clear signs in *Hoyptshtet* that indicate the transitional stage in Der Nister's literary evolution. All three sketches contain striking elements of transgressing norms of socialist realism by phantasy. In *Kharkov*, the narrator imagines himself flying on the newly built government building Gosprom to Kiev. Der Nister's 'shikerer monolog' (pp. 17–44), the monologue of a drunkard, describes this surreal journey recalling Hans Christian Andersen's *The Flying Suitcase*, the Ukrainian folk tale *The Flying Ship*, or, as part of the Utopian visions of avant-garde art, El Lissitzky's *prouns* or Malevitch's *architectones*. In *Moscow*, the Kremlin walls remember the cruel tsarist oppression as if they were human beings. In *Leningrad*, the boundaries between life and death are constantly transgressed.

In the following, I am examining *Leningrad* in the light of the so-called 'St Petersburg text' concept.[16] Vladimir Toporov, a Russian theoretician of the Tartu–Moscow School of Semiotics and a colleague of famous Yuri Lotman, convincingly suggests that the Russian city on the Neva generated a special category of texts. Deeply saturated with intertextual and topographical references, redemptory and at times apocalyptic, they merge into one '*hypertext*' (sverkh-tekst).[17] Der Nister repeatedly refers to basic texts, literary devices, and tropes of that 'St Petersburg text'. Reading *Leningrad*, we become acquainted with the rich tradition of the St Petersburg literature. The aesthetic principles of the Russian classical canon of Pushkin, Gogol, and Dostoyevsky undermine the new normative Soviet form of *ocherk*, which, in turn, has its origins in the so-called Natural School of early Russian realism developed in St Petersburg.[18] Among the first examples of that genre are socially oriented descriptions of the town in the 1845 almanac *Fiziologiya Peterburga* (The Physiology of Petersburg).[19] Both the city and its literary representation have an impact on Der Nister's conceptualization of Leningrad and perhaps on the formation of the *fartseykhenung* genre in Yiddish literature. The city that was the cradle of the Russian Revolution as well as of the *ocherk* genre stimulates Der Nister simultaneously to adapt the genre to Soviet Yiddish literature and to transgress its socialist realist aesthetic norms.

Der Nister's *Leningrad*: Content, Composition, Code

Leningrad is written by a first-person narrator visiting the town for the first time. This narrative voice seems to belong to a journalist who writes a report about Leningrad. His style is sober, with a slight tendency towards using *leitmotifs*, lyrical elements, comparisons, and metaphors.[20] The narrator directly appeals to the reader by focusing on facts and objective description. The sketch is composed of four chapters: *Denkmeler* (Monuments), *Aspektn* (Aspects), *Virklekhkayt* (Reality), and *Vayse nekht* (White Nights). In every chapter, the description of Leningrad is dialectical. The chapter 'Monuments' examines the dialectics of progress versus standstill by opposing the famous monument of Peter the Great, the so-called Bronze Horseman by Maurice-Étienne Falconet, to the monument of the reactionary tsar Alexander III by Paolo Trubetskoi. The chapter further explores the dialectics of socialism versus autocracy through the opposition between the tsarist residence of the Winter Palace and the prison in the Peter and Paul Fortress on the opposite bank of the Neva. 'Aspects', the second chapter, continues in this vein by juxtaposing two historical dates, 1709 and 1917. In 1709, about 40,000 workers from all over Russia were forced by Peter the Great's order to move to the construction site of the new capital. St Petersburg is said to be built on their bones.[21] In 1917, the year of the Great Socialist Revolution, the working class that had once been sacrificed for the tsarist whim of creating a city out of nothing was liberated.

Leningrad is presented as a *museum*. It is an urban body which unites two historical epochs, those of aristocracy and socialism.[22] Der Nister translates these historical dialectics into urban spatial imagery. Having decoded the moribund traits of the autocracy and the life-inspiring ones of the revolution, he leaves the centre of power, the Winter Palace on Uritskii Square,[23] for the Smolny building, a Mecca for every Leninist. The former tsarist Institute for Noble Maidens designed by the Italian architect Giacomo Quarenghi in 1805–09 became the headquarters of the October Revolution, in which 'Khaver Lenin', Comrade Lenin, spent 124 days.[24] The final note in these dialectics of the dark past and the bright future is heroic. The chapter ends with the memory of Lenin as a fervent orator, of faithful communists singing the Internationale, and a soldier weeping for joy like a child.[25]

Suffocated by the illusionary splendour of tsarist Petersburg, the narrator recovers fresh breath in today's *Lenin-shtot*, Lenin's city. In 'Reality', the third and most 'socialist' chapter of the sketch, Der Nister perfectly meets the exigencies of representing Leningrad as the ideal Soviet city. The author who used to explore the Jewish tradition of numerology and *gematria* in his symbolist writings now soberly describes the growth of the city and its industry using the habitual socialist Newspeak and statistics. Leningrad is presented as an anti-Babel, as a place where there is no division into different national and linguistic entities, and which all brotherly socialist peoples can call their home. Insurrection Square and the adjacent October Station (today Moscow Station) are depicted as the ideal Leningrad representations of the socialist myth. The station is the multiethnic Soviet state's entrance gate to the city. Gypsies, Jews, Mongols — everybody finds their home in this socialist paradise of brotherhood and development. The narrator visits Soviet factories and the famous dockyard and describes enthusiastically Leningrad's overfulfilment of the Five Year Plan. The Leningrad workers are characterized by their insatiable thirst for education, by their will to overcoming their national roots (Der Nister uses the term *race*), in order to achieve a political-ideological rebirth as socialist working *class*.

To complete the picture of the new society in Leningrad, Der Nister employs another cliché of socialist dialectics. In a tram, he admires a Stakhanovite shock worker studying mathematics after work. The ideal representative of the Soviet 'new man' displaces an old monk who symbolizes the old order. Atheism and faith in science defeat religion and prayers about Abraham or Daniel in the Lion's Den.[26] Religion is all but forgotten: a young boy does not even know what a monk is, and does not follow any religious code in his behaviour. The worker, on the contrary, is sacralized. Der Nister endows him with a halo, one of the most fantastic images in the text bordering on socialist kitsch.[27]

The title of the final chapter, 'White Nights', perfectly prefigures the ambivalence of its content. It refers to the time of the year in June and July when it hardly gets dark in St Petersburg. In 1848, Dostoevsky published his sentimental novel *Belye nochi* (White Nights), subtitled *Iz vospominanii mechtatelia* (From the Recollections of a Dreamer). Der Nister shifts his point of view and contrasts dreamlike fiction and reality. Documentary journalism turns into literary criticism on behalf of socialism. The chapter evolves into the settling of scores with Dostoevsky and his critical parody of the socialist movement in his novel *Besy* (The Demons, 1871).[28] Der Nister accuses Dostoevsky of becoming a henchman of tsarist autocracy and a follower of the reactionary thinker Konstantin Pobedonostsev, the head of the Holy Synod from 1880 to 1905 and one of the most influential political figures in the Russian Empire of that time. By misinterpreting the creative energy of the future-oriented socialist movement, Dostoevsky betrayed his own genius and deceived his young avid reader Der Nister. Eventually, Der Nister argues, history triumphed over Dostoevsky's anti-socialist literary vision.[29] Dostoevsky's idea of power turns out to be a relic of the past.[30] The Peter and Paul Fortress where Dostoevsky was imprisoned in 1848 awaiting a death sentence as a member of a pro-socialist circle is now a museum. The perverse inversion of the revolutionary ideal of freedom by the grotesque character of the novel, who wanted to establish a world-wide dictatorship of slavery through ignorance, is debunked by a group of young komsomol members from Uzbekistan visiting the Hermitage. Der Nister explains how diligently they acquaint themselves with world culture by studying Leonardo da Vinci's *Madonna and Child*.³¹ The Italian Renaissance masterpiece contributes to the rebirth of these 'barbarian people' through education.

Of course, the dialectical structure of *Leningrad* is a tribute to ideology and its dialectical materialism. But it is also a result of the antithetical character of the city itself, its division into two entities: St Petersburg and Leningrad. This 'split personality' allows Der Nister to introduce literary devices which open the documentary narrative up to a magic realism. As a result, Der Nister's *Leningrad* constantly oscillates between text and topography. The Russian-American poet Joseph Brodsky identifies St Petersburg as the place of origin and the nucleus of Russian literature: 'There is no other place in Russia where thoughts depart so willingly from reality: it is with the emergence of St. Petersburg that Russian literature came into existence.'³² The *genius loci* of St Petersburg strongly stimulates Der Nister's imagery. The surface of Der Nister's hyperrealistic, at times didactic, at times pathetic Soviet model *fartseykhenung* is blurred by strange perturbations of reality. Alongside realistic depictions of the city, fantastic visions of dead men or hypostasies of the man of the future appear in the text. Fantastic elements, quotations, and literary devices reveal that Der Nister's perception of the city is double-edged. On the one hand, it is oriented towards the city, its architectural language and urban landscape. On the other hand, Der Nister's *Leningrad* engages in a constant dialogue with St Petersburg literature. Its main features are intertextuality, complex intercultural coding, and a fantastic-illusionary, surreal, sometimes apocalyptic quality.

Flying workers, hovering revolutionaries: Intertextuality and Irreality in *Leningrad*

From the very beginning, myths and legends accompany the mystery and mirage that St Petersburg has always been. A vivid oral culture preserved the hopes and fears of a city that arose from the genius mind of Peter the Great. Some perceived him as a godlike creator, others, like the Russian Old Believers, as Anti-Christ. They put a spell on the town: 'Peterburgu byt' pustu' (May St Petersburg be waste) which goes back to Jeremiah's foreseeing the end of Babylon (Jer. 51. 42f.).³³ Der Nister is aware of these ardent fights between believers and non-believers in Peter the Great's demiurgic reinvention of Russia and quotes the spell using 'Petrograd', the city's name from 1914 to 1924.³⁴ Der Nister strongly supports Peter's modernizing project by referring to Pushkin and the panegyric opening of his poem *Medny vsadnik* (The Bronze Horseman, 1834), a literary double of Falconet's monument mentioned before. Der Nister ignores the critical ambivalence in Pushkin's poem regarding Peter the Great. He needs Pushkin's positive panegyrical *laus urbis* (praise of a city), not the critical and uncanny story that unfolds later in his poem. Der Nister depicts Peter the Great as the incarnation of a strong-willed ruler, as a modernizer and ideal precursor of the heroic socialist leaders, contrasting him with Alexander III as a mere caricature of power. Der Nister juxtaposes monuments of the two tsars. *Leningrad* opens with a depiction of the ugly and unshapely monument of Alexander III, which in the vernacular is called *begemot* (hippopotamus) or *pugalo* (scarecrow).[35] When Der Nister arrived in Leningrad, the statue stood on the Znamenskaia Place (today's Insurrection Square) in front of the October Station.[36] The narrative then shifts to the heroic representation of Peter the Great by Falconet. While Falconet's monument inspired Pushkin's masterpiece, the scarecrow Alexander III merely served as an occasion for a satire by the Soviet proletarian poet Demyan Bedny.[37]

Accidental encounters in the street are an important motif in the St Petersburg text. They form the fabric of Dostoevsky's novel *Crime and Punishment* (1865–66). In *Leningrad*, the narrator meets both dead and living people in the streets of the city. These encounters enable Der Nister to include fantastic uncanny elements in his sketches. As in his earlier symbolist stories, these accidental encounters break up the realistic flow of narration by introducing another dimension of reality. All these literary visions are politically correct from the Soviet point of view. One night the narrator meets a 'red person', an image of socialist uprising, or a strange figure which might have sprung straight out of Andrey Bely's symbolist novel *Petersburg* (1913–14/1922). This fantastic figure evokes the atmosphere of death, bringing to mind the line from Osip Mandelstam's 1916 poem, *V Petropole prozrachnom my umrem* (We shall die in the translucent Petropolis). This episode makes the narrator evoke the sense of the *umheymlikhkayt* (uncanniness) and *toyte eynzamkayt* (dead loneliness; p. 52) of tsarist Petersburg.

Encounters with the dead enable the narrator to see the pain and tragedies caused by the tsarist regime. In the street next to the Winter Palace, he points to a building on the opposite side of the Neva, the Trubetzkoy Bastion prison for political prisoners in Peter and Paul Fortress, where at different times were detained literary celebrities and political activists, such as Dostoevsky, Maxim Gorky, and Leon Trotsky.[38] One of its inmates, the Russian revolutionary Maria Fedosyevna Vetrova (1870–97), burnt herself in this prison in protest against the inhuman conditions in tsarist jails.[39]

A friend of the author, formerly an architect and now a theatre director, proposes a guided tour through Leningrad. He demonstrates to Der Nister the astonishing architectural harmony of the Admiralty, one of the first buildings in Peter's town. Leningrad/St Petersburg appears as a stronghold of beauty. The way in which the two *flâneurs* discover and appreciate the town is reminiscent of Konstantin Batyushkov's essay *Progulka v Akademiyu khudozhestv* (A Stroll to the Academy of Arts, 1814).[40] Like Batyushkov, Der Nister's excitement about the town is overwhelming. But left by himself, the narrator counterbalances the seduction by imperial St Petersburg with his tours through revolutionary Leningrad and visits of the sites related to the Great October Revolution, such as the building of the Duma, the first parliament, founded in 1905. This revolutionary wandering route brings him to the émigré philosopher Alexander Herzen.[41] In Herzen's view, St Petersburg was the city of despotism and suppression, but at the same time it harboured a certain revolutionary potential.[42] This is Der Nister's message as well, with a heroic tinge of socialist propaganda.

St Petersburg/Leningrad provides Der Nister's reportage with literary shadows. Gogol makes an appearance, quoting his tale *Nevsky Prospect* (1831–34) and revealing the essence of St Petersburg and its text: 'My God! What is our life! An eternal battle between dream and reality!'[43] Wandering between dream and reality through the city and encountering authors and characters from famous St Petersburg texts, Der Nister nevertheless remains in control of the political correctness of his imagination. Be it Gogol's 'little man', a prostitute reminiscent of Dostoevsky's Sonya in *Crime and Punishment* or his 'man from the underground', or the critic Vissarion Belinsky, the poets Nikolai Nekrasov or Alexander Blok (the only symbolist author in the sketch) — every intertextual allusion remains within the confines of the officially approved Soviet interpretation of these authors.

Der Nister refrains from using any of the metaphysical or religious allusions with which Dostoevsky's and Gogol's works are replete. Writing in 1932, he had good reasons to do so. He evokes the aesthetic legacy of his predecessors, not their religious-philosophical ideas. It is therefore hardly surprising that one of the phantoms that make an appearance at the end of Der Nister's *fartseykhenung* is a Rasputin-like caricature of an Orthodox monk. Indeed, after Rasputin was murdered in 1916, there were rumours that he was still alive, which makes him a fitting figure for the St Petersburg mythology of the 'undead dead'. Since Leningrad chose socialism over the 'opium for the masses', the phantom monk, an outdated relic of the bygone era, turns his back on the city and disappears at the end of Der Nister's sketch. His rival, an oversized image of the proletarian worker studying mathematics after work, hovers high above the heads of the living on his way back from the Smolny to the city centre. This harbinger of the bright socialist future will find fulfilment not in eternity, as promised by religion, but in infinity. The worker is fascinated by the mathematical miracle that 1 divided by 0 equals infinity.[44] Der Nister 'paints' him into the sky above Leningrad like Jesus in the Ascension.

The ideological battle is resolved in favour of socialism and the Revolution: the monk leaves, the worker remains. At the fantastic end of *Leningrad*, Dostoevsky's spectre returns to the 'grave' of his 'museum apartment' on Yamskaya Street (today Dostoevsky Street). The narrator remains with Dmitry Karakozov, the moving spirit of the revolutionary cause. Since his revelation to the Hidden One in the hotel Znamenskoe on the eponymous square, the revolutionary assassin has been accompanying the narrator. Der Nister witnesses the ideological duel between Karakozov and his opponent Dostoevsky. In 1866, Karakozov failed to kill Tsar Alexander II, to whom Dostoevsky, by then a reactionary author boldly promoting Russian messianism and autocracy, was close.[45] Der Nister's description of the ascension of the proletarian worker and of Dostoevsky's 'descent into hell' (i.e. his own apartment) is a hidden statement about himself: he has chosen the revolutionary man of action over the reactionary man of thought.

Literary Metamorphosis after the Great Break

At a book presentation of *Hoyptshtet* in Kharkiv in 1935, Der Nister told the audience about 'the daunting challenge of "liberating himself" from his previous literary style'.[46] Der Nister characterized his panoramic documentary narratives about Kharkiv, Leningrad, and Moscow as 'an already accomplished stage in the process of his artistic development, aimed at understanding of the "Great Epoch"'.[47] So far the official Pinkhes Kahanovitsh. The unofficial one expresses himself in an often-quoted letter to his brother, the artist and art-dealer Max (Motl) Kaganovitch, in 1934, the year when *Hoyptshtet* appeared:

> Simbolizm hot in ratnfarband keyn ort nit. Un ikh, vi dir iz bavust, bin fun ale yorn a simbolist — ibergeyn fun simbolizm tsu realizm iz far a mentshn, vi ikh, velkher hot a sakh gehorevet af tsu farfolkomnen zayn metod un oyfn fun shraybn — zeyer shver. Dos iz nisht keyn frage fun tekhnik, do muz men vi af s'nay geboyrn vern, do muz men iberkern di neshome af di andere zayt.
>
> [There is no place for symbolism in the Soviet Union. And I, as you know, have for all these years been a symbolist. To switch from symbolism to realism for someone like me, who has worked so hard to perfect his method and style of writing, is very difficult. This is not a question of technique, for this one has to be born anew, one has to turn his soul inside out.][48]

Der Nister's official confession is also a result of his trying his hand at the genre *fartseykhenung*. In fact, Der Nister then turned his soul inside out in his sketches. After 1929, when he was no longer able to publish fictional texts, Der Nister faced enormous inner and external pressures while reinventing himself as a Soviet Yiddish writer. He was exposed to difficult and destructive mechanisms of censorship and self-censorship, of conformity and non-conformity (cf. the case of Mandelstam who wrote both a pungent epigram on and an ode to Stalin). The fact that his sketches are documentary and fantastic at the same time, i.e. the strange kind of fantastic realism they display, is a product of the schizophrenic state of existence under Stalin's regime. Der Nister's *fartseykhenungen* were a serious attempt at a creative and ideological metamorphosis in order to overcome Symbolism. Nevertheless, they were harshly criticized. Already the editors' brief introduction did not fail to point out the deficiencies and mistakes of Der Nister's sketches 'that show that the comrade Nister has to work harder on himself in order to master Marxist-Leninist ideology'.[49]

In Der Nister's *Leningrad*, the gigantic proletarian personifies the so-called 'Great Epoch'. His splendour outshines the shadows that were cast on that epoch: the *Great Break* of 1929 and the *Great Purges* of the 1930s. In 1929 the cultural revolution was instituted from above. It 'marked the watershed between the period of relative stylistic and thematic freedom and the new year of the ideological dictate in Yiddish literature'.[50] In 1929, Der Nister's symbolist period ended. After severe attacks on his obscure, multi-layered writings, branded as *nisterizm*, Der Nister was forced to align his literary productions with socialist aesthetic doctrines. As a result, the allegorical-symbolist system 'that formed the core of his aesthetic beliefs before 1929' disintegrated.[51]

From 1929 on, deviant literary movements and authors like the Russians Boris Pilnyak, Mikhail Zoshchenko, Anna Akhmatova, Osip Mandelstam or the Yiddish literati Leyb Kvitko, Dovid Hofshteyn, or Lipe Reznik were severely attacked, censored, and repressed. In the 1931 VOAPP's (All-Soviet union of Associations of Proletarian Writers) resolution Yiddish proletarian writers were praised for unmasking the reactionary, nationalist essence of works by Itsik Kipnis, Lipe Reznik, Shmuel Halpern, and Der Nister.[52] In 1932, while Der Nister was writing his urban sketches, the Central Committee's resolution 'dissolved existing artists' associations and replaced them by centralised organisations'.[53] Consequently, literary criticism controlled literary production.[54] Parallel to the events on the Russian-Soviet literary stage, by 1934 socialist realism became the one and only official aesthetic doctrine.

Der Nister's sketches *Hoyptshtet* are, of course, a largely technical work.[55] They were written at a turning point of the author's literary career,[56] when he had to earn his living and to find literary means of co-existing with the new Soviet reality. He attempted his rebirth as a writer of journalism. The 'neo-mystic', as Shmuel Niger characterized him, had to toil in the Socialist 'vort-fabrik' (factory of words).[57] He did so after having lost his aesthetic and ideational reference system, which originated in symbolism, mystical allegory and a modernist paraphrasing of the traditional Jewish style of interpretation known as *Pardes*.[58] After Der Nister's hermetic literary pieces, be it symbolist poetry, symbolist prose with its complex embedded plot structures or enigmatic animal tales, he switched to literary journalism. Instead of creating a sophisticated narrative point of view with puzzling metamorphoses and mimicry, he opted for a voice which guides the reader through a new reality. After having written highly aestheticized and anti-mimetic texts, he chose a genre where referentiality to the world outside the text and its realistic, mimetic representation prevail. From the heights of allegoric storytelling in the footsteps of the Hasidic master Nakhmen Braslaver he turned to the nether realism of socialist documentary literature. Yet his sketches are the only texts narrated in the first person between his last symbolist story *Unter a Ployt* (Under a Fence, 1929) and the realist historical novel *Di Mishpokhe Mashber* (The Family Mashber, 1939–47). In contrast to his translations, Der Nister can at least in them raise his own voice as a domesticated narrator of an *ocherk*.

Der Nister carefully observed the rules of Soviet political correctness of that time and operated within the framework of the genre. He left the ivory tower of symbolism: no mysticism, no Aesopian language, no folklore stylization (*folkstimlekhkayt*). Not a word in *Leningrad* about Vyacheslav Ivanov's tower and its famous Wednesdays symbolist gatherings, not a word about the blossoming of Russian modernism at the turn of the twentieth century, not a word about Dmitry Merezhkovsky or Osip Mandelstam. Der Nister did not mention by a single word Jewish and Yiddish cultural activities in St Petersburg, such as Granovsky's theatre studio, S. An-sky and the Jewish Historical-Ethnographic Society, or Jewish relief agencies.[59] Not a word about Zakhari Mirkin, the hero of Sholem Asch's *Peterburg*, or the journal *Voskhod* (Sunrise). In the chapter 'White Nights' Der Nister writes nothing about religious concerns that St Petersburg is no place for Jews since it is impossible to start and finish Sabbath when the sun does not set, which are reported by Saul Ginzburg in his memoir *Amolike Peterburg* (St Petersburg in the Old Days).[60] The only Jewish presence in *Leningrad* is provided by two Jews at the railway station and the episode with a worker who — in a happy multi-ethnic homeland — is successfully transformed from an uneducated Jew into a cosmopolitan, Russian-speaking proletarian.[61] Thus, Der Nister dutifully fulfilled the requirements of *klassovost'* (class consciousness) prevailing at that time. The time of *narodnost'* (national consciousness) had not yet come. It was to start around 1935 and would mean an important ideological shift towards Jewishness in *Di mishpokhe Mashber*.[62] Yet at no point in his sketches does Der Nister criticize *yidishkayt*, either Jewish culture in the secular sense or religious Judaism. He ridicules the orthodox priest, not the rabbi.

But what about the torments of a symbolist writer trying to overcome the old literary system of symbolism and the new one of socialist realism at the same time? What about the ambivalences between what is ideologically correct, but aesthetically not attractive, and what is aesthetically attractive, but ideologically not correct? In Der Nister's case, this is not a mere question of taste. It arises from the need to survive in a double sense: within the system, dominated by imposed outside constraints, and within his literary self, dominated by his internal demands.

A Wanderer in Aesthetics

In *Hoyptshtet* in general, and especially in *Leningrad*, I suggest we differentiate between two conflicting ideological-philosophical and aesthetic forces: *wandering versus building*. In all three sketches, the first-person narrator admires the achievements of socialism which consist of building a new multi-ethnic state, a new class system, a new economics with socialist production methods, and a new man.[63] The new order is depicted with biblical pathos: 'loyt undzere binyomin vet undz di geshikhte mishpetn' (History will measure us by our buildings; p. 5), echoing Matthew 7. 16: 'Ye shall know them by their fruits!'. In the first of the three sketches, Der Nister stresses the proximity of building and social transformation, of material and spiritual *boy* (building), of constructing and reshaping a society and its members. The construction of a new world and its inhabitants cannot be separated.[64] Der Nister has valid ideological and etymological reasons for his approach: In Yiddish as in Russian 'to build' and to 'transform the existing order' have the same root: 'boyen' and 'iber-boyen' ('um-boyen') or 'stroit' and 'pere-stroit' (hence Gorbachev's famous formula *perestroika*).[65]

The editors of *Hoyptsthet* extend the concept of *iberboy* to the author himself: 'Eyns kon men ober shoyn zikher zogn, az ot di "fartseykhenungen" zaynen gevis a vikhtiker trit foroys in Nisters sheferishn iberboy' (Yet one thing can be said with certainty, that these 'sketches' are surely an important step forward in Nister's creative transformation).[66] But does Der Nister meet these expectations? The first-person narrator of *Hoyptshtet* observes various forms of socialist building, construction, shaping, remodelling of people and the society, and describes the material, mental, and moral *iberboy*, but he himself does not take part in it. To narrate means to keep a distance. Der Nister's narrator comes and sees — to use his own reference to

The Song of Songs (3. 11) in *Leningrad*[67] — in order to go on wandering. In *Kharkov*, he characterizes himself as a 'nakht-vandler' (somnambulist), a 'halb-shikerer un troymer' (half-drunkard and dreamer),[68] very much like Dostoevsky's protagonist in *White Nights*. As he strolls around the city in *Leningrad*, he confesses: 'Fremd, kh'blondzh on a veg, on a plan' (A stranger, I wander around aimlessly and without a plan).[69] During his perambulations, the narrator admires the process and the result of the big socialist project and has uncanny encounters at the same time. Wandering around the city, he opens up the socialist *fartseykhenung* genre to fantastic elements, adding a phantom dimension to it. All these techniques can be described using the Bakhtinian terms *chronotope*, *polyphony*, and *carnivalization*.[70] The narrator's walk through the town turns into a journey through the historical chronotope of St Petersburg and the Revolution. Using elements of polyphonic montage technique, Der Nister inserts different voices into his reportage. He combines voices glorifying the revolution, such as Lenin and Stalin, or excerpts from *Ten Days that Shook the World* by the American communist John Reed,[71] along with voices from the noble literary past, such as Gogol and Dostoevsky.

Like Raskolnikov in *Crime and Punishment* or Golyadkin in *The Double* (Dvoynik, 1846) by Dostoevsky, Der Nister's narrator is accompanied by a visible or invisible double as he walks the streets of St Petersburg/Leningrad. Thanks to these encounters, the narrator becomes a wanderer between revolution and literature, between reality and fiction, between this world and the world to come. It is the act of wandering that enables him to *carnivalize* the genre. As a *flâneur* in Leningrad, he discovers in the St Petersburg texts what is *politically not correct*, but forms an essential part of the St Petersburg tradition in Russian literature — and an integral part of his own poetics: a blurring of reality and fantasy, of materiality and spirituality, of things uncovered ('nistar') and revealed ('nigle'). In these aesthetic rambles of the 'professional pilgrim' (after all, the narrator is a journalist on a business trip, cf. p. 93), Der Nister undermines the socialist *ocherk* by perceiving and depicting the world that goes beyond ordinary logic and destabilizes the new order. Der Nister's first-person narrator is a wanderer in disguise, a socialist version of the modern *flâneur* that Walter Benjamin described in detail, and an echo of the wandering *tsadik* (rabbi) of Hasidic stories.[72]

In *Hoyptshtet*, Der Nister is wandering through the textual world which is violently reduced to ideological, non-aesthetic, and non-literary functions, to mono-semantic content, to a simplistic rhetoric and socialist clichés. By masking himself as a socialist author, he turns the genre into a phantom, while by masking the genre as ideologically correct, he turns himself into a phantom. But inventing, together with other writers, the *fartseykhenung* genre in Yiddish literature, he successfully reinvents himself as a storyteller, albeit for the time being only within the factual narration of *Hoyptshtet*. Within this genre pertaining to the Procrustean system of Soviet literature, Der Nister, in *Leningrad*, meets spectral Dostoevsky and Gogol, and, with them, a fabulous imagination that overcomes the confines of time and space, of life and death, and of socialist realism.

After *Hoyptshtet*

After *Hoyptshtet*, the way to an ideologically accepted fiction was open. On the one hand, this became possible thanks to the changes in the ideological system of Soviet literary production during the mid-1930s. Historical themes 'were not deemed escapist anymore. Rather, they were welcomed as works that helped illuminate the "genealogy of the revolution".'[73] On the other hand, this was also the result of Der Nister's efforts with inventing different literary masks.[74] In *Hoyptshtet*, he offers an almost magic reading of time in space: the Kremlin wall in *Moskve*, for instance, functions as a gate into a dreamlike chronotope. His topographical wandering around mirrors his inner search for a new aesthetics. The result is Der Nister's breakthrough with *Di mishpokhe Mashber* (1939) where his symbolist and his realist conception of literature merge.

With his magnum opus, Der Nister shifts from the capital cities to the peripheral space. The novel takes place at Berdytshev, a Hasidic centre in Volhynia, even though Der Nister does not mention the town by name, and moves in time from the heroic post-revolutionary present to the Jewish pre-revolutionary past, and from the literature of facts to epic fiction. In *The Family Mashber*, Der Nister quietly shifts from socialist realism to 'kinstlerishn realism' (creative realism), as he states in his introduction.[75]

After the forced wandering through various aesthetic modes and contemporary socialist reality, class-oriented *Hoyptshtet* laid the ground for Der Nister's rebirth as an author and return to the Jewish cause and to Jewish narratology in *The Family Mashber*. What at first sight might seem incompatible reveals hidden links. Be it Kharkiv, Leningrad, or Moscow, these capitals are perceived and evaluated in a Gogolian manner. The setting of *The Family Mashber*, a town named 'N.', refers directly to Gogol's *Dead Souls*. Dostoevsky, a St Petersburg author *par excellence* and a spectral shadow in *Leningrad*, is present in *The Family Mashber* as an important source of inspiration for the depiction of scandals, coincidental encounters, psychological states of holy excitement or epilepsy, debates about doubt and faith. The stranger and wanderer of the *fartseykhenungen* is transfigured into the stranger figure of his late epic.[76] However, in *Hoyptshtet*, Der Nister describes his wandering *within* Stalin's megalomaniac and teleological construction of the Soviet Union. With *The Family Mashber*, he designs a literary Jewish space *beyond* Stalinist rebuilding. *The Family Mashber* is a book about the decay of Moshe Mashber, but, first of all, it is a book about the spiritual evolution and elevation of his brother Luzi, a very Nisterian version of the wandering Hasidic *tsadik*. The *wanderer motif* is the link that connects his early symbolist tales, his sketches of the socialist capitals, and his last novel masterpiece. According to the Yiddish critic Shmuel Niger, Der Nister was able 'to adjust to the new goals, but not to the new means' (tsupasn zikh tsu naye tsiln, ober nit tsu naye mitlen).[77] After examining *Hoyptshtet* as a turning point of Der Nister's literary evolution and in the light of *The Family Mashber*, I would put this statement the other way round: Der Nister was able to adjust to the new means, but not to the new goals. Wandering was and remains the key model of spiritual and ethical evolution which Der Nister cherished more than any revolution, including the socialist one. Strange as it may sound, Sruli and Luzi, the two pilgrims in the footsteps of Rabbi Nakhmen, continue Der Nister's own wanderings through the capitals, with one decisive difference. After his difficult socialist mimicry and eye to eye with the impending Nazi and Stalinist destruction, Der Nister's wanderers move on with the Jewish God in their heart. This implies redemption and a quest for the divine that transcends the historical time and ontological space on a way 'far velkhn di himl- un erd-randn zaynen far zey keylekhik anplekt un tseefnt . . .' (whose borders, heaven and earth, appear to them round uncovered and unfolded . . .).[78]

Notes to Chapter 6

1. The volume includes *Tsum tog* (To the Day), a cycle of shorter reportages about Jewish settlement in the Crimea (*Shnit/Harvest*, *A nokht mit a tog/A Night and a Day*, *Eyns a shtetl/A Shtetl*). For a discussion of Der Nister's treatment of architecture in *Hoyptshet* see Mikhail Krutikov's article in this volume. Harriet Murav deals with the complex visions of time in essays by Bergelson and Der Nister related to Moscow.
2. See *Uncovering the Hidden: The Works and Life of Der Nister*, ed. by Gennady Estraikh, Kerstin Hoge, and Mikhail Krutikov (London: Legenda, 2014).
3. Der Nister, *Hoyptshtet. Fartseykhenungen* (Kharkov: Literatur un kunst, 1934), p. 194. All subsequent quotes follow this edition. Translations are my own unless otherwise stated. My thanks go to Petra Huber and Holger Nath for helping me to translate this essay into English.
4. The Yiddish term *fartseykhenung* comes from Russian *ocherk*, a popular genre in Russian literature and journalism in the late nineteenth-twentieth century which can be approximately translated into English as 'sketch' or 'reportage'.
5. Sholem Asch, *Peterburg. Ershter bukh fun 'Farn mabl'. Roman* (Buenos Aires: Tsentral-farband fun poylishe yidn in Argentine, 1949), p. 321.
6. Sholem Asch, *Three Cities*, trans. by Willa and Edwin Muir (New York: Carroll & Graf, 1983), p. 242.
7. According to the editors, the aim of the reportages is to show the socialist reconstruction of some of the big cities in the Soviet Union (Der Nister, *Hoyptshtet*, p. 3).
8. See *Mapping the Jewish World. 1929*, ed. by Hasia R. Diner and Gennady Estraikh (New York: New York University Press, 2013).
9. Mikhail Krutikov, 'Desire, Destiny, and Death: Fantasy and Reality in Soviet Yiddish Literature around 1929', in *Mapping the Jewish World. 1929*, pp. 217–33 (p. 218). *Unter a ployt* first appeared in the Kharkov-based literary monthly journal *Di Royte Velt* (*The Red World*) and was also included in the collection *Gedakht*.
10. Der Nister, *Hoyptshtet*, p. 3. See also Moyshe Zilbertsvayg, 'Hoypt-dates in lebn un shafn fun dem Nister', in *IKUF-Almanakh 1967*, ed. by Nakhman Mayzl (New York: IKUF, 1967), pp. 347–51 (p. 349).
11. *Literaturnaia entsiklopediia v 11-i tomakh*, VIII (Moscow: izdatelstvo Kommunisticheskoi akademii, Sovietskaia entsiklopediia 1929–39, 1934), cols 381–88.
12. Ibid. Apart from Belinsky, the classic prose writers Vladimir Korolenko and Aleksandr Kuprin or the Soviet writers Marietta Shaginian and the better-known Dimitri Furmanov excelled in writing documentary narratives. For Soviet travelogues to the West see Evgenij Ponomarev, *Sovetski putevoi ocherk 1920–1930-ch godov. 'Puteshevstvie na zapad' v literature mezhvoennogo perioda*, 2nd edn (St Petersburg: Izdatelstvo SPbGUKI, 2013).
13. *Hoyptshtet*, p. 145.
14. The narrator, witness of the new socialist order, stands face to face to Nikolai Andreevich Andreev's monument of Gogol from 1909. In 1932/36, the monument has been removed from Gogol Boulevard into an inner court because of its pessimistic, mystic expression and replaced with a new monument by Nikolai Vasil'evich Tomski; see Vladimir Paperny, *Kultura dva* (Moscow: Novoe Literaturnoe Obozrenie, 1996), pp. 167–69.
15. Der Nister had returned from Berlin and Hamburg in 1925. In 1928, he settled in Kharkov

'following a stint in Kiev as an editor at the Kultur-Lige publishing house'; Gennady Estraikh, 'Der Nister's "Hamburg Score"', in *Uncovering the Hidden*, pp. 7–26 (p. 17). Hence the detailed comparison between Moscow and Hamburg in the sketch about the Russian capital and his eye-witnessing of Kharkov's (re-)construction as a socialist 'model city'.

16. For a documentary and photographic survey of the town of that time see *Vremya nesbyvshikhsia nadezhd: Petrograd-Leningrad. 1920–1930*, ed. by Vladimir Nikitin (St Petersburg, Limbus-Press [u.a.], 2007), and Alexander Chistiakov, *Petrograd–Leningrad. 1920–1930 gody v fotografiach i dokumentakh* (St Petersburg: Liki Rossii, 2010).
17. See Vladimir N. Toporov, 'Peterburgskii tekst russkoi literatury'. *Izbrannye trudy* (St Petersburg: Iskusstvo-SPb, 2003), esp. pp. 7–118. A precursor of Toporov's theory is the long-prohibited study *Dusha Peterburga* (The Soul of Petersburg) written in the early 1920s by the Russian scholar Nikolai Antsiferov, who developed a special methodology of excursions through the city. It was published after the breakdown of the Soviet Union in 1991 under the title *Nepostizhimyi gorod . . . Dusha Peterburga* (Leningrad: Lenizdat).
18. Renate Lachmann, *Erzählte Phantastik. Zu Phantasiegeschichte und Semantik phantastischer Texte* (Frankfurt am Main: Suhrkamp, 2002), p. 243.
19. The title refers to the literary tradition of the French *physiologies*, cf. Balzac's *Physiologies* or Louis-Sébastien Mercier's *Tableaux de Paris* (1781). Among its contributors were leading Russian writers, linguists, and literary critics like Nikolai Nekrasov, Vladimir Dal, and Vissarion Belinsky.
20. See especially *Hoyptshtet*, pp. 60 and 91.
21. Der Nister puts it more ideologically: 'Ir shteyt un kukt af peters shtibele un dermont zikh: Af vemen beyner hot es di rusishe selbsthershung ir tsukunft geboyt' (You are standing and looking at Peter's hut and you remember on whose bones Russian autocracy built its future, p. 59).
22. *Hoyptshtet*, p. 60.
23. Palace Square, renamed in 1918 after Moisei Uritskii, the fearsome head of the Petrograd Cheka (Bolshevik secret police) whose murder initiated the wave of 'Red Terror'. The old name Palace Square was restored in 1944.
24. Dietmar Neutatz, *Träume und Alpträume. Eine Geschichte Russlands im 20. Jahrhundert* (Munich: C. H. Beck, 2013), pp. 152–58.
25. *Hoyptshtet*, p. 84.
26. Ibid., p. 106.
27. Ibid.
28. Stavrogin and Verkhovensky appear as demoniacal psychopaths who 'fantazirndik onanirn' (are masturbating while fantasizing), p. 111. Hersh Remenik's analysis of this chapter in *Sovetish heymland* is partly simplified and misreading. See Hersh Remenik, 'Dostoevsky and Der Nister', *Soviet Studies in Literature*, 8.4 (1972), 405–19 (originally published in *Sovetish heymland*, 11 (1971)).
29. *Hoyptshet*, p. 119.
30. Ibid., p. 117.
31. Ibid., pp. 119–20.
32. 'Guide through a Renamed City' in *Less than One: Selected Essays* (New York: Farrar, Straus and Giroux, 2001), pp. 69–94 (p. 76).
33. See Nikolai Antsiferov, *Nepostizhimyi gorod . . . Dusha Peterburga*, p. 302. Tsarina Avdotia (properly Evdokia Fiodorovna Lopukhina), the first wife of Peter I, who was banished to the Uspensky monastery in Suzdal, is said to have cursed the city with these very words. The Russian poetess Anna Akhmatova, who, like der Nister and many other Russian and Russian-Jewish intellectuals, was evacuated to Tashkent in the early 1940s, makes the spell and the rumour part of her late masterpiece *Poem without Hero* (1940–1962/65), see Anna Akhmatova, *Poema bez geroya/Poem ohne Held* (Leipzig: Reclam, 1993), pp. 174–75 and 293.
34. Ibid., p. 51.
35. *Hoyptshtet*, p. 48.
36. The monument has been removed in the 1930s by the Soviet Government. Today it is located in the interior courtyard of the Marble Palace. See David Sittler, 'Snamenskaja Platz — Platz des Aufstands: Ein (Schau-)Platz des Alltags und der "Revolution"', in *Sankt Petersburg. Schauplätze*

einer Stadtgeschichte, ed. by Karl Schlögel, Benjamin Frithjof, and Ackeret Markus (Frankfurt and New York: Campus, 2007), pp. 273–85.
37. *Hoyptshtet*, p. 48.
38. See Olga Reznikova, 'Tiurmy Peterburga-Petrograda-Leningrada' <http://urokiistorii.ru/node/227; 20 July 2015>.
39. *Hoyptshtet*, p. 55.
40. Batyushkov was a friend of Pushkin's. His *A Stroll through the Academy of Arts* is one of the first Russian sketches and a cornerstone of the image of Petersburg in Russian literature. See Antsiferov, *Dusha Peterburga*, p. 57.
41. *Hoyptshtet*, p. 75.
42. See his 1842 pamphlet 'Moskva i Peterburg' (Moscow and Petersburg) in *Sochinenia v tritsati tomakh*, II (Moscow: Izdatelstvo akademii nauk SSSR, 1954), pp. 33–42, and Antsiferov, *Dusha Peterburga*, pp. 84–85.
43. For the Russian original see 'Nevski Prospekt', in Nikolai Gogol, *Izbrannye sochinenia* (Moscow: Izdatel'stvo Pravda, 1985), pp. 469–503 (p. 488). The English translation is quoted after *The Complete Tales of Nikolai Gogol*, 2 vols (Chicago and London: The University of Chicago Press, 1985), I, 207–38 (p. 225).
44. *Hoyptshtet*, p. 106.
45. In 1878, Dostoevsky even became the tutor of two of the tsar's sons, the Grand Dukes Sergej and Pavel. According to David Goldstein, see *Dostoevsky and the Jews* (Austin: University of Texas Press, 1981), p. 90, no other writer in nineteenth-century Russia 'was on such intimate terms with the ruling aristocracy'.
46. Gennady Estraikh, 'Der Nister's "Hamburg Score"', in *Uncovering the Hidden*, pp. 7–26 (p. 17), according to Der Nister's questionnaire.
47. Ibid. See also the biographical sketch in *A shpigl oyf a shteyn. Antologye. Poezye un proze fun letste farshnitene yidishe shraybers in ratn-farband*, ed. by Khone Shmeruk and Benjamin Harshav (Jerusalem: The Magness Press, The Hebrew University, 1964; 2nd edn 1987), pp. 737–41 (p. 739).
48. The Yiddish original and the English translation are quoted after Mikhail Krutikov, '"Turning My Soul Inside Out": Text and Context of *The Family Mashber*', in *Uncovering the Hidden*, pp. 111–44 (p. 113).
49. Der Nister, *Hoyptshtet*, p. 3.
50. Mikhail Krutikov, 'Desire, Destiny, and Death: Fantasy and Reality in Soviet Yiddish Literature around 1929', in *Mapping the Jewish World. 1929*, pp. 217–33 (p. 218).
51. Delphine Bechtel, *Der Nister's Work. 1907–1919. Study of a Yiddish Symbolist* (Berne, Frankfurt am Main, New York, Paris: Peter Lang, 1990), p. 269. See also Gennady Estraikh, *In Harness: Yiddish Writers' Romance with Communism* (Syracuse, NY: Syracuse University Press, 2005), pp. 130–31.
52. See *A shpigl oyf a shteyn*, p. 739, and Estraikh, *In Harness*, p. 138.
53. Hans Günther, 'Education and Conversion: The Road to the New Man in the Totalitarian Bildungsroman', in *The Culture of the Stalin Period*, ed. by Hans Günther (Houndsmill: Macmillan, 1990), pp. 193–209 (pp. 193–94).
54. See Hans Günther, *Die Verstaatlichung der Literatur* (Stuttgart: Metzler, 1984).
55. *A shpigl oyf a shteyn*, p. 739, and Krutikov, 'Turning My Soul Inside Out', p. 112.
56. See Remenik, 'Dostoevsky and Der Nister', p. 407.
57. *Yidishe shrayber in Sovet-Rusland*, ed. by the Shmuel-Niger book Committee and the International Yiddish Congress of Culture, (New York: Alveltlikher Yidisher kultur-kongres, 1958), pp. 368–80 (p. 370).
58. See Bechtel, *Der Nister's Work*, pp. 197–200, and Krutikov, 'Turning My Soul Inside Out', p. 112. Shmuel Niger ignores Der Nister's literary production between 1929 and 1939 (p. 371).
59. For a general description of Jewish St Petersburg see Mikhail Beizer, *The Jews of St. Petersburg: Excursions through a Noble Past* (Philadelphia and New York: The Jewish Publication Society, 1989).
60. See Seth L. Wolitz, Brian Horowitz, with Zilla Jane Goodman, 'Cities in Ashkenaz: Sites of Identity, Cultural Production, Utopic or Dystopic Visions', in *History of the Literary Cultures of East-Central Europe. Junctures and Disjunctures in the 19th and 20th Centuries*, 4 vols, ed. by Marcel

Cornis-Pope and John Neubauer (Amsterdam and Philadelphia: John Benjamins Publishing Company, 2006), II, 182–212 (pp. 195–200).
61. *Hoyptshtet*, pp. 93–94. In *Moskve*, we find another ethnic marker: a German engineer who fled Germany after the economic breakdown in 1929 is married to a Jewess. This fact underscores his liberalism (p. 185).
62. Krutikov, 'Turning My Soul Inside Out', p. 127.
63. Der Nister exemplifies the '*um-boy*' (re-building) of the worker, the student by education by various examples.
64. *Hoyptshtet*, p. 5.
65. A terrifying shift from this utopian rebuilding of world into its dystopian counterpart is Andrei Platonov's short novel *Kotlovan* (The Foundation Pit, 1929/30).
66. *Hoyptshtet*, p. 3.
67. Ibid., p. 92.
68. Ibid., p. 27.
69. Ibid., p. 61.
70. Hersh Remenik in his article 'Dostoevsky and Der Nister' mentions Der Nister's affinity to Dostoyevsky's literary devices that are examined by Mikhail Bakhtin, pp. 415–16. Nevertheless, his analysis remains within Soviet ideological confines and touches upon aesthetic dynamics only marginally.
71. *Hoyptshtet*, p. 82.
72. See Krutikov, 'Turning My Soul Inside Out', pp. 134–35, and Dan Miron, *The Image of the Shtetl and Other Studies of Modern Jewish Literary Imagination* (Syracuse, NY: Syracuse University Press, 2000), p. 31
73. Estraikh, 'Der Nister's "Hamburg Score"', p. 17, and n. 45 (p. 25).
74. For the concept of narratological masks see Roland Gruschka, 'Symbolist Quest and Grotesque Masks: *The Family Mashber* as Parable and Confession', in *Uncovering the Hidden*, pp. 145–60 (pp. 149–50).
75. Der Nister, *Di mishpokhe Mashber. Roman*, 2 vols (New York: Folks-farlag, 1943), I, 21.
76. See Krutikov, 'Turning My Soul Inside Out', pp. 132–34.
77. Niger, *Yidishe shrayber in Sovet-Rusland*, p. 370.
78. Der Nister, *Di mishpokhe Mashber. Roman*, 2 vols (New York: YKUF, 1948), II, 267.

CHAPTER 7

From Facts to Symbols: Space and Architecture in Der Nister's *Hoyptshtet*

Mikhail Krutikov

Der Nister's collection *Hoyptshet* (published in 1934, written between 1931 and 1933) is remarkable in several aspects. It is an experiment in 'realistic' depiction of the new Soviet urban reality, an attempt to conquer new stylistic and thematic territories and to catch the dynamic characters of three capital cities, Kharkov as the new capital of Soviet Ukraine, Moscow as the new capital of the Soviet Union, and Leningrad as the former Russian imperial capital. Unabashedly enthusiastic about the Soviet present and communist future, and scathingly critical about the Russian imperial past, this series of reportages also offers an intellectual reflection on the historical role of art and the artist. Der Nister's desire to adjust to the newly shaped norms of socialist realism is obvious; but no less obvious is his attempt to expand these norms by incorporating elements of fantasy and symbolism into the realist master narrative. I would argue that it could be regarded as a preparatory stage to his magnum opus, the novel *The Family Mashber* (Di mishpokhe mashber, 1939–47), in particular with regard to the literary representation of space and architecture.

From what is known about Der Nister after his return to the Soviet Union in 1926, there is little evidence to suggest that he was a conscious opponent of the Soviet ideology and practice. He certainly resented his own marginality, which became especially painful after 1934, when the capital of Soviet Ukraine was moved from Kharkov to Kiev, and Der Nister was stuck in the provincial backwater while most of his colleagues and former associates had moved to Kiev and Moscow. He also had enemies, real or imaginary, most notably the Minsk group of proletarian writers such as Khaskl Dunets, Yasha Bronshtein, and Ber Orshansky, as well as Itsik Fefer in Kiev, whom he blamed for many of his misfortunes. But his overall attitude to the Soviet project as a form of radical reconstruction of imperial Russia, for which he clearly had little sympathy, seems to have been positive. The year 1929 was critical for Der Nister. Following sharp criticism of his book *Gedakht* by Dunets, he realized that he had to change his style and produce a major novel, or else he would disappear from Soviet literature. In a frequently quoted statement from a letter to his brother he wrote that his future as a writer depended on his ability to write a big realistic novel dealing with the fate of his generation, and explained that symbolism was an 'opgefregter artikl' (unsaleable article) in the Soviet Union. Whether Der Nister sincerely believed that symbolism was outdated or was forced to accept this as a fact, we will probably never know, but he evidently felt a deep anxiety about his survival in literature.

To a certain degree this anxiety informs *Hoyptshtet*, which became Der Nister's first attempt to depict reality 'as it is'. Der Nister speaks here in the first person and describes his own impressions, creating a new narrative voice, but we of course should be careful not to identify the narrator with the author who continues to guard his 'hidden' persona. Another important feature of the new book are the references to other writers and their works, which can serve as a guide for understanding Der Nister's sphere of interests of that time and help identify sources of his artistic inspiration. *Hoyptshtet* is also Der Nister's least 'Jewish' work. It has only few episodic Jewish characters and cultural references which play no major role in the narrative. The genre of *fartseykhenung* — a literally translation from the Russian *ocherk*, popular in the Russian literature — is a hybrid between personal impressions and objective report. It is based on a personal experience of the author, which can be related in a mixture of subjective and objective tones. In Yiddish literature this genre was inaugurated by Peretz in his *Bilder fun der provintsrayze*, a series of highly subjective reports about a journey through the Lublin region of Poland as a member of a statistical expedition. The genre of travelogue had become especially popular in Yiddish literature with the development of the Yiddish press during the interwar period.

Contrary to Der Nister's symbolist tales which had no relation to reality, *Hoyptshtet* offers very detailed and careful depictions of urban spaces. Images of landscape and architecture have several functions in the narrative: at the most basic level they depict the location and help the reader visualize the physical environment and the author's position in it; they also have an aesthetic dimension which is a product of the imagination of their creators; finally, and importantly for Der Nister's agenda, they function as a material embodiment of historical time, a multi-layered repository of different epochs of the past. Every building, street, and square is a container of stories about historical events. But architecture also preserves the present for the future. Der Nister declares in the opening of the book: 'History will judge us according to our buildings: how our order is built, on what kind of moral foundations, what political, socio-economic and cultural-customary forms did it take' ('Loyt undzere binyonim vet undz di geshikhte mishpetn: vi azoy undzer ordenung iz geboyt, vos far a morale gruntn zaynen unter ir untergeleygt, un in vos far a politishe, sotsial-ekonomishe un kultur-shteygerishe formen zi hot zikh ongekleydt').[1] The process of socialist construction creates not only new buildings, but transforms the builders as well: 'by participating in the building process, builders are rebuilt themselves' ('boyendik, ze ikh, boyen zikh aleyn di boyer iber'), which echoes the Zionist slogan 'livnot ve lahibanot ba' — 'to build up [the Land of Israel] and to be built by it'. By laying down the contours of our buildings, we lay down the foundation of our future: 'the conviction gave us security to imagine our future reality in fantasy and to fulfil our fantasies step by step' ('di ibertsaygung hot undz festkayt gegebn vegn undzer tsukunftiker virklekhkayt tsu fantazirn un undzere fantasies trit nokh trit take tsu farvirklekhn').[2] Thus, architecture serves as an embodiment of imagination which can run ahead of its time and become reality only in the future.

Kharkov: A Capital *ex nihilo*

The immense scope and dizzying speed of the Soviet construction process disorients the author:

> and in my head different images from different ages are disorderly mixed up, and analogies and comparisons between then and now suggest themselves, and the times of Catherine II come to my mind, and right next to them the Tractor Factory for instance and I want to compare them but there is no comparison.
>
> [un in kop mishn zikh mir in umordenung farsheydene bilder fun farsheydene, epokhes, un analogies betn zikh un farglaykhungen fun amol mitn haynt, un s'kumt mir Ekaterine der tsveyters tsaytn afn zinen, un bald take — trakterboy, lemoshl, un ikh vil farglaykhn un s'iz fort keyn farglaykh nit.][3]

The massive construction sites of socialist industry are new altars or temples where the future is being built, and to highlight the contrast between the past and the present, Der Nister draws upon religious symbolism. Under Catherine's rule building was the labour of slaves, as a kind of pagan fetish worship of wood and stone in ancient Egypt; the communist construction is a religious ritual of 'self-worship of the masses that have grown up to the new needs and requirements of their own' ('zelbstfarerung fun groyse masn, vos zaynen tsu eygene groyse naye foderungen un baderfenishn dervaksn').[4] The combination of self-worship and self-sacrifice produces new creation, 'a nay bashefenish', which carries a new name. The socialist builders 'are building an edifice for the name such as Ts. K. [Central Committee], Tractor Factory, etc.' ('boyen binyomin far dem nomen, vi Ts. K., traktor-boy u az'v.').[5] The mysterious power of those names makes the enemies sleepless and the friends happy. These somewhat incoherent musings belong to the intoxicated narrator who got drunk celebrating the fourteenth anniversary of the October Revolution, perhaps as a way to defuse the mystical association that might be too ideologically dangerous in the mouth of a sober Soviet author.

An intoxicated character was not unusual in Der Nister's symbolist tales, which are set in an abstract mythological landscape outside real time and space. Now he tries to transpose this familiar type onto the real ground of Soviet cities, using drunkenness as a licence for fantastic representation of Soviet reality by stressing its 'surreal', meta-historical aspect. The three capital cities form a sort of a dialectical triad: Kharkov is a construction site of the communist future, Leningrad embodies Russia's imperial past, whereas Moscow brings the past and the future together in a grand apocalyptic revelation on Red Square. Kharkov has no remarkable past: the willpower of the Soviet regime can create a new capital out of any city.[6] The new capital of Ukraine emerges miraculously like a new creation ex nihilo ('vi fun a nisht vert a yesh') by the command of the Communist Party.[7] Der Nister ridicules the previous unsuccessful attempts by the imperial Russian government and local administration, beginning from Catherine II on, to turn this provincial backwater into a city of any significance. Only the Soviet regime, which defeated its enemies in the bloody civil war, was able to build a truly modern, future-oriented capital of the new Soviet Ukraine out of 'garbage' ('mist'). Construction is going on around the clock under electric lights, which are changing the way of nature by turning night into day. The new city magnetically attracts people from its vicinities, 'and so entire provincial shtetlekh have moved here, and the provinces have built their colonies here' ('un azoy hobn gantse provints-shtetlekh aher ibergevandert, un azoy hobn provintsn gantse do kolonies gebildet').[8] In fact, however, the book came out at the time when the capital was moved to Kiev, so Der Nister's enthusiasm appears in retrospect misplaced (in a footnote he notes that the text was written in 1931–32). Perhaps even less appropriate for 1934 was Der Nister's excited praise for the new Soviet Ukrainian culture, which by that time had already been cruelly decimated by Stalin. And needless to say, there are no hints at the Soviet-orchestrated famine that took millions of lives of Ukrainian peasants in 1932–33.

The architectural centrepiece to the future age is the complex of Gosprom buildings (the seat of the Soviet Ukrainian government which opened on 7 November 1928). Located at the large central square of the new Ukrainian capital, it was perhaps the grandest building of the Soviet constructivist style. The narrator was delighted that the new structure had no history: 'It is good that especially those kinds of buildings without a past and a tradition now make you happy' ('Gut, vos dafke azoyne binyonim on nekhtn un on traditsyes makhn dikh itst freyen').[9] Another structure on the same square, the yet unfinished building of the Central Committee of the Communist Party of Ukraine, appeared to him as a giant musical instrument which contains 'rare melodies' within its walls ('di muzik un zeltene melodies in zayne vent bahaltn'), which is another variation on the theme of architecture as a repository of the future.

The description of Kharkov's new central square is followed by a personal memory of the narrator's experience at the Party purges in the summer of 1929, when Der Nister was subject to severe ideological criticism. As a result, he was not allowed to publish his creative works for about five years and was only allowed to do translations and editing. Now, in his first published work since that episode, he exalts the purges as a festive ritual, a public performance of confession by party members before large audiences. Notwithstanding certain elements of obligatory criticism, the purge appears to be mainly a celebration of the past heroic achievements of respected party old-timers. When a man with a scar on his forehead appears on stage, the audience enthusiastically greets him as 'zhid!', which at first glance sounds as an inappropriately derogatory word for a Jew. It turns out, however, that the man was captured together with other Red Army soldiers by Petlyura's Ukrainian nationalist army during the civil war. When Jews were ordered to step aside from others, he, although not a Jew, joined his Jewish comrades. The enraged captors cut the word *zhid* on his forehead, and since then this word became his honorary *nom de guerre*. This episode may have some real basis, but it reads like a response to the famous story 'Der tseylem' (The Cross) by the American Yiddish writer Lamed Shapiro, in which the Jewish protagonist bore on his forehead the sign of the cross that was cut by the pogromists. In both cases, the symbolic word-scar has a fortifying effect on the character's personality: it made Der Nister's *zhid* a stronger communist, and turned Shapiro's hero into a determined pursuer of antisemites.

The empty square between the grand buildings of Gosprom and the Party's Central Committee becomes the site of the narrator's bizarre and surreal experience that forms the core of the Kharkov chapter. Impersonating a lonely drunken man on the eve of the fourteenth anniversary of the October Revolution (that is, 6 November 1931), the narrator engages in a conversation with a policeman guarding the empty new square. The narrator tells the policeman about a peculiar vision that was probably the product of his drunken imagination. One night the entire structure of the Gosprom buildings, with the participants of the purges on its roof surfaces, took off like a dirigible, flew over peacefully sleeping fields, woods, and villages of Ukraine, and landed on St Sophia Square in Kiev. As a welcome gift, St Sophia Church invited the guests to play with its domes. The passengers, among them *zhid*, took out straws and began to blow soap bubbles which grew into St Sophia's domes. Inside each one of those bubble domes was a church cleric of a certain rank. When one of the guests coughed, the bubbles began to burst one after the other together with the clerics, re-enacting metaphorically the collapse of the old regime.[10] To console Kiev for the loss of the golden domes, the guests advise her to look forward, not backward, and throw a fishing net into the Dnieper three times. The first catch brings back remnants of the ancient and medieval ages, the second one brings fragments of the most recent, pre-revolutionary past, and the third catch lands a golden fish of the future, which is ready to fulfil desires for the future, 'a tsukunft-fishele, a fil-tsuzogndiks'.[11] Kiev thanks the guests for remembering the older relative, and the entire Gosprom crew sets off on the return flight, to be back in its usual place for the numerous office workers who will come to work in the morning.[12] The unusual story ends where it started: 'Here we are, comrade policeman, and you are again at your post, and I am still a little . . . not quite sober yet' ('Un ot zaynen mir gekumen, khaver militsioner, un du bist oyf dayn post vider, un ikh nokh alts abisl . . . nokh nisht ingantsn oysgenikhtert').[13]

The unreality of that vision, the narrator explains, should not be surprising because now, when radio and aeroplanes are familiar to every village boy, 'no novelty is a novelty anymore' ('itst zaynen keyne khidushim keyn khidushim') and therefore 'such a gigantic construction, an entire street of buildings, with twelve- and fourteen-floor buildings which are connected through corridors that look like long train carriages, can also fly in the air' ('kon shoyn oykh aza machine, a gantser gasn-binyen, mit moyern, mit tsvelf- un fertsn-shtokike korpusn, mit koridorn, vos zeen oys vi lange tsug-vagones, velkhe fareynikn a korpus mit a korpus, inderluftn flien').[14] The encounter between the two signature buildings of the new and the old capitals represents symbolically a meeting between the past and the future, as the new capital of Soviet Ukraine comes to pay a visit to the ancient 'mother of Russian cities'. This bizarre fantasy mixes elements of Pushkin's famous 'Tale of the Fisherman and the Fish' with the avant-garde fantastic projects of 'flying cities' by the early Soviet architects and artists of the suprematist school such as Lazar Khidekel, Ladovskii, and his disciple Georgii Krutikov, whose design of a flying city caused a stir when he presented it as his diploma project at VKhUTEIN (Higher State Institute for Arts and Technology) in 1928.

Leningrad: Urban Museum of Imperial History

The first thing the narrator sees upon his arrival in Leningrad is the famous monument to Alexander III by Paolo Trubetskoi (erected in 1909, removed in 1937) in the middle of the square next to the Moscow Train Station. As he tries to cross the busy traffic to come closer to the monument, he is stopped by a vigilante worker and fined for violating the traffic regulation despite his protests that that he is a provincial journalist and not familiar with the big city regulations. The worker retorts: 'you will write about the monument and make some money'.[15] Indeed, Der Nister depicts the monument in great detail, setting the tone for his critical investigation of the city's rich architectural legacy. His description is typical for that time:

> a typical assistant policeman [pristav-gehilf], or a gendarme, with broad trousers, short boots, shaven, in a round sheep Kuban Cossack fur hat [. . .] a pug dog face that looks and doesn't see, a broad comic bottom of a coachman, which could be swapped around with his face.

In short, concludes the narrator, 'a better caricature of autocracy even its worst enemy could not imagine'.[16]

Der Nister contrasts the Alexander III monument with the famous Bronze Horseman, the monument to Peter the Great, seeing in them an artistic expression of the opposition between the early dynamism and later stagnation of the imperial epoch. Peter's monument captures the man who embodies the historical momentum:

> Apart from personal features of the horseman, the artist has also conveyed here, consciously or not, the appearance of his young historical class, his wild expression, his drive to conquer new land and sea routes for the trade with Europe and the world.
>
> [der kinslter hot do — bavust oder umbavust far zikh aleyn — oyser di perzenlekhe eygnshaftn fun rayter, oykh dem oysdruk fun zayn yung-geshikhtlekhn klas gegebn — zayn vilde ekspresye, zayn shtrebn tsu velt- un eyrope-handl, tsu naye yaboshe- un vaser-vegn derobern.][17]

Der Nister's understanding of Peter's historical role follows the theory of Mikhail Pokrovsky, who until 1934 was the leading authority in Soviet Marxist history. According to Pokrovsky, Peter's reforms were driven by the energy of Russia's young and vigorous trade capital, which sought access to new European markets. As a result of Peter's victory over Sweden in 1721, the 'mechanism' of the Romanov Empire took its final shape as a 'combination of two powers, serf labour and trade capital'.[18] Peter's historical role was therefore progressive for the age of the emerging trade capitalism, but this brief period was followed by the long moral and intellectual decline of the ruling classes of the Russian Empire.

Der Nister's Leningrad is populated by ghosts of the past, who fall into two categories: the oppressors and the oppressed. There are also whole ghost streets and neighbourhoods that people try to avoid, especially at night. One of them is the space between what Der Nister calls 'Palace Street' (Millionnaya, at that time Khalturina),[19] which goes from the Winter Palace parallel to the Neva river, and the Palace Embankment, formerly the abode of aristocracy. The narrator comes there from Senate Square and finds the area dark and eerie even at a light summer night. Using an imagined passer-by as a 'centre of consciousness', he weaves a web of visions of the past, in which political prisoners in the Peter and Paul Fortress across the river are contrasted with the nobility dancing at the balls in the palaces on the embankment. He imagines today's Leningrad inhabited by the 'shadows' of the past, which reside among architectural elements of the buildings: 'these shadows, they have no rest. They are wandering, and one can see them appear on the roofs, walking between the roofs and building entrances, looking down from cornices, friezes, masks, roof vases, stairs and balconies' ('zey ruen nit, ot di shotns. Zey lebn umvandlerish un me ken zey, dakht zikh, oft af di dekher zen, fun eyn dakh afn andern umshpatsirn, fun eyn moyer-arayngang tsum andern, un fun di karnizn, frizn, maskes, dakh-vazes, trep un ganikes aropkukn').[20] The area around the Winter Palace is the most appropriate place for the ghosts who walk around the netherworld ('oylem-hatoyhu', literally the world of chaos, in which souls of the dead must wander until they atone for a misdeed and earn their place in heaven),[21] and ought to be turned into a museum, 'because one cannot think of it otherwise, and one cannot perceive it other than as a museum' ('vayl andersh vi a muzey kont ir zi nit denken, andersh vi a muzey kont ir zi nit onemen un nemt zi take nit on, ot di gas').[22]

The ghosts whom the narrator encounters during his walks can be ordinary, nameless people as well familiar historical personalities. These apparitions can exist only in the appropriate architectural environment, like Peter's house, which looks 'simple and very ordinary, even poor by our time's standards' ('prost un gvaldik-geveynlekh, un far undzer tsayt — afile oremlekh')[23]. By walking for fifteen minutes from Peter's house to Kadetskaya Liniia one moves into a different historical age, from the imperial past to the beginning of the communist future. In the red corner building Lenin famously proclaimed on 4 June 1917 that the Bolsheviks were ready to take power.[24] The principal Marxist dichotomy between the slavery of the past and the promise of the future liberation is imprinted in every piece of Leningrad architecture, which is saturated with history. Its variety of architectural styles reflects the progressive decline of the empire, from the imposing originality of Baroque and Classicism of the eighteenth and early nineteenth centuries to the late nineteenth–early twentieth-century derivative mock-Byzantine, mock-Gothic, and mock-Russian styles.[25]

On Nevsky Prospect the narrator runs into an old acquaintance of his who shows him around the city. The man was trained as an architect but became a theatre director, and the combination of two professions enables him both to tell the history of the city and to impersonate the types of its former inhabitants, such as a Tsarist officer or the petty official Akaki Akakievich, the protagonist of Gogol's story 'The Overcoat'. This character pulls the ghost of its creator, who appears draped in a black Spanish coat walking on Nevsky Prospect and whispering, in Russian, from his story 'Nevskii prospect': 'our life is an eternal strife between dream and substantiality [sushchestvennost']'.[26] One cannot understand St Petersburg without Gogol and other Russian classical writers because the city exists for us thanks to their imagination, the narrator tells us, or, in Gogol's words, the city's 'substantiality' is a product of the writer's dream.[27] Trying to absorb the city, the narrator gets dizzy from the 'cinematographic' speed of changing historical names and places. Standing next to the Admiralty, he feels intoxicated and has a strong desire to retain in his memory 'the entire building and its every detail' ('dem gantsn binyen un yeder detal').[28] The architectural memorials to the cruel imperial past, such as the buildings on the Palace Square, also provide 'a bit of consolation', a 'relief from everything that was hard, and a sure promise of a happy future' ('derlaykhterung fun ales shvern un ales gevezenem, un a zikherer tsuzog af vayterdikn un af shtendik gliklekhn').[29] Observing the panorama of the city from an embankment on a light June night, he sees the city emerging and then disappearing with a 'light airiness of a dream' ('a shtot antshteyt, a shtot vert farshvundn mit der laykhter luftikayt fun a kholem').[30]

The promise of the future is embodied in the revolutionaries who sought to bring about liberation ahead of time. Such is the apparition of a revolutionary terrorist who waits for his victim for hours in winter, then slips on ice and blows himself up. The main figure from this set is the ghost of Dmitry Karakozov, the failed assassin of Alexander II in 1866 who missed the shot and was eventually hanged. The ghost appears to the narrator in his room in the Znamenskaya hotel where Karakosov stayed before the assassination attempt. Together they visit historical sites in search of indications of the future revolution. In the Tauride Palace, which was the seat of the State Duma, the narrator imagines himself amidst the political debates of the past. He is especially fascinated by the former seat of Purishkevich, the infamous leader of the anti-Semitic and monarchist Black Hundred movement. The narrator is unable to leave this seat, 'like a gravestone (matseyve) of a lover'. Thinking about the past, he laughs with one eye and weeps with the other one, thus internalizing the contradictory character of the city.

From the 'dead' Tauride Palace the narrator walks, accompanied by Karakozov and 'intoxicated' (shiker) by the beauty of the city, to the Smolny Palace. Built originally as an Institute for Noble Daughters, this architectural complex was taken over by the Bolsheviks as the headquarters of the uprising in October 1917. Architecturally, Smolny is the opposition to the Tauride Palace, which reflects their opposite roles in the revolution. Admiring the Smolny building, Der Nister formulates his view of art and its historical purposefulness:

> Genuine art remains a long-living remarkable masterpiece, regardless of the artist's own intentions and purposes at the time of its creation. If they were artistically thorough, I mean if the artist committed all his energy to his work, then it will outlive his time and his purpose, and it remains relevant and pleasing aesthetically for other times, and even for purposes that are contrary to those of the artist.
>
> [emese kunst iz un blaybt a langdoyerndiker un tsu bavunderndiker muster, vos far a kavones un vos far a tsiln der kinstler hot zikh in zayn tsayt bam shafn dos

verk nit geshtelt, nor oyb er hot zey kinstlerish-oysshepndik geshtelt, kh'meyn, oyb er hot mit zayn gantser im gegebener kinstler-energye getray dem verk gedint, lebt er dernokh iber zayn tsayt un zayn tsil, un es blaybt giltik un a sheferisher genus un fargenign oykh far andere tsaytn un afile far kegnzetslekhe tsum kinstlers tsiln.]³¹

In other words, the criterion of 'genuine' art is its ability to outlive its time and social conditions, and retain its aesthetic and practical utility at later ages. Such a view echoes the position of the 'despitists' ('voprekisty') against the 'thankists' ('blagodaristy') in the heated polemics about the validity and worth of artistic works of the past in Soviet criticism during 1932–34. The former, represented by Georg Lukács and Mikhail Lifshits, 'argued that in the case of a literary genius [. . .] a writer is liable to produce a telling critique of his society *despite* his political position or class identity'.³² Their opponents 'believed that a truthful depiction of reality was possible only thanks to the author's (correct) worldview'.³³ The latter view was defended by the prominent Marxist critic Isaac Nusinov who promoted Der Nister's work — despite the fact that ideologically it did not conform to the tenets of proletarian realism.

Der Nister interprets the Smolny building, built in 1806–08, according to the 'despitist' view:

> You stand in front of this work in 1932 and see that there is no disagreement with 1932 and the interests which this building serves now. On the contrary, you think: that's exactly what the artist had in mind; he intended his work somehow to pass over the past century and, most importantly, reach to the present and fulfil its main purpose.
>
> [Ir shteyt far dem verk in 1932tn yor un zet, vi s'iz gor keyn stire nit tsu 1932 un tsu di interesn, vos badint itst. Farkert, ir trakht: grod dos take hot der kinstler gemeynt, dertsu, eygntlekh, hot er getsilt, zayn verk zol far yenem yorhundert vi nit iz farbay, un der iker zol tsum iker, tsum itst un zayn hoypt-baruf, ariberkumen.]³⁴

Thus, each work of art — a book, a sculpture, or a building — relates simultaneously to two different historical moments, one in which it was created and the other one for which it was intended and in which it fulfils its purpose, and the distance between the two can be as long as several centuries. The contrast between the intended purposes of the Tauride Palace and the Smolny Institute is inherently built into their architectural forms:

> Nothing in common! While the former one bends, from its old age, to the ground, to calm obliteration and to the stillness of a museum or a cemetery, the latter rises vigorously, with its high entrance stairs, its whole front and annexes, up into air, to a dynamic and life-awakening activity.
>
> [keyn moshl un keyn dimyen! Ven yents bet zikh shoyn, vi fun elter, opgelebt, tsu der erd, tsu shtil, fartishkevetkayt un tsu muzey-un matseyve-ru, rayst zikh op dos geboy, mit di hoykhe oyfgang-trep, mit gantsn front un mit di zaytn-geboyen — in luft, inderhoykh, tsu muntern un tsu lebnvekndiker tetikayt.]³⁵

The dominant horizontal outline of the Tauride Palace is opposed to the verticality of Smolny. The former has fulfilled its historical purpose and has become a museum (or a gravestone) to its age, while the latter is thriving under the new regime. It was not accidental that the two different 'class representations' ('klasn-forshteyershaftn') had chosen these two different architectural structures as their 'historical tribunes' to reveal their 'class substance' ('klasn-mehus').

Of course, the Bolsheviks were motivated in their choice of Smolny primarily by their 'social and political strategy', ('gezelshaftlekhe un politishe strategie'), but post-factum, when 'whatever had to happed did happen' ('dos gesheene iz geshen'), one realizes that 'regardless of all the motives, the events had to take place here and only here' ('epes oyser ale motivn hobn di gesheenishn take do, un dafke do gedarft geshen').[36] This observation leads Der Nister to a conclusion that captures the essence of his new literary style, which brings together realism and symbolism: 'the fact becomes a symbol' ('der fakt vert a simvol').[37] In other words, history follows its own course which is, in accordance with Pokrovsky's theory, fully determined by dynamic socio-economic forces and class interests, but eventually, sometimes in a distant future, these forces take accomplished symbolic forms in the works of art. This way of thinking might have helped Der Nister reconcile the troublesome reality of his time with the larger sense of artistic purpose. By capturing the key progressive features of his own epoch, an artist created a long-lasting work of art that would be speaking to future generations.

While Kharkov is portrayed as a newly built industrial capital which embodies the stormy development of the formerly backward Ukraine, Leningrad represents an urban museum where even new industrial facilities, such as the Red Triangle rubber factory, are located in old buildings. Moscow is portrayed as a place where the imperial past and the Soviet future actively interact, preparing the future communist utopia-cum-apocalypse. Like Bergelson in his 1926 essay 'Moskve', Der Nister contrasts the moribund city that he encountered at the end of the Civil War with its present dynamic state.[38] He first saw Moscow in 1920, when he was working in the Jewish orphanage in Malakhovka near Moscow. Back then the city was 'half-dead, a kind of Pompeii' ('halb-toyt in a min Pompeye')[39]: its main trade street Ilinka looked like a cemetery with glass show windows.[40]

By 1920 the young Soviet regime had already eliminated the past imperial order but was as yet unable to build a new one. This was a critical historical period of transition, a moment of twilight between the old and the new. The division was strikingly evident in the Kremlin: the seat of the Soviet government was guarded by the revolutionary soldiers, but the surrounding areas were still largely populated by the 'bitter enemies' ('farbisene sonim') of the revolution who inhabited the numerous monasteries and churches, such as the Iverskaya Chapel and St Basil's Cathedral.[41] Equally dire was the situation with education, culture, and trade that was conducted mainly on dirty and dangerous street markets ('tolkuchka').

The narrator's visit to new Moscow begins, as in Leningrad, with a monument, this time to Pushkin. The great poet looks 'much older and more melancholic', not recognizing the busy streets around him which are filled with crowds of people and traffic.[42] Some of the old church buildings, such as Iverskaya, have been demolished to free up space for parks, streets, and traffic, while others were turned into museums. A lot of 'traditional mould' ('traditsioneler shiml') was removed 'to reveal what is valuable from the layers of different epochs' ('dos vertfule fun di onshikhtungen fun farsheydene epokhes aroystsushayln').[43] Now people can experience the horrors of medieval religious practices in the new Atheism Museum in the building St Vassily's Cathedral and get a relief by looking thankfully at the Lenin Mausoleum as they come out[44].

Moscow is a meeting place not only between the old and the new, but also between East and West, North and South, where one sees 'all sorts of types, people, dresses of wild ethnographic mixture and variety' ('tipn, mentshn, kleyder fun a vildn gemish un etnografishn alerley').[45] But all these diverse elements merge into a 'charming harmony of the old and the new' ('alt-nayem khen'), complementing each other, 'without any conflict or dissonance, just the wonderful harmony and authenticity' ('nisht keyn vidershprukh, nisht keyn disonans, nor vunderlekhe harmonie un ekhtkayt').[46] 'Harmony and authenticity' find their fullest expression on Red Square, where the commercial shopping complex as a representation of Imperial Russia's trade capital is absorbed and redeemed by the new construction that promises 'hope and security' ('hofenung un zikherkayt') for the future.[47] The new spatial focus of the square, Lenin's Mausoleum, attracts visitors from all parts of the country. This is a quiet temple in the midst of the busy square where people come to see their new deity. A Chinese family comes to see Uncle Lenin ('feter Lenin'), and their child asks, in Russian, whether he is alive ('zhivoy'). The response comes like an echo, not clear whether from his parents or the narrator, as the same word but written with Yiddish characters.[48]

At night the Kremlin wall dreams about the cruel times in the past, when the busy market place at Red Square doubled up as a site of public executions. Now the wall looks hopefully at the Mausoleum from where Lenin sends his call to representatives of the people from the entire world to gather at Red Square. In this apocalyptic vision,

> Red Square will be full. Large crowds will come to see the representatives. The entire city will climb, stand, and lie on balconies, roofs, and church tops, every street pole and gutter will be covered with youths like flies. Everybody will want to see those who have prevailed in the last struggle, who have cracked down on the last remnants of crime, who have erased the last borders between countries, and united all countries into one and all peoples into one working people, and whose representatives have now gathered here, on Red Square.
>
> [Der royter plats vet ful zayn. Hamoynim, hamoynim veln af di forshteyer kumen kukn. Di gantse shtot af ganikes, af dekher, af shpits-kloysters vet shteyn, lign, krikhn, ale gasn-stoypes, ale rinves mit yungvarg, vi mit flign badekt. Ale veln viln zen ot yene, vos hobn dem letsn kamf oysgekemft, yene, vos hobn di letste reshtlekh farbrekhn gebrokhn, yene, vos hobn di letste grenetsn fun land tsu land opgevisht, un fun ale lender — eyn land, un fun ale felker — eyn arbet-folk, un vos di forshteyer fun zey ale zaynen itst do, afn roytn plats, farzamlt.][49]

The celebration of the final victory of the working class will commence with the performance of the Internationale for the last time, 'and it will become quiet, and the entire people will cry with joy, and join in singing, crying and rejoicing' ('un shtil vet vern, un dos gantse folk vet fun freyd veynen, un veynendik un yoyvlendik der muzik mit gezang tsu hilf kumen').[50] And although the present reality is still different from that apocalyptic vision, one must firmly believe that the dream will come true. Der Nister supports his point by a reference to Lenin's article, which in turn quotes the radical positivist Russian critic Dmitry Pisarev, which calls on people to work persistently on turning their fantasies into reality[51]. Following this call, the narrator's dreaming of the bright future joins in the dream of the wall: 'I dream together with it, I dream its great and bright dream of the future that is already close' ('ikh troym mit ir mit, kh'troym mit ir vor, afn bodn vor — ir groysn un likhtikn, shoyn noentn tsukunft-troym').[52] At this culminating moment of the book Der Nister resuscitates his symbolist style and casts his narrator as a new communist prophet. He is careful enough to legitimize this revival of visionary symbolism by a quotation from Lenin, at the same time implicitly using the allegory form to Prophet Zachariah's vision of the final gathering of all nations in Jerusalem.

Conclusion

Like many Russian modernists who wanted to stay in Soviet literature, Der Nister had to go through a painful process of adaptation to the new stylistic and ideological requirements at the turn of the 1930s. Clarity and simplicity were required attributes of the emerging doctrine of socialist realism. The critical campaign of 1929 made Der Nister painfully aware of the changing situation, and forced him to rethink his position in Soviet literature. In *Hoyptshet*, his first attempt to write about 'reality', he developed a variety of elaborate techniques, which enabled him to transpose Symbolist and neo-Romantic stylistic elements from his previous period into the new realist mode of narration. Along with detailed depictions of the urban landscapes of the three capital cities, each chapter contains surreal fantasies which grow out of architectural imagery. In such episodes, which are seamlessly integrated into the narrative, such as the night flight of the Gosprom building from Kharkov to Kiev, the appearance of Karakozov's spectre in Leningrad, or the apocalyptic dream of the Kremlin wall, Der Nister reflects on the questions that were of paramount importance for him during that transitional period. The main problem that apparently preoccupied his mind at that time concerned the ability of an artist to transcend the socio-political limitations of his time and to speak to the future generations, perhaps over the heads of his contemporaries. Der Nister addressed this issue explicitly in the much-quoted letter to his brother, but also revisited it implicitly in the fantasies that transported his imagination to different times and allowed him to take a viewpoint outside his real position in space and time.

An important feature of Der Nister's new realist style is the attentive depiction of the urban environment. Buildings, streets, and squares function on the one hand as markers of objective reality which identify the place of the action, and on the other hand, as material embodiment of historical time. Architecture preserves memories of the past, but it also contains seeds of the future, although the proportion between the two can vary. Some new buildings, such as the Kharkov Gosprom, carry no weight of the past, and therefore are literally barely attached to the ground.

Others, like the Tauride Palace of Leningrad, have already fulfilled their historical mission and have no future apart from being a museum, which is reflected in their structure dominated by horizontal lines. Only very few architectural units, such as the Smolny or Red Square, have both a rich past and a future. The ultimate purpose of a work of architecture is not necessarily known to its creator or patron, and can fully manifest itself under very different historical circumstances in the future; however, a discerning eye can recognize its destiny in some of its formal features. The architectural ensembles of the central squares of Kharkov, Leningrad, and Moscow are parts of a certain dialectical triad. The Kharkov Gosprom is the positive 'thesis' of socialist construction, a new creation that emerges out of nothing. Leningrad Palace Square is a negative 'antithesis', a perfect material embodiment of Russian imperialism, which is now turned into a museum. Finally, Moscow represents a communist 'synthesis', both utopian and apocalyptic, which brings the past and the future together. The Red Square preserves layers of different historical epochs, from medieval Rus' to the late nineteenth-century trade capitalism, but its true purpose can only be fulfilled in the envisioned communist future, when the representatives of the toiling masses from the whole world gather at Lenin's Mausoleum to proclaim the end of history. And although this event is yet to come, it is already prefigured in certain architectural forms that can be detected by the perceptive eye of a writer with the special ability to see symbols through facts.

Notes to Chapter 7

1. Der Nister, *Hoyptshtet (fartseykhenungen)* (Kharkov: Literatur un kunst, 1934), p. 5.
2. Ibid.
3. Ibid., p. 25.
4. Ibid., p. 28.
5. Ibid.
6. Ibid., p. 14.
7. Ibid., p. 8.
8. Ibid., p. 11.
9. Ibid., p. 16.
10. The trope of the church lost in time and space after the October revolution was popular among Yiddish writers depicting new Soviet reality; see also Harriet Murav's chapter in this volume.
11. *Hoyptshtet*, p. 43.
12. Ibid.
13. Ibid., p. 44.
14. Ibid., p. 38.
15. Ibid., p. 48.
16. Ibid.
17. Ibid., p. 50.
18. M[ikhail] N. Pokrovskii, *Russkaia istoriia v samom szhatom ocherke*, 4th edn (Moscow: Partizdat, 1933), p. 70.
19. Der Nister refers to it, apparently by mistake, as 'Street of the Ninth of January'; in fact, it was the Palace Embankment that until 1944 was named after 9 January.
20. *Hoyptshtet*, p. 55.
21. Ibid.
22. Ibid., p. 56.
23. Ibid., p. 57.
24. Ibid., pp. 59–60.

25. Ibid., pp. 60–61.
26. Ibid., p. 61.
27. Ibid., p. 64.
28. Ibid., p. 79.
29. Ibid., p. 73.
30. Ibid., p. 74.
31. Ibid., p. 80.
32. Katerina Clark and Galin Tikhanov, 'Soviet Literary Theory in the 1930s: Battles over Genre and the Boundaries of Modernity', in *A History of Russian Literary Theory and Criticism: The Soviet Age and Beyond*, ed. by Evgenii Dobrenko and Galin Tikhanov (Pittsburgh: University of Pittsburgh Press, 2011), pp. 109–43 (p. 117).
33. *Hoyptshtet*, p. 80.
34. Ibid.
35. Ibid., p. 81.
36. Ibid.
37. Ibid.
38. On Bergelson's essay see Harriet Murav's chapter in this volume.
39. Ibid., p. 128.
40. Ibid., p. 131
41. Ibid.
42. Similar metaphoric imagery can be found in Moyshe Olgin's impressions of Moscow, see Harriet Murav's chapter in this volume.
43. Ibid., p. 147.
44. Ibid., p. 144.
45. Ibid., p. 145.
46. Ibid., p. 148.
47. Ibid., p. 149.
48. Ibid., p. 209.
49. Ibid., p. 213.
50. Ibid.
51. Ibid., p. 214.
52. Ibid., p. 216.

CHAPTER 8

Did Mikhail Epelbaum Study at Warsaw Conservatoire? The Early Years of an Eminent Yiddish Singer

Alexander Frenkel

The question posed as the title of this chapter is not prompted by mere curiosity or unhealthy fascination with the minutiae of stars' lives. Musical education is an aspect that we *must* take into account while trying to understand the phenomenon of Mikhail Iosifovich Epelbaum, the 'Jewish Chaliapin' as his admirers used to call him, the singer who once enjoyed unprecedented popularity amid the Jews of the Soviet Union and who served as an inspiration for a whole generation of Soviet Yiddish vocalists, being, as one of them (Zinovy Shulman) phrased it, 'the pioneer of the genre'.[1]

It should be emphasized that in its significance the 'Epelbaum Phenomenon' goes beyond being yet another sample of the thorny path of a Yiddish artist. The words 'the pioneer of the genre' are not just a ritual laudatory formula, but a precise definition. Of course, Epelbaum was by no means the first to tour cities and shtetls performing Yiddish songs. Yet he was the first one to make this commitment in the new historic reality, in the post-revolutionary period. Moreover, he was the first one to carve his own niche within the Soviet entertainment industry, exactly as the promoter and interpreter of the Yiddish songs. For him these performances were not a way to supplement his income as an actor, cantor or opera singer, as it had been for most of his predecessors, but they became his main mission in life. It was in his concert practices of the early 1920s that the concept of the 'Yiddish folk song' as a genre of Soviet popular music gradually began to emerge, to be fully shaped only in the mid-1930s.[2]

However, Epelbaum was neither a scholar nor an ideologist; as we will show further, he had not even received a systematic musical education. He left us neither any mission statements nor memoirs or lengthy interviews; besides, he never joined the heated debates on Jewish music that often raged in the press in the days of his youth.[3] And yet the analysis of Epelbaum's life, of his changing repertoire and of the controversial media responses to his performances gives us enough data to trace the

FIG. 8.1. Group of Yiddish actors (right to left): Mikhail Epelbaum, Clara Young, and Samuil Goldberg. Ca. 1934
From the collection of Isaak Kofman, Santa Clara, CA

FIG. 8.2. Announcement of the first night of Franz Lehar's *Khave* (*Eva*) at the Warsaw's Elizeum theatre. Der fraynd, 2 November 1912

stages of the formation of Soviet Jewish music and, to an extent, of Soviet Jewish culture as a whole. But the task of this chapter is less ambitious — it will focus on the origins of the 'Epelbaum Phenomenon', on the artist's first steps on stage in the years before the First World War.

Should We Trust the Encyclopaedias?

The entries on Epelbaum in the Russian-language Jewish encyclopaedias claim that 'from home-schooling he went on to studying at a private gymnasium, then at the Warsaw Institute of Music',[4] or that he 'studied at the Warsaw Conservatory'.[5] In both entries the establishment in question was a musical college that in the late nineteenth–early twentieth centuries was known as the Warsaw Institute of Music (*Warszawski Instytut Muzyczny*), and in 1918, after Poland became independent, received the official name of the State Conservatoire (*Konserwatorium Państwowe*). Since the same encyclopaedias mention Epelbaum's success on the Russian opera stage, we are left with an image of an acclaimed opera singer who had received his vocal training at one of the best conservatoires of Europe and, at a certain stage of his career, turned to the heritage of his own people, to the Yiddish songs. Such was the path taken by his younger colleagues, the pre-war Soviet Yiddish singers Saul Liubimov, a graduate of Moscow Conservatoire, and Zinovy Shulman who had been trained at the Opera Department of the State Institute for Theatre Arts (GITIS).[6] Yet Mikhail Epelbaum's career was completely different, and the false image created by the encyclopaedias falls apart the moment we make an attempt to analyse it.[7]

Let's take a closer look at his 'success' on the Russian opera stage. One of the encyclopaedias states that he 'made his debut at Kiev Opera House, in Anton Rubinstein's *The Demon*'.[8] The source of this data is not mentioned, but it is easily guessed; it is an essay by the Soviet Yiddish journalist Zalmen Kahan: much later, in the mid-1950s, he worked, for a brief period, as the literary editor of Epelbaum's programmes at the Lengosestrada state concert agency. That's how the debut of the future celebrity is described in the essay: looking for an income, the sixteen-year old Epelbaum left his native Odessa for Kiev, and there took a menial job at the opera house; once the voice of the gifted young man was heard there, he was invited to perform on stage, first as a supernumerary, then in the choir, and finally as a soloist in *The Demon*. According to the journalist, the only thing that had prevented him from pursuing this promising career was his own restlessness, his urge to travel.[9] We can only marvel at the fact that the encyclopaedia compilers took this preposterous story seriously.[10]

'The singer's strong voice (dramatic baritone) allowed him to perform opera arias. [. . .] On the invitation of Kiev Opera House he performed, more than once and with unfailing success, the part of the Demon in Anton Rubinstein's opera of the same name', states yet another encyclopaedia.[11] Once again, the 'source of information' is easy to guess. It is the memoirs of the above-mentioned Zinovy Shulman — quoted (without acknowledgement) almost verbatim, yet with the original sense distorted. Actually, the memoirist, while listing the traits of

Epelbaum's artistic personality, mentioned, among other things, 'his strong voice (dramatic baritone) that allowed him to perform opera arias (he was invited more than once to Kiev Opera House and enticed to sing the part of the Demon)'.[12] To rephrase, he *was* invited and enticed, but did he ever actually sing? Apparently Shulman himself did not know the answer.

And here are the real facts. In the mid-1920s Epelbaum, by then a renowned artist named in the playbills as 'A famous singer of Yiddish folk songs', would once in a while perform on the Russian-language stage; not in opera, but in operetta. More than once, while on tours in various cities, such as Rostov, Vitebsk and Kherson, he performed the part of Edwin in Emmerich Kálmán's *Die Csárdásfürstin* (as *Silva*), together with the local Russian casts.[13] Once he did perform it in Kiev Opera House, named at the time after the founder of the German Communist Party Karl Liebknecht.[14] In those years, the singer would once in a while include Russian opera arias (in Russian, as well as in the Yiddish translations), romantic songs by the Russian composers (Sergei Rachmaninov, Modest Mussorgsky, Sergei Prokofiev, Alexander Gretchaninov), and Neapolitan songs in the programmes of his Yiddish concerts. His intentions were quite obvious: to highlight his vocal potential, to demonstrate 'internationalism', and, in a way, to promote the Jewish music by placing it side by side with the Russian and world classics.

As for the part of the Demon, he did not perform it 'more than once and with unfailing success'. Epelbaum sang the part of the Demon in Kiev only once, on a special occasion, and not the whole of it either. In the spring of 1924, the Gubrabis (the local Trade Union of Artists) organized in many of the city's theatres the so-called 'Day of the Rabis': special, often unconventional shows were staged in order to raise money for the Union's relief fund. One of those performances took place on 14 April at the Liebknecht State Academic Opera House; it was *The Demon* with a rotating cast. The advertisement said,

> The Day of the Rabis. Gala Show THE DEMON. New cast in each act, 5 Demons, 3 Tamaras, 3 Angels, 3 Synod Servants etc.[15]

In order to attract a larger audience, the popular Yiddish singer was enlisted amid the '5 Demons'. The city's newspaper emphasized that 'in one of the acts, Epelbaum will make his first appearance as the Demon on the opera stage'.[16]

In any case, for him it was triumph. A Yiddish singer had performed in one of the country's most prestigious opera houses together with the renowned celebrities, such as Pavel Andreev, a soloist of St Petersburg's Mariinsky Theatre. No doubt, Epelbaum would remember the occasion for the rest of his life, recall it quite often, and share the story with his friends and colleagues. Apparently, a distorted version of this episode had found its way into their memoirs. Strictly speaking, thanks to the joint efforts of the entrepreneurs, the journalists, the memoirists and, finally, of the encyclopaedias compilers, we have ended up with a badly mangled, inaccurate, misinterpreted version of Epelbaum's biography. Obviously, the singer himself also had had a hand in mythologizing it — mythologizing that was both inherent to his profession and served as a survival strategy in the atmosphere of Russia that had never been particularly favourable for a Yiddish artist. Impressive titles, eloquent epithets, overstatements of achievements easily found their way into the playbills, concert programmes and newspaper announcements, to be firmly implanted into the public consciousness. In the late 1930s, in keeping with the requirements of the Soviet propaganda of the period, he was even reported to be 'from a working class family' and to 'have spent two years employed as a turner'.[17] As we will see later, his alleged two years as a turner are actually missing from his biography, and neither could the singer boast of proletarian descent. And still, his career, as befalls a Yiddish artist in Russia, was striking and dramatic — and *this* is not an overstatement.

The Beginning

Even his birthplace is obscure. According to the Soviet files, he was born in 1894 in Odessa.[18] Almost all the published sources give the same information. Yet, the entry on Epelbaum in the fundamental *Leksikon fun yidishn teater* (Lexicon of the Yiddish Theatre) claims that he 'was born in Brest-Litovsk [. . .] in a tailor's family'.[19] There is a possibility that this statement is actually correct. A Soviet citizen always had a wide range of reasons to tamper with his own background. Here's at least one valid reason: in the interwar period Brest-Litovsk was outside the Soviet Union, being part of the 'bourgeois' Poland.

Even though the Lexicon is by no means a reliable historical source, this entry needs to be meticulously studied. It is based on an 'oral interview' that the artist gave to the compiler while touring the Western countries in the late 1920s. In effect, we have here, in a way, the only autobiography by Epelbaum available to us:

> [He] studied in a heder until the age of eleven, then in a private school, and after his parents had moved to Odessa, where they opened a sartorial accessories store, he was enrolled in a gymnasium.
>
> His friends introduced him to an amateur drama group that was staging in Odessa the play *God, Man, and Devil*, where he was given the role of Uriel Mazik. The drama group went on a provincial tour with other plays. Mishurat engaged him in his professional troupe, where he acted at first in dramatic and then in singing roles. Later Epelbaum acted in the troupes of Korik, Genfer, and Kompaneyets (in Warsaw's Elizeum theatre). From there he accepted Rappel's engagement to come to Odessa, and then returned to Warsaw, to the Elizeum, where he performed in modern operetta repertoire. Here he was engaged to Fishzon in Odessa, [then] participated as a soldier in the [First World] War; he was wounded and after his release from service, he joined Lipovsky's [company] in Kharkov; [then] for six years he was touring, performing Yiddish folk songs [. . .][20]

This is, obviously, a sketchy outline. What is remarkable, though, is that no conservatoire is mentioned. Another important detail is that here his stage career begins not with operas or operettas, but with drama — and, naturally, not in Kiev, but in Odessa (his debut was in a play by Jacob Gordin). The chronological boundaries are not specified, but we can fathom them from other sources: Epelbaum made his debut on the professional stage in 1910.[21] He was just sixteen at the time — here the Soviet journalist Zalmen Kahan is right; however, this brilliant career took flight not in the Russian opera, but in the Yiddish troupes that toured the south of the Ukraine.

The early 1910s were a turning point, a fairly controversial one at that, in the history of the Yiddish theatre. Almost unanimously, the theatrical activists claimed that the Yiddish theatre was in a deep crisis, and even predicted its complete and speedy demise. There were both external and internal reasons for this pessimism. After the First Russian Revolution, the legal restrictions on the 'jargon' performances had been de facto removed, yet the decisions still depended on the whims of the local authorities. As before, the Yiddish actors had to perform in the guise of 'German-Yiddish troupes'; besides, they had to secure a *tsenzurka* (permit) for each play. Predictably, the mechanism tended to stall without bribes and connections. To boost the sales, the lion's share of the repertoire had to consist of uncomplicated operettas targeting the undemanding audience. The intellectuals, irrespective of their political orientation, regarded the theatre as a key element of the Jewish cultural agenda, and thus tended to show impatience with the 'domination of lowly plays', 'profiteering on the audience's bad taste', and 'exploitation of the masses' base instincts'. The financial failure of the playwright and stage director Peretz Hirschbein, who had made the most consistent attempt at 'renovation', was a bitter disappointment for many enthusiasts. His troupe, which focused on 'literary' repertoire (plays by Sholem Asch, Sholem Aleichem, Semen Yushkevich, and Hirschbein himself), had existed for eighteen months only, and had to be dissolved in the summer of 1910. The breakthrough ideas of the stage director were alien to the general public, and no major patrons ever stepped in.

And yet dozens of Yiddish troupes toured the cities and shtetls of the Pale of Settlement and of the Kingdom of Poland. Despite all the challenges, their numbers were constantly growing. Young talents were joining the casts, those who saw in the Yiddish theatre an opportunity of pursuing their artistic and national agendas. The repertoire was also growing; plays by Leon Kobrin, Zalmen Libin and, primarily, by Jacob Gordin (as per the Lexicon, Epelbaum made his debut in one of them) were securing their permanent places therein. At the time they seemed to be a major step ahead, in comparison with the vaudevilles and the operettas, the ones that were known under the derogatory name *shund* (trash). The opposition of operetta and drama was one of the manifestations of the differentiation between popular and high culture that was taking place in all the spheres of Yiddish culture, including the theatre. The striving to merge 'art' and 'entertainment' was becoming a general trend. Most troupes would define themselves as drama-and-operetta or operetta-and-drama ones. The existing conditions made the Yiddish theatre a synthetic one, requiring universality from an actor, who had to possess drama, vocal, and dancing skills.[22]

Meyer Mishurat, the first one to engage Epelbaum, was, according to a contemporary, an entrepreneur who deserved the following description, 'a smug, completely uncultivated whip-cracker'.[23] Still, he was apparently a rather audacious person, for he would willingly take up the young and the inexperienced — a number of actors who subsequently rose to fame began their careers with Mishurat. His third-rate troupe was touring the remotest provinces, and thus, as a rule, did not catch the attention of the press. It seems that Epelbaum's involvement with this company has not been covered at all. We know that in August 1910 Mishurat's Yiddish-German

Troupe was performing Gordin's *Mirele Efros* in the shtetl of Novaia Odessa outside Nikolaev.[24] However, it is mere guesswork whether Epelbaum was part of the cast.

Once he moved to Ilya Korik's troupe, he was immediately spotted by the press. On 12 November 1910, the Yiddish theatre began its guest programme in Kherson with Gordin's *Man and Devil*. Korik himself played the part of Uriel Mazik, and received a laudation from a local critic. Epelbaum, too, got his share of praise: 'We would like to single out the fairly impressive acting of Epelbaum (Drakhme) and Miss Weinstein (Tsipenyu).'[25] Roza Weinstein had made her debut in Hirschbein's troupe.[26] She was soon to become Mrs Epelbaum.

From that point on, the life of the aspiring actor is chronicled by the records of his tours. What had been changing, were the entrepreneurs, the provincial stages, and the rooms at the provincial hotels. The stock of plays had hardly been changing at all, a mix of the operetta *shund* with Gordin's dramas and Goldfaden's classical plays. In the summer of 1911, he was performing in Kherson, Mariupol and Lugansk, with the German-Yiddish Drama-and-Operetta Troupe directed by A. Lifshits and V. Shumsky; in the autumn it was Aleksandrovsk and Ekaterinaslav with Moisey Genfer's troupe. Then he rejoined Korik, and in February–April 1912 they were performing together in Melitopol and Aleksandrovsk. In May, he came to Elisavetgrad with Aba Kompaneyets's troupe. In July, his name appeared briefly in the newspaper announcements for David Sabsay's troupe that performed in the Moldavanka district of Odessa. By the end of August he was in Vitebsk, again with Kompaneyets. Then, with the same company, he went to Dvinsk.

In all the casts mentioned, the young man played rather prominent, sometimes even the leading parts, and the press was fairly benevolent. 'The young, but undoubtedly gifted actor Mr Epelbaum', was the assessment by an Aleksandrovsk reporter.[27] After the operetta *Dos pintele yid*, a Melitopol newspaper praised him: 'Mr Epelbaum seems to have given a lot of consideration to his part, and thus his acting was very good, if not brilliant.'[28]

At times he was even singled out by a petulant reviewer, generally displeased by the show: 'The only one in the entire cast to make a good impression was Mr Epelbaum, he is definitely capable of enacting strong dramatic moments, [yet] he should rather do it in a more natural way, in a less affected style.'[29] Once in a while, though, the reviewers were quite harsh: 'Unlike Mr Shumsky, his partner, Mr Epelbaum was quite lacklustre.'[30] Or, 'Mrs Weisman was quite stunning, while Mr Epelbaum was rather bleak.'[31]

He was gradually earning popularity with the public. After one of the shows in Aleksandrovsk, the reviewer reported that 'Mr Korik and [Mr] Epelbaum received the warmest reception and got an impressive number of curtain calls'.[32] Ilya Korik was a renowned actor, who gained notoriety primarily through his tragic parts. The reviewers compared him with the stars of the Russian-language stage, such as Pyotr Radin and Pavel Orlenev. As for Epelbaum, he was still a beginner. And yet, sometimes his name was used to attract the public. Thus, a promo for Genfer's troupe stated: 'featuring Miss N. G. Nadina and Mr Epelbaum, the renowned actors from the theatres of Warsaw, Lodz and Odessa'.[33] By that time the 'renowned actor' had spent only a year on the professional stage and had never performed either in Warsaw or in Lodz.

Incidentally, the early reviewers perceived Epelbaum primarily as a drama actor. A critic from Lugansk wrote, after having seen Gordin's *Mirele Efros*, 'Mr Epelbaum was not at all bad as Shalmen'.[34] His colleague from Kherson, reviewing Libin's *The White Slave*, shared his enthusiasm, 'Mr Epelbaum, who played the part of Daymants, was very good in certain episodes'.[35] A reviewer from Vitebsk pointed out, in earnest, in his piece on a popular *shund* operetta *Shloyme Khokhem, or My Wife's Friend*: 'Mr Epelbaum (Jacob, the music teacher) plays with great finesse and sincerity the part of the unfortunate husband and father who has to recognize that his happiness is gone'.[36]

On seeing the comedy *Semka Lets*, a connoisseur from Aleksandrovsk made this lengthy and rather critical assessment of the young actor's performance:

> It seems that Mr Epelbaum is a good actor, yet the part of Ezriel is not right for him. He is not a tragedian. That's why his rendition of the dramatic part of 'the luckless Ezriel' is not particularly successful. His involvement and diligence were quite obvious, but to no avail. He was obviously overtaxing himself, yet in vain. He was screaming, gesticulating, he looked overexcited, yet he failed to impress the public. It was rather funny to watch a tragedian out of his element.[37]

And here is a rare testimony on his vocal skills of that period, from a Vitebsk review of Goldfaden's *Shulamith*:

> Mr Kompaneyets (the Old Monk) and Mr Epelbaum (Absolom) were brilliant as always; the latter had to do a fair amount of singing, and did it quite successfully, revealing impressive vocal faculties and good command of those.[38]

Apparently, he had acquired certain vocal skills in his early years in Odessa.

First Time in Warsaw

Epelbaum toured Vitebsk and Dvinsk with a company called Warsaw Yiddish-German Operetta-and-Drama Troupe directed by A. G. Kompaneyets. Its leading lady was an actress and a singer Nadezhda (Esther) Neroslavskaya who had once performed at the Italian opera stage, yet gained fame as a Yiddish actress. The word *Warsaw* on the billboards was a common promotion gimmick of the period, yet this entrepreneur's use of it was more or less justified — back in 1906 Kompaneyets had settled in Warsaw, rented the so-called Muranov Theatre, assembled the best cast possible and managed to sustain it on the banks of the Vistula for several years. Now, in the fall of 1912, having toured the towns of Russia's North-Western Region (*krai*), he planned to re-establish a resident theatre in Warsaw. Epelbaum followed him to the Jewish 'cultural capital' of the Russian Empire.

It was almost purely an operetta venture, but not a run-of-the-mill, rather a breakthrough one, offering its own solution to the crisis of the Yiddish theatre. Instead of focusing on the traditional Yiddish plays — the *shund* that outraged the intellectuals, the company planned to concentrate on the European ones, tested out on the various stages, in various languages, including Russian and Polish. The ambitious plan fitted into the framework of the up-and-coming Yiddishism: the Jews have to avail themselves of the world's cultural treasures not in foreign languages, but in translations into their mother tongue. The idea was to please everyone — both the refined connoisseurs and the mass audiences that preferred the 'light' genre. Having rented the Elizeum theatre, well known to the Jewish audience of Warsaw (Lazar Rappel's troupe had performed there for a few years), Kompaneyets joined forces with the composer Peretz Sandler (Neroslavskaya's husband) and the acclaimed actor Yankev Libert.[39]

On the first night (2 November 1912) the 'truly European operetta' *Khave* by Franz Lehar was presented. To highlight its European origins, the billboards featured the original title, *Eva*, in brackets, next to the title in Yiddish.

The first night was reviewed by all the three Yiddish dailies of the city, in a most appraising way. Menakhem Kipnis, a music and theatre critic from *Haynt*, wrote:

> The most important thing is that the new management of the Elizeum has introduced us, for the first time in Yiddish, to a purely European classical operetta, and we should emphasize that it is a most significant step ahead in our young and scanty theatrical history. [. . .] For the present, the most immediate work to be done for the progress of Yiddish theatre is to yiddishize [*faridishn*] the European operetta. It is also the best compromise between the Jewish intellectuals and the masses.[40]

The same opinion was shared by a *Der moment* staff writer, a renowned proponent of Yiddishism, the lawyer and philologist Noah Prylucki:

> Since currently the Yiddish stage cannot do without the light repertoire, let it at least be not downright trashy. Let it not lag behind the European operetta. Let's make it possible for an intellectual to sit through the performance from the beginning till the end without feeling disgusted, but experiencing an aesthetic pleasure. [. . .] Let people see on stage a glimpse of real life; even though presented in a superfluous and unsophisticated way, it is fine as long as it is not clumsy, melodramatic, or silly. It does not matter whether it is Jewish life or not. One *Lehar* is a thousand times better than a hundred *Latayners*.[41] After all, the main thing here is *the music*.[42]

Even the caustic A. Mukdoni, a theatre critic from the 'intellectual' daily *Der fraynd*, seemed to be happy:

> We should rejoice that the new theatre has not opened with *Dos pintele yid* or *Yidishe neshome*.[43]
>
> It opened with an excellent alien operetta. An alien one with a thousand virtues is better than a home-bred cripple and native ugliness.
>
> All in all, it was a happy night in the small Elizeum theatre.
>
> Everything was trim and neat, both on stage and in the audience.
>
> Neat in the European way![44]

Epelbaum, too, took part in *Eva*.[45] Yet he is not mentioned in any of the reviews. He was obviously playing a small support part, to say nothing of the fact that he was overshadowed by the other actors. There were a number of celebrities in the cast. Apart from Neroslavskaya, the lead lady, the reviewers singled out Samuel Landau, Lev Braun, Adolf Berman, Herman Berman, and Lazar Fried. All of those were experienced, renowned actors, local for the most part, i.e. Warsaw residents; they had long been popular and caught the attention of the press. Thus, Landau had been singing for years in Polish operas and operettas, but then he moved to the Yiddish theatre and performed successfully in Kaminsky's Literary Troupe and in Yitskhok Zandberg's Grand Theatre in Lodz. In Lehar's *Eva*, he was not only playing one of the leading parts, he was also the stage director.

However, in the theatre's second 'European' production, Jean Gilbert's *Die keusche Susanne* (as *Di tsnue Shoyshane*), Epelbaum, still playing a support part, managed to catch the reviewers' attention. The first night was on 11 January 1913. 'Mr Epelbaum is not at all bad in the comic part of Alexis the Kelner', reported Kipnis.[46] Prylucki was didactic, like a schoolmaster: 'The young Mr Epelbaum looks quite satisfactory as the Kelner. He has a chance to become a useful member of the family of Yiddish actors'.[47] Even Mukdoni admitted, with his typical sarcasm:

> Mr Epelbaum is not at all bad in the role of Alexis, the Ober Kelner. However, his is not a Frenchman, even less a Parisian waiter. He is more of a Russian valet from a provincial club; still, he is quite funny, dynamic, with a lot of inventions.[48]

This part apparently was the young actor's major success. Yet when six weeks later Franz Lehar's other masterpiece, *Gypsy Love* (as *Tsigayner libe*), was first shown to the public, Epelbaum, who played the village lad Miklós, went unnoticed by the press.

Meanwhile, the market dictated the demands. Apart from the 'European' ones, the company was showing a lot of standard Yiddish plays, mostly on Saturdays at daytime, at reduced prices. The Elizeum had to offer the 'lowly operettas' that the intellectuals detested: *Zayn vaybs man* (His Wife's Husband), *Di amerikanerin* (American Woman), *Sura Sheyndl*, etc. Goldfaden's pieces were staged too, *Shulamith*, *Koldunye* (The Sorceress), *Tsvey Kuni-Lemls* (Two Kuni-Lemls), and even Gordin's plays, *Di shvue* (The Oath) and *Der fremder* (The Stranger). Kompaneyets had to withstand fierce competition with Warsaw's other Yiddish company, Kaminsky Theatre, which often staged the same plays. There were some downright comic situations: two versions of one and the same operetta, *Dr Zeyfnbloz* by Yehuda-Leyb Boymvol, were first presented on the same night. Mukdoni the critic rallied, 'With unprecedented humdrum, with truly competitive vigour the two theatres attacked the soap bubble [*zeyfnbloz*]. This bitter competitive struggle resulted in casualties on both sides. In both theatres, some actors lost their voices from tireless rehearsing'.[49]

Epelbaum was cast in all the troupe's shows. Apparently, one of his most significant parts was that of Hotsmakh in *Koldunye*. The entrepreneur, Aba Kompaneyets, also played in this Goldfaden classic.[50] In those years he would act but rarely, yet Bobe Yakhne was still his key part, and he loved to enact it a couple of times a year.

Most shows went unnoticed by the press, and the few reviews would only mention the names of the lead actors or the beneficiaries. Epelbaum, described in the advertisements as 'the popular and talented actor and singer', had his benefit night on 30 April 1913. American comic opera *Di shpil-foygelekh* (Singing Birds) was being performed — the same advertisements announced that it had enjoyed 'smashing success in the New York theatres'. Neroslavskaya played the lead part. Apart from the beneficiary, those taking part in the long divertissement at the end of the show were opera singer Jacob Kelter, 'the favourite of the Warsaw public' Lev Braun, Roza Weinstein (Epelbaum) who had joined the cast early in the year, and a dancer 'Fraulein Nadya'.[51] Yet the night, the 'star hour' for the young actor, failed to stir the interest of the press. It was the time when Clara Young, an American star, came as a guest actor to the Kaminsky Theatre, and obscured the Elizeum in the eyes of the journalists.

It seems that Epelbaum was only mentioned one more time, in an anonymous review of *Uriel Acosta*, penned, undoubtedly, by the same Mukdoni. The review was hardly complimentary: 'Mr Epelbaum who was playing the Rabbi was a real caricature, a scarecrow that people put out to keep the birds away'.[52]

Young Epelbaum was 'bypassed' in yet another way. At that time, the gramophone industry was booming in Russia. Amid the others, the voices of many Yiddish actors from Warsaw were recorded, including Epelbaum's Elizeum colleagues Neroslavskaya, Braun, and Fried. To please the public of the day, they were mostly recording arias from the popular Yiddish operettas (the above-mentioned *shund*) plus, rather rarely, folk songs.[53] Yet Epelbaum, whose name was still obscure, failed to impress any of the fiercely competitive labels. His first disk would only be presented fifteen years later, in New York.

And still, the months spent in Warsaw turned to be a very important formative period for Mikhail Epelbaum the singer, the artist, the advocate of Yiddish heritage; it was the period when his taste, his professional criteria, and his attitude to art in general and to Jewish art in particular were shaped. The troupe headed by Kompaneyets, Sandler, and Libert was the most serious stage project he had participated in in the pre-revolutionary years; it gave him a great opportunity to perfect his acting skills. For the first time ever he was a part of a resident theatre, with seamless rehearsal process, high-quality stage directing and scenography, with the best European standards used as a target. His partners were highly experienced opera and operetta singers, the shows were reviewed by the most qualified Yiddish critics of the time, and all the Yiddish literary celebrities of Warsaw, including Yitskhok Leybush Peretz, attended the performances.

Among the Warsaw critics who had mentioned the young man from Odessa in their reviews, Menakhem Kipnis should be singled out, a singer and a folklorist, who is considered to be the first true interpreter of the Yiddish folk songs, the one who managed to preserve 'the original character of the songs while making them accessible to the contemporary audiences'.[54] Through his concerts, articles, and books he achieved tremendous popularity in interwar Poland and was the only Yiddish folklorist who managed, rather than just tried, to find a way 'to sweeten Jewish lives, to raise a consciousness of Jewish nationalism with Yiddish folklore'.[55] Unlike Kipnis, Epelbaum, as stated above, was not a writer, a visionary, or a music expert. Still, as a performer and an interpreter of Yiddish folklore he carried on the tradition set by Kipnis, even though it was reoriented towards the new audiences of Soviet Russia. Moreover, a significant part of Epelbaum's repertoire would consist of the songs that one can find in Kipnis's famous collections published in Warsaw in 1918 and 1925. It seems very possible, though not obvious, that in the post-revolutionary years, when Epelbaum was embarking on his Soviet career, the first collection was already available to him. What is obvious is that Kipnis, both as a public figure and as a performer, just like the entire Warsaw milieu of the early twentieth century, had a strong influence on Epelbaum.[56]

Back on the Road and Back to Warsaw

Each of the first nights of the 'truly European' productions was a special event in the Jewish cultural life of Warsaw, yet its preparation required considerable time and considerable investment. Competition and the struggle for survival pushed the entrepreneurs towards the established practices of all the Yiddish troupes. Gradually American operettas, *Borg mir dayn vayb* (Lend Me Your Wife), *Dos pintele yid* (The Essence of the Jew), *Di amerikanerin* (The American Woman), etc., performed by all and sundry, began to dominate the repertoire of the Elizeum. The company also tried to stage 'literary material', namely such pieces as Sholem Aleichem's *Tsezeyt un tseshpreyt* (Scattered and Dispersed) and *Di dray matones* (Three Gifts) based on Y. L. Peretz's short stories, yet without much success[57]. By the summer of 1913, the management hired a number of new actors, vesting its hopes in the foreign celebrities. On 2 June, 'the famous American actors Mr Natanzon and Mrs Natanzon' were presented to the Warsaw audience in the above-mentioned production of *Uriel Acosta*. Meanwhile, the members of the old cast began to leave.

The last glimpse of Epelbaum's name in the announcements published by the Warsaw newspapers dates back to the beginning of August, while on the 15th he already appeared on the stage of Odessa New Theatre, as a member of Lazar Rappel's operetta troupe. A little later he participated in its tour to the nearby Akkerman. His former Elizeum colleagues, Lev Braun and Jacob Kelter, were also part of the cast; the repertoire featured not just the good old *Borg mir dayn vayb* and *Di amerikanerin*, but the pieces that had made a sensation in Warsaw, *Eva*, *Gypsy Love*, and *Die keusche Susanne* (as *Di tsniedike Shoyshane*). Of course, the lead parts were played by a different lady, the entrepreneur's wife Zina Rappel. Years later she would recall that her Susanne had a smashing success in Odessa and enjoyed numerous performances.[58]

In the spring of 1914, Braun, together with Max Rappel, the entrepreneur's brother, established, without informing Lazar Rappel, their own 'Warsaw German-Yiddish Operetta' and lured away some actors, including the Epelbaums. A tour to Elisavetgrad, Kishinev, and Belts ensued, with the routine stock of plays including *Zayn vaybs man*, *Khantshe in Amerika*, *Der kleyner milioner* (The Little Millionaire), and *Sure Sheyndl*. These pieces that not only Prylucki and Mukdoni, but many provincial critics, found disgusting were spiced up by *Di tsniedike Shoyshane*, which was advertised as 'the new addition to the Yiddish stage', rather than as 'a European operetta'.[59] To all intents and purposes, Menakhem Kipnis's dream came true — the Yiddish theatre had *yiddishized*, digested, adapted the works by Lehar and Gilbert, transforming them into an organic and, seemingly, blended-in segment of the repertoire of the Yiddish troupes that toured the country far and wide. This time Susanne was played by Epelbaum's wife, 'a famous variety show soubrette Miss Rosette Weinstein'. The lead actor was also Mikhail Epelbaum himself. The announcements for his benefit night in Kishinev called the twenty-year-old actor 'the King of the Yiddish stage baritones' and 'the favourite of the local public'.[60] The newspaper reviewers seemed to praise both spouses unanimously, sometimes to a point of exuberance. Their Belts colleague was the only one to add a fly to the ointment:

> Mr Epelbaum has a most rewarding vocal material. Yet his voice, fairly powerful, orotund and rich, is still rather rough, and the actor cannot use it to its best advantage. If trained properly, Mr Epelbaum would hardly make it to the 'King of the Baritones', but would probably hold a prominent place. He has a fairly vivid temperament and knows how to captivate the public.[61]

Yet the critical acclaim was not a guarantee of commercial success — the box office takings were meagre. The same critic, while acknowledging the high quality of the production, lamented:

> It is a shame that our public is still unable duly to appreciate the truly good and talented productions. Feldman Theatre [of Belts] is empty, as always. Discouraged, Rappel and Braun would hardly feel like coming here again, and the same had happened to a number of others who had the misfortune of becoming our ill-fated guests. All the entrepreneurs are bound to fail in Belts, consistently and inevitably.[62]

The affairs of the breakaway entrepreneurs were indeed in dire straits. According to Zina Rappel's memoirs, Braun, panic-stricken, cabled her husband from Kishinev: 'Help, we are starving!' Despite his grievance, Lazar Rappel had to send the money to bail out his reckless brother and all the cast. His interference allowed them to break even and get out of Bessarabia.[63]

The Belts tour ended in early June 1914, and soon the Epelbaums were back in Warsaw. The new Elizeum management hired a new cast, and opened on 17 June with the production of a French play *Madame X*, with Malvina Lobel from New York playing the lead part. It was a real throwback: the 'favourites of the public' Mikhail Epelbaum and Roza Weinstein, who had just basked in the light of their provincial fame, were again overshadowed by their more eminent partners. The newspapers admired the prima donna and praised the famous actors Nathan Dranov, Aizik Samberg, Itskhok Fishelevitsh, and Adolf Berman. However, three weeks later, while reviewing the resuscitated *Di tsnue Shoyshane*, Kipnis made a favourable mention of Epelbaum, who was still playing the part of the Ober Kelner.[64]

Yet this new Warsaw episode of Epelbaum's biography turned out to be rather brief. The First World War began. Theatres closed down all over Poland. That's how Sholem Schwartz, a theatre reviewer from Odessa (who later became Shalom Ben-Baruch, the prominent Israeli journalist and writer), described the situation:

> The storm of war ravished the centres of the Yiddish (as well as Polish) theatre arts. Warsaw, Lodz, Vilna and Minsk used to have 2–3 troupes performing simultaneously, sometimes even more. Now the large Jewish centres that used to have their own cultural life, their own press and theatres, are no more. The Jewish masses turned into an endless stream of fugitives — and Yiddish actors are fugitives too. Odessa is one of the main, if not the main, centre where members of the Yiddish stage family now find refuge.[65]

Epelbaum and his wife also left Warsaw. By mid-September 1914 he was singing in the Yiddish operettas staged by the Novosti Theatre in Odessa, with the troupe under the direction of Nina (Chana) Dashkevitsh.

Conclusion

In the Soviet questionnaires, Epelbaum would write 'incomplete higher musical education'.[66] We do not know what he meant — and whether he meant something specific. As we trace his life course starting with the age of sixteen, with all his interminable touring, we find it hard to locate a period when he might have attended some higher education institution. It is true both regarding those months he had spent in Warsaw — between November 1912 and July 1913, and mid-June to mid-August 1914. Throughout this time, almost every night (as well as in the daytime on Saturdays) he was performing at the Elizeum theatre, and almost every week (and sometimes more often) would take part in a new production. He could possibly find time to be tutored by a private voice instructor, or to attend short-term private musical courses. Still, we can confidently assume that the Merited Artist of the Russian Federation had no conservatoire education, whether complete or not. Like most Yiddish actors of the early twentieth century, he was, to all intents and purposes, a self-trained genius.

What, then, was at the core of his success, of his unique singing career? Let us once again resort to Zinovy Shulman's memoirs and quote his testimony about his friend and colleague in full:

> His strong voice (dramatic baritone) that allowed him to perform opera arias (he was invited more than once to Kiev Opera House and enticed to sing the part of the Demon), his extraordinary stage talent, his distinguished appearance, height, mimics, unrestrained expressiveness and temperament made M. I. Epelbaum a luminary of the Yiddish singing. [. . .] I turned into an Epelbaum fan, and remained one forever, even after I acquired more finesse in the understanding of art and became aware that he had certain flaws.[67]

Possibly it was the lack of the vocal schooling and technique that the memoirist refers to as 'flaws'. Listening to Epelbaum's recordings, we have to admit that the particular charm of his singing is primarily due to his dramatic skills, his emotional and inclusive approach to any kind of material, be it recruits' songs, an anti-Hasidic satire, or Soviet pieces about the Jewish collective farms. He managed to preserve the continuity with the pre-revolutionary Yiddish theatre, democratic, improvisational, close to the folk style, and yet to bring Yiddish singing to a new level through his cooperation with the pianists, the composers, and the arrangers who had a solid musical background and impeccable taste; he united the Yiddish songs with the traditions of the European and Russian vocal art. Lastly, he was the first Soviet Yiddish performer to put together a balanced repertoire: 'acceptable' for the Communist authorities and yet diverse, full of ethnic colour, congenial to the Jewish audience. That's what turned him into the 'pioneer of the genre'.

We have left the twenty-year-old Epelbaum in Odessa in the early autumn of 1914. His rises and falls, his achievements and tribulations still lay ahead. He would

Fig. 8.3. Mikhail Epelbaum's tombstone at the St Petersburg Jewish Cemetery
Photograph © David Frenkel 2013

Fig. 8.4. Mikhail Epelbaum. New York. 1927
From the Archives of the YIVO Institute for Jewish Research

soon be drafted to the Russian Imperial Army and, as we already know, sustain an injury at the front in the First World War; after his discharge, he would rejoin the Yiddish troupes that criss-crossed the Ukraine. In 1919, he would have a narrow escape in the course of a pogrom in Cherkassy carried out by the gangs of Ataman Grigoriev, and soon afterwards, while the Civil War was still raging, he would begin to tour with solo recitals. In 1922–23, his concerts of Yiddish songs would cause a sensation in Moscow and Petrograd. In 1926, he would be touring in the West, performing on the Yiddish stages of Riga, Berlin, Paris, Buenos Aires, and New York. In 1929, he would be back in the Soviet Union, settle first in Kiev, then in Leningrad, and travel far and wide singing Yiddish songs, from Birobidzhan to Białystok. In 1937, he would receive the title of the Merited Artist of the Russian Federation from the Soviet government, and in 1949 ten years of labour camps, with property confiscation. In 1954, he would be released, poor in health, but strong enough in spirit to return to the stage. He would be one of the first Yiddish artists in the post-Stalin Soviet Union to resume touring the country, just two years after the dictator's death — and thus he would bring joy and hope to the terrorized, anguished Soviet Jewish audiences.

Mikhail Iosifovich Epelbaum died of cancer on 15 April 1957, and was buried at the Jewish Cemetery of Leningrad.[68] We can still play the old records with his enchanting voice and his catching laughter. He has recorded thirteen gramophone discs that feature twenty-five songs — a fraction of the great master's extensive repertoire.[69]

Notes to Chapter 8

1. See Zinovy Shulman, 'Onheyb veg', *Sovetish heymland*, 3 (1967), 108–33 (p. 133).
2. On the replacement of scientific ethnomusicological work with propaganda and the establishment of state control over the composition, publication and performance of Jewish music in the Soviet Union see Jeffrey Veidlinger, 'Klezmer and the Kremlin: Soviet Yiddish Folk Songs of the 1930s', *Jews in Eastern Europe*, 1[41] (2000), 5–39.
3. However, his partners would sometimes take part in such debates. Thus, in 1924, while on tour in Simferopol, Epelbaum's accompanist Jascha Fisherman (1895–1976), a pianist and an arranger from Kiev, joined a fierce discussion on the ways of development of modern Jewish music that raged in a local newspaper. He showed himself to be an ardent admirer of Moicei Milner and the other composers from the St Petersburg Society for Jewish Folk Music of the early twentieth century — his opponent even accused him of 'belligerent Zionist ardour' (see *Krasnyi Krym*, Simferopol, 9 August 1924).
4. *Kratkaia evreiskaia entsiklopediia*, x (Jerusalem: The Society for Research on Jewish Communities, The Hebrew University, 2001), col. 661.
5. *Rossiiskaia evreiskaia entsiklopediia*, III (Moscow: Russian Academy of Natural Sciences, The Israel-Russian Encyclopedia Center, 1997), p. 462.
6. The only and, unfortunately, rather unreliable publication on the life of Saul Liubimov (Leibman; 1900–68) is the essay on him in Simon Kopelman, *Ugasshie zvezdy* (Springfield, MA: n.p., 1992), pp. 7–18. As for Zinovy Shulman (1904–77), his artistic career is related in his own memoirs: Zinovy Shulman, 'Onheyb veg', pp. 108–33; idem, 'Zhivi, moia pesnia: Zapiski artista', *Druzhba narodov*, 2 (1969), 215–35.
7. Overall, both encyclopaedia entries on Epelbaum are hopeless. Here are some of the most obvious blunders: erroneous claims that he took part in S. An-sky's ethnographic expedition, visited Africa while touring the Western countries in 1926–29, worked at the Leningrad State Musical Comedy Theatre, personally arranged Jewish folk tunes, held the title of the People's Artist of the Russian Federation (in fact, he was Merited Artist, which was a lower title), having spent several years in the GULAG, was rehabilitated (i.e. cleared of all charges) as early as 1954 (two years before the ground-breaking 20th Congress of the Communist Party!), and had his title reinstated (in fact, he was *released* from the GULAG in 1954, 'for medical reasons' according to the documents, rehabilitated in late 1956 only, and never lived to see his title of the Merited Artist officially returned to him by the Soviet government).
8. *Rossiiskaia evreiskaia entsiklopediia*, III, 462.
9. See Zalmen Kahan, 'Moyshe Epelbaum — der yidisher Shalyapin', *Sovetish heymland*, 8 (1977), 102–04 (p. 103). This unreliable article includes other downright wrong or questionable details. In particular, it is open to doubt whether Epelbaum's original (Jewish) name was Moyshe. More likely he was Mikhoel (see, for instance, his obituary: 'Geshtorbn der sovetish-yidisher artist Mikhoel Epelboym', *Folks-shtime*, Warsaw, 8 May 1957).
10. It seems that the fictitious story presented by Zalmen Kahan was of literary origin. The theme of a young Jewish man who, having discovered his God-given voice, decided to leave his patriarchal environment and to join the Russian or Polish opera permeates Yiddish theatre. Thus, it was the subject of Mark Arnshteyn's classic play *Der vilner balebesl* (1905). On this motif

as a reflection of 'the clash of modernity and tradition' caused by Jewish musical and theatrical performances at the turn of the twentieth century, see Jeffrey Veidlinger, *Jewish Public Culture in the Late Russian Empire* (Bloomington: Indiana University Press, 2009), pp. 215–16.
11. *Kratkaia evreiskaia entsiklopediia*, x, col. 661.
12. Shulman, 'Zhivi, moia pesnia', p. 232.
13. See *Trudovoi Don*, Rostov-on-Don, 5 June 1923; *Izvestiia Vitebskogo Gubispolkoma i Gubkoma RKP(b)*, Vitebsk, 27 October 1923; *Khersonskii kommunar*, Kherson, 27 May 1924.
14. See *Proletarskaia pravda*, Kiev, 27 June 1924.
15. Ibid., 13 April 1924.
16. Ibid., 12 April 1924.
17. See the programme of Epelbaum's concert in the Pillar Hall of the House of the Unions in Moscow on 25 December 1937 (Russian National Library, *Fond gruppovoi obrabotki*, IS 90/3, package 1).
18. For instance, that's what was filed in Epelbaum's criminal case, opened by the Leningrad Region Department of Ministry of State Security of the USSR in May 1949. For more on this, see Alexander Frenkel, '"Sonim af tsulokhes" — "Vragam nazlo": Evreiskaia estrada v Leningrade epokhi ottepeli', *Iz istorii evreiskoi muzyki v Rossii*, III, ed. by Galina Kopytova and Alexander Frenkel (St Petersburg: Evreiskii obshchinnyi tsentr Sankt-Peterburga, Rossiiskii institut istorii iskusstv, 2015), pp. 191–242 (p. 201).
19. 'Apelboym, Misha', *Leksikon fun yidishn teater*, ed. by Zalmen Zylbercweig, I (New York: Elisheva, 1931), col. 84.
20. Ibid., cols. 84–85. Further the article claims that Epelbaum took part in an expedition together with Kiselgof, which is quite improbable. Possibly, in his 'oral interview' the singer tried to explain that he had included in his concert programmes some folk songs recorded by the Leningrad folklorist Zinovii Kiselgof during his ethnographic expeditions, but the Lexicon compiler misinterpreted his answer.
21. See, for instance, Isai Fail', *Zhizn' evreiskogo aktera* (Moscow: Vserossiiskoe teatral'noe obshchestvo, 1938), p. 81.
22. See Nokhem Oyslender, *Yidisher teater: 1887–1917* (Moscow: Der emes, 1940), pp. 261–73; Evgeny Binevich, *Istoriia evreiskogo teatra v Rossii: 1875–1918* (Baltimore: Seagull Press, 2009), pp. 102–75; idem, *Evreiskii teatr v Peterburge* (St Petersburg: Evreiskii obshchinnyi tsentr Sankt-Peterburga, 2003), pp. 31–98; Nahma Sandrow, *Vagabond Stars: A World History of Yiddish Theater* (Syracuse: Syracuse University Press, 1996), pp. 203–13.
23. Fail', *Zhizn' evreiskogo aktera*, p. 72. Mark Myodovnik, who had acted in Mishurat's company several years before Epelbaum, left a detailed description of its mores in his memoirs: unceremonious attitude to the actors and contemptuous one to the public, little, if any, stage directing, plundering of the till by the entrepreneur together with the ticket collectors (see Mark Myodovnik, 'Mayne teater-zikhroynes', *Shtern*, 4 (Minsk, 1926), 32–36 (pp. 33–35)).
24. See *Trudovaia gazeta*, Nikolaev, 1 September 1910.
25. *Iug*, Kherson, 14 November 1910.
26. See 'Apelboym, Rozalia', *Leksikon fun yidishn teater*, I, col. 85.
27. *Aleksandrovskie novosti*, Aleksandrovsk, 2 September 1911.
28. *Melitopol'skie vedomosti*, Melitopol, 21 February 1912.
29. *Elisavetgradskie novosti*, Elisavetgrad, 11 May 1912.
30. *Mariupol'skaia zhizn'*, Mariupol, 15 June 1911.
31. *Elisavetgradskie novosti*, Elisavetgrad, 22 May 1912.
32. *Aleksandrovskii golos*, Aleksandrovsk, 28 March 1912.
33. *Aleksandrovskie novosti*, Aleksandrovsk, 31 August 1911. See also *Pridneprovskii krai*, Ekaterinoslav, 16 September 1911.
34. *Donetskaia zhizn'*, Lugansk, 13 August 1911.
35. *Khersonskaia gazeta Kopeika*, Kherson, 7 June 1911.
36. *Vitebskii vestnik*, Vitebsk, 24 August 1912.
37. *Aleksandrovskii golos*, Aleksandrovsk, 11 March 1912.
38. *Vitebskii vestnik*, Vitebsk, 4 September 1912.
39. In his memoirs, written in New York in 1929, A. Mukdoni, a theatre critic, claimed that he

was the one to come up with the idea of renewing the repertoire of the Yiddish theatre through adding several European operettas in Yiddish translations, and that he was the one who talked Neroslavskaya and Sandler into it (see A. Mukdoni, 'Zikhroynes fun a yidishn teater-kritiker', *Arkhiv far der geshikhte fun yidishn teater un drame*, I, ed by Yakov Shatski (Vilna and New York: YIVO, 1930), pp. 341–421 (p. 411). It is important to keep in mind, while assessing this statement, that the memoirs are full of factual errors.

40. Menakhem Kipnis, 'Fun teater "Elizeum". "Khave"', *Haynt*, 5(18) November 1912.
41. Yozef Latayner (1853–1935) was a playwright, one of the most prolific suppliers of unsophisticated plays for the early Yiddish theatre.
42. Noah Prylucki, 'Teater-felyeton', *Der moment*, 16(29) November 1912; reprinted in Noah Prylucki, *Yidish teater: 1905–1912*, II (Białystok: A. Albek, 1921), pp. 116–19 (p. 117).
43. *Dos pintele yid* and *Yidishe neshome* are names of Yiddish operettas. They are used here as samples of *shund*.
44. A. Mukdoni, 'Eva', *Der fraynd*, 5(18) November 1912.
45. Apart from the announcements in newspapers, we have memoir testimonies for that. Describing his impressions on the show, Zygmunt Turkow mentions that 'Misha Epelbaum, a young actor with great appearance and incredible bass' took part in it (Zygmunt Turkow, *Fragmentn fun mayn lebn* (Buenos Aires: Tsentral-farband fun poylishe yidn in Argentine, 1951), p. 238). The same is confirmed by the less-than-reliable memoirs by A. Mukdoni, who adds: 'The singer was still young and more dynamic, while his voice was softer' (Mukdoni, 'Zikhroynes fun a yidishn teater-kritiker', p. 411). Apparently, this caustic statement was provoked by Epelbaum's performances in New York in 1927.
46. Sfinks [Menakhem Kipnis], ' "Di tsnue Shoyshane"', *Haynt*, 16(29) January 1913.
47. Noah Prylucki, 'Teater-felyeton', *Der moment*, 21 January (3 February) 1913; reprinted in Prilutski, *Yidish teater: 1905–1912*, II, 122.
48. D"r A. M. [A. Mukdoni], ' "Di tsnue Shoyshane"', *Der fraynd*, 17(30) January 1913.
49. Dr A. M. [A. Mukdoni], 'Teater-notitsn. "Dr. Zeyfnbloz"', *Der fraynd*, 4(17) December 1912.
50. See, for instance, the announcement in *Haynt*, 18(31) January 1913.
51. See, for instance, the announcement in *Der moment*, 30 April (13 May) 1913.
52. ' "Uriel Akosta", teater "Elizeum"', *Der fraynd*, 4(17) June 1913.
53. See, for instance, *Katalog evreiskikh plastinok Russkogo aktsionernogo obshchestva grammofonov v S. Peterburge* (Warsaw: n.p., [1913]). See also the discography of another recording company, Syrena Record, <http://www.russian-records.com/details.php?image_id=9834&l=russian>. The catalogues of the records give us a unique insight into the repertoire of the professional Yiddish singers of that period. Strictly speaking, the challenge of introducing the Yiddish folklore to the concert stage, as well as of its adaptation for the needs of contemporary audiences, still had to be tackled. Menakhem Kipnis began working on it in Warsaw in the pre-First World War years, Epelbaum in the Ukraine in 1917, when the February Revolution eliminated all the restrictions, and the Yiddish artists gained freedom in their concert activities.
54. Natan Meir, 'Kipnis, Menakhem', *YIVO Encyclopedia of Jewish Eastern Europe*, I (New Haven and London: Yale University Press, 2008), pp. 897–98.
55. Itzik Nakhmen Gottesman, *Defining the Yiddish Nation: The Jewish Folklorists of Poland* (Detroit: Wayne State University Press, 2003), p. 65. For detailed analysis of Kipnis's activity, see ibid., pp. 56–66.
56. Thus, practically throughout his entire career Epelbaum would include in his repertoire macaronic Yiddish folk songs (i.e. songs in a mix of languages). In the posters and programmes for his concerts, these songs used to comprise a special section under the title '*Ukrainizirovannaia evreiskaia pesnia*' (Ukrainized Yiddish Song). As early as the beginning of the 1920s, he would already perform such songs as *Khezhbn tsedek*, *Der tate un di kinder*, *Mikitke* (see *Iskusstvo*, 7 (Kiev, 1922), 14; *Zhizn' iskusstva*, 43 (Petrograd, 1923), 18). In November 1923, *Mikitke* and *Katerina-moloditsa* performed by Epelbaum were phonographed by the folklorist Zinovii Kiselgof (see Liudmyla Sholokhova, *Fonoarkhiv ievreiskoyi muzychnoyi spadshchyny* (Kiev: Natsional'na Akademiia nauk Ukraïny: Natsional'na biblioteka imeni V. I. Vernads'koho, 2001), p. 696; see also tracks 24 and 25 at the CD 'Historical Collection of Jewish Musical Folklore: 1912–1947. Vol. 3. Materials from the Zinovii Kiselgof Collection' that was issued by the Vernadsky

National Library of Ukraine in Kiev in 2004). All the above-mentioned songs were first published by Menakhem Kipnis in a special chapter 'Yudish-ukrainishe folks-lider' (Yiddish-Ukrainian Songs) of his first collection (see *Folks-lider fun M. Kipnis un Z. Zeligfelds kontsert-repertuar* (Warsaw: A. Gitlin, [1918]), pp. 127–40; see also Gottesman, *Defining the Yiddish Nation*, p. 62). There is an obvious continuity between the repertoires of the two singers. However, Epelbaum's versions, as recorded on the phonograph cylinders, are markedly different from Kipnis's versions, to say nothing of the fact that as early as 1923 the repertoire of the Soviet singer included more macaronic songs than one can find in the collection of his Warsaw predecessor. That means that we are dealing not with a straightforward imitation, but with the continuity of ideas, of the overall approach to the folk material.

57. For the review of Peretz's staging see Menakhem Kipnis, 'Dray matones', *Haynt*, 23 July 1913.
58. See Nechemias Zucker, *Fir doyres yidish teater: Di lebns-geshikhte fun Zina Rapel* (Buenos Aires: n.p., 1944), p. 302.
59. See, for instance, *Bessarabskaia zhizn'*, Kishinev, 11(24) April 1914.
60. See ibid., 17(30) April and 18 April (1 May) 1914.
61. *Beletskaia mysl'*, Beltsy, 25 May 1914.
62. Ibid.
63. See Zucker, *Fir doyres yidish teater*, pp. 306–07.
64. See Menakhem Kipnis, 'Teater-notitsn. Di tsnue Shoyshane', *Haynt*, 6(19) July 1914.
65. Shv. [Sholem Schwartz; Shalom Ben-Baruch], 'Teatr Bolgarovoi. "Dvosia sufrazhistka"', *Odesskie novosti*, 9(22) October 1915.
66. At least, this was the data on Epelbaum's education as filed in his criminal case. For more details see Frenkel, '"Sonim af tsulokhes" — "Vragam nazlo"', p. 201.
67. Shulman, 'Zhivi, moia pesnia', p. 232.
68. For more details on Epelbaum's biography see Alexander Frenkel, 'Pioner evreiskoi narodnoi muzyki Mikhail Epelbaum', *Evreiskie pesni iz repertuara Mikhaila Epelbauma dlia golosa i fortepiano* (St Petersburg: Evreiskii obshchinnyi tsentr Sankt-Peterburga, 2014), pp. 5–16.
69. For Epelbaum's discography see ibid., pp. 113–18 (all the twenty-five songs recorded by Epelbaum with US and Soviet labels between 1927 and 1939 are included into the CD supplement to the book).

CHAPTER 9

Warsaw, St Petersburg, and Moscow in the Life of the Yiddish Actress Clara Young

Galina Eliasberg

Clara Young is known as one of the most brilliant actresses of the Yiddish theatre of the first half of the twentieth century. Her performances in the first decade of the twentieth century, and later in the 1920s and 1930s, went all over the wide geography of the Jewish diaspora in Europe and America from Argentina and Brazil to Canada. But two countries played a special role in her life: the United States, where she started her professional career as an actress in the Yiddish-American theatre and musical comedy, and the Russian Empire, later the Soviet Union, where she spent the last decades of her life. Clara Young 'led the Jewish musical comedy from the quarters of the poor to the rich stages of the European capital cities', as was noted by the Russian American journalist Simon Kopelman in his short biography of the actress.[1]

The history of Clara Young's life and theatrical career was truly remarkable. Theatre critics from the United States, Poland, Russia, England, France, Romania, Austria, and Germany wrote about her art. Great Yiddish writers, such as Mendele Moycher-Sforim, Y. L. Peretz, H. N. Bialik, Mordechai Spector, S. An-sky, and David Frishman, attended her performances in Warsaw and Odessa. Famous Russian theatre actors from Moscow and St Petersburg, such as Vasily Kachalov, Ivan Moskvin, Olga Knipper-Chekhova, Maria Blumental-Tamarina, Vera Yureneva, the stage director and playwright Nikolay Popov, as well as political figures as diverse as Anatoly Lunacharsky, Karl Radek, and Grigory Rasputin, admired her talent.

During her long theatre career Clara Young played in approximately 300 musical comedies and plays written by Jewish and European playwrights. The most popular among them were *Dzhekele-blofer* (Jeykele the Bluffer), *Di zekste vayb* (The Sixth Wife), and *Leybele Odesit* (Leybele from Odessa), written specially for her by her husband Boaz Youngvitz. Clara played brilliantly in Joseph Rumshinsky and Anshl Shor's operetta *Di Amerikanerin (Dos meydl fun der vest)* (The American Girl (The Girl from the West)), in Moyshe Shor's *Di Rumeynishe hasene* (The Romanian Wedding), and in Abraham Shomer's *Olraytnikes* (Allrightniks). In the 1920s she played in many of Israel Rosenberg's musical comedies, notably *Berele tremp* (Berele, the Vagabond Boy), *Shoshana, Dem farmers tokhter* (The Farmer's Daugther), *Dos holander vaybl* (The

Dutch Woman) *and Dos ungarishe meydl* (Hungarian Girl), and in Nahum Rakov and Joseph Rumshinsky's operetta *Hantshe in Amerike* (Hanche in America). Several manuscripts of these plays are preserved in her personal file in the Russian State Archive for Literature and Art in Moscow (RGALI, File 2682).

The book of memoirs of Clara Young's husband, the stage director and actor Boaz Youngvitz *Mayn lebn in teatr* (*My Life in Theatre*, New York, 1950), remains the most important source for the biography of the actress, but it provides information only up to the mid-1930s. Additional sources are newspaper and magazine reviews of Clara Young's tours in Warsaw, St Petersburg, and Moscow, as well as archival materials such as her Russian autobiography (1938), which is composed in according to the formal Soviet template, the unpublished memoirs (1966) by ballet actor Akiva Dinner, a Russian article by Yeshua (Ovsey) Lubomirsky (1930s), and a chapter from his 1976 Yiddish memoirs *Af di lebnsvegn* (*On the Roads of Life*), which describes the last decades of her life in the Soviet Union.[2]

Clara Young was the stage name of Khaya-Risye Shpikolitser. As she mentions in her 1938 autobiography, her father's family name is derived from the name of a small shtetl in Galicia. She states: 'I was born on 10 December 1886 in the town of Złoczew (Galicia) in a poor Jewish family', but the date is crossed out. The question about the year of birth was always difficult for her biographers. In other sources one can find that she was born 1876, 1877, 1878, 1882, and 1888. Boaz Youngvitz wrote that his wife descended from a Jewish religious family which was dominated by her merchant grandfather. His only son, Clara's father, was a *maskil*, a close friend of the poet Naftali Hirsh Imber, the author of the famous poem 'Hatikvah', which became the anthem of Israel.[3] In the hall of her grandfather's house Clara saw Polish amateur theatricals and plays staged by Jewish companies. She was six years old when she saw a musical performance with the Yiddish actress Rokhl Akselrod. Her autobiography contains a detailed and emotional description of that episode, and later Clara said that from that very moment she was caught by a passion for the theatre.

After her father's death Clara, who was only seven years old, was sent to New York to the family of her aunt. In New York she studied at school and started to play in mass scenes in the Yiddish theatre. Her sister helped her to join the *Goldfaden Dramatic farain* (Goldfaden Drama Union), where she made her debut as a singer with a song *Heyse babkelekh yidelekh koyft* (Jews, Buy Hot Sweet Cakes) in the role of a homeless boy — a seller of hotcakes at the scene *At the market* in Abraham Goldfaden's comedy *Di kishefmakherin* (The Sorceress). Later on she got the main role — Mirele — in this play, and was invited to Sigmund Feinman's Yiddish People's Theatre. At this period she studied at Feinman's Dramatic Club. Also she studied the art of dance at the Brother's Keralfa Studio. In the article published in the Warsaw newspaper *Literarishe bleter* (31 October 1924) under the title 'Vi azoy Klara Yong is gevorn an operetn-aktrise' (How Clara Young Became an Operetta Actress) and in the 1938 autobiography the actress mentioned that she studied with the prominent American director David Belasco and started to play small roles in English theatre.

Her life made a real switch in 1896, when she became acquainted with Boaz

Youngvitz, the 26-year-old Yiddish actor. Later in his memoirs *Mayn lebn in teater* (My Life in Theatre) Boaz wrote that at this time she was already married and had a child: 'Her blue eyes were pure as crystal and full with fire of youth and hypnotic strength, but deep in her eyes one could see that she was unhappy.'[4] Her first husband was an entrepreneur named Heinman who was sixteen years older than Clara. After some public scandals she finally left her husband to marry Boaz. The new couple travelled to New York, where Boaz started to work in the People's Theater with Jacob Adler and Boris Tomashevsky, but there was no place for Clara. Only in 1903 was she invited to the Music Hall, where she sang her famous songs — 'Di dame fun Broadway' (Dame from the Broadway) and 'Libe mayne' (My Love) — and immediately received great success. As a result she was invited to the People's Theater where she played in Joseph Lateiner's plays on Jewish everyday life and in classical repertoire. Here Clara also played alongside the famous German-Jewish actor Rudolph Schildkraut when he toured in New York. In his productions of Shakespeare Clara Young played Cordelia in *King Lear* and Jessica in *The Merchant of Venice*. In her autobiography 1938 she stressed that Schildkraut's tours on the Jewish scene became a major theatrical event in New York. She also played in Alexandre Dumas's *Kean*, in Friedrich Schiller's *The Robbers*, and Karl Gutzkow's *Uriel Acosta* alongside the famous German actor Moritz Morrison on his tour in the People's Theater.

An important change in her life took place in 1909 when she started to play the Yiddish drama repertoire, although she was not engaged in leading roles. Clara and Boaz worked with David Kessler's Thalia Theater on the Lower East Side, where the actress played a number of roles in Jacob Gordin's plays. Clara played with the famous Jewish dramatic actress Esther-Rokhl Kaminska on the latter's tour in New York. They played together in Hermann Sudermann's *Homeland* (Clara as a younger sister Magda) and Jacob Gordin's *The Kreutzer Sonata* (as Celia). During this period she received an invitation from representatives of the American theatre, but decided to stay on the Yiddish stage. Her colleagues were surprised. 'While the temptation to work on the American scene was great (and the working conditions were very tempting), I chose to remain a Jewish actress', noted Clara Young in 1938.

Her position in the theatre changed in 1910 due to Boaz Youngvitz's new version of H. Maizel's musical comedy *Bigamiste*, which was remade specially for Clara.[5] In the version now called *Zayn vaybs man* (His Wife's Husband) she got the main role, which became her great success. It was the first time when she performed as a soubrette. Clara and Boaz started to play it on tours in Boston, Chicago, and Philadelphia, and then crossed the ocean and played in London where they signed a contract with the Warsaw entrepreneur Hershl Eppelberg.

In the article 'Mayn ershter oyftrit in Varshe' (My First Performance in Warsaw), published in the Yiddish newspaper *Varshe* (1 January 1930), the actress described her first visit in 1910 to the office of the Elysium Theatre. At that time the famous actor Maurice Moscovitch performed in August Strindberg's play *The Father*. The theatre director was confused when he saw Clara in a raincoat because she didn't look like other American actresses with their expensive make-up and dresses. Eppelberg refused to allow her to play in Warsaw and sent the young actress on tour to Lodz.

In 1938 Clara Young explained this curious occurrence. Being still very young but already successful on the stage she had tried throughout to be modest as befits a 'great actress'. In America a decent actress dressed up modestly and did not stand out in the community. 'But I'm too overzealous in his modesty and paid for it'. So, the director sent her with part of his troupe to Lodz. The first two performances in Lodz she played in Zandberg's theatre on the Sabbath day (morning and evening) to full houses. On Sunday morning, the formidable Eppelberg unexpectedly arrived from Warsaw and warmly applauded her during the play. On Tuesday she appeared on the stage in Warsaw and played there for six weeks.

The success in Warsaw was so great that the historian of Yiddish Theatre Michal Weichert compared her first performance with the success of Goldfaden at the beginning of the 1880s and with An-sky's play *The Dibbuk* performed by the Vilna Troupe in the 1920s. Her tour in 1911 was no less successful. Those who had previously ignored the Yiddish scene started to visit her performances.[6] Alexander Mukdoni also recalled the impression that Young made on the Warsaw audience. For the first a soubrette represented not an image of a poor and unfortunate simpleton, but of a hero full of vitality, temperament, and humour. Audiences in Warsaw acknowledged her talent when she was not widely known in the theatre world. Mukdoni stressed that at that time the art of the operetta flourished on the Polish stage and Warsaw's operetta actress successfully performed on many stages in Russia and Europe. He noted Young's personal modesty and simplicity in communication and stressed that she continued to gain success in Warsaw in 1920s and 1930s, but the success of her tour in Russia, which he had witnessed himself in Moscow in 1916, was even more grandiose. She managed to charm not only ordinary spectators, but also intellectuals.[7]

In the summer of 1912 Clara Young travelled to Warsaw with Rumshinsky and Shor's play *Di amerikanerin*. Once again she had a great success. The audience of her viewers was very wide, including Jews and Poles, Hasidim and assimilated intellectuals. Not only Jews, but also Catholic Poles sang Rumshinsky's music and songs. She was praised by the Yiddish and Hebrew writers Jacob Dinezon, Mordechai Spector, and David Frishman (the latter's lithographic portrait is preserved in Young's archive in Moscow). In the article '*Di yidishe subretin*' (The Jewish Soubrette), published on 27 August 1912 in the Warsaw Yiddish daily *Der Moment*, Mordke Spektor wrote that Clara Young brought to Yiddish a new word, *subretin*, because after her performances the Jewish audience started to understand the real meaning of this notion.

Clara Young published her memoir article in the Warsaw weekly *Literarishe bleter* (17 October 1924) under the title 'Perets als dzhentlemen' (Peretz as a Gentleman) in which she described her meeting with the great writer. Boaz Youngvitz also mentions in his memoirs their visit to Peretz's flat and their conversation on Yiddish theatre and Yiddish actors, and the Russian, Polish, and American stages. It is noteworthy that Y. L. Peretz, the author of the famous symbolist dramas *The Night at the Old Marketplace* and the *The Golden Chain*, a sharp critic of the second-rate plays that formed the stock repertoire of the Jewish stage, had admitted at that evening that the Jewish audience also needed operetta and musical comedy. At the same time, he stressed that the main problem he saw in the lack of professionalism of the actors and their bad artistic taste. The actress recalled that after the performances Peretz called her on the phone and warmly thanked her for the high aesthetic pleasure and particularly for her Yiddish, which sounded charming in her voice.[8] In an interview with Anita Blumenthal for *Der yidisher froyen zhournal* (Jewish Women's Journal, 1922) Clara Young recalled her meetings with Y. L. Peretz and emphasized his spiritual strength and inner nobility.[9]

After a short visit to the United States the actors returned to Warsaw in 1912, where Boaz Youngvitz's actors performed their comedy repertoire in Kaminsky's theatre. For the first time he put on the Yiddish stage the new German operetta *Puppchen* (*Puptshik* in Yiddish) by Jean Gilbert (pen-mane of Max Winterfeld). In 1913 Clara Young successfully performed in Warsaw in their new comedy *Alma, vu voynstu?* (Alma, Where Do You Live?), based on the play of the Broadway composer and writer Adolf Philipp. Newspapers stressed the brilliant talent of the actress. Clara and Boaz toured a lot in Warsaw in the 1910s and 1920s, presenting their new comedies: *Hayke in zibetn himl* (Hayke on the Top of the World; music by Joseph Tantsman) and Boaz Youngvitz's *Sha, der rebe fort!* (Hush, the Rebbe is Coming!), written in 1927 and performed in Warsaw in 1929 and 1930.[10] The poet Peretz Markish, who lived in Warsaw before he moved to the Soviet Union in 1926, admired her 'delicate theatrical skills'. According to him, frivolity in operetta somehow was effaced as soon as Clara Young touched it. She played without a trace of cynicism and did not pursue a cheap effect. Instead, her performances turned into a manifestation of 'deep artistic revelation'.[11] Mukdoni wrote that in the 1910s the Warsaw theatrical community was well aware that Clara was not the first star in the American Yiddish Theatre, but, as often happens, fame comes to an actor not at home but away from home. From the retrospect of the mid-1950s, he wrote that Clara Young wasn't an actress of a modern operetta, but her art was based on the old American school and she deserved the special gratitude of audiences in Russia and Poland as a wonderful actress, who was able to create a wonderful theatrical atmosphere of real art.[12] Warsaw reviewers focused on Clara Young's musical and theatrical art and the well-understood conventions and boundaries of the operetta as a genre, while in the Russian capitals, and especially during the Soviet period, her funny musical performances not infrequently gave rise to ideological criticism.

The outbreak of the First World War caught Young and Youngvitz in Warsaw soon after their tours in London, Vienna, and Berlin. From Warsaw they decided to travel on tour to Odessa, at that time one of the important centres of Jewish theatrical culture. Boaz Youngvitz wrote that in Odessa they became acquainted with the Yiddish writers Yoel Linezky, Mendele Moycher-Sforim, and H.-N. Bialik, who were in the audience. Like Y. L. Peretz in Warsaw, Mendele was highly inspired by her wonderful voice and the sound of her Yiddish. In Odessa they staged for the first time the musical comedy *M'lle Goplya* (Mademoiselle Hoopla), based on Georges Feydeau's play *La Dame de Chez Maxim* (The Girl from Maxim's).[13]

For their second visit to Odessa after their tour in Romania, Boaz Youngvitz prepared a new comedy, *Dzhekele-blofer*, with music by Fishl Kanapov. This play would become Clara's theatrical visiting card. It was a story about a girl and a

FIG. 9.1. Clara Young in Moscow, at the Pillar Hall of the House of the Unions, 1937. Courtesy of the RGALI, file 2682

wealthy barber, Aizik Pipik, who made his fortune in New York. Mr Pipik wants to marry his son Moritz to a girl from the respectable family of Mr Kutzik. But Moritz is in love with Iva, the daughter of Zilberberg, with whom Mr Pipik quarrelled because of some 10,000 dollar bills, which should be paid back to him. Learning from Moritz that his father intends to sell their summer cottage at auction, Iva decides to act. In order to get into Pipik's house, she dresses up in a suit impersonating a shoeshine boy named Jeykele. After a series of metamorphoses Jeykele (Iva) manages to steal her father's bills out of Pipik's locker. And then with the assistance of Mr Pipik himself the girl manages to organize her own wedding with Moritz. The plot of this play reflects many recognizable features of the musical comedies staged by Boaz Youngvitz for Clara.

After the performances in Odessa and Ekaterinoslav Boaz Youngvitz decided to play in Moscow. But it was rather complicated, because most of the actors did not have the *pravozhitelstvo*, a permit to reside beyond the Pale of Jewish Settlement. Boaz Youngvitz wrote in his memoirs about a discussion between S. An-sky and David Frishman in the famous cafe Fankoni in Odessa. An-sky hoped that Young and Youngvitz's tour would be possible because of the expectation of political reforms, to which Frishman ironically responded that the artists certainly could play in Moscow, but for an overnight rest they would have to travel to Berdichev.[14]

In July 1916, with the help of the Russian actor Leonid Leonidov (Volfenzon) from The Moscow Art Theatre and by paying bribes to relevant officials, they received a permit to play in Moscow, but only four of the troupe's sixty actors were allowed to stay in the city. The others stayed in the suburbs of Moscow, slept on the benches near the Pushkin monument in the city centre by day, and spent the nights tramping the streets. In early August the *Teatralnaia gazeta* (Theatrical Newspaper, nos 32 and 33), edited by Emmanuel Beskin, published two reports from Ekaterinoslav about the 'quite exceptional success of the two-month tour of the troupe of Boaz Youngvitz': 'A significant percentage of visitors of the Jewish operetta are not Jewish. Interest focused almost exclusively on the versatile actress Clara Young. She was not only an operetta actress, but also a comedienne', wrote the correspondent, comparing her 'noble style on the stage' with the famous Russian comedy actress Elena Granovsky.

> Clara Young is well known in America, Western Europe and in the Russian provinces, but she remains completely unknown in the capitals of Russia, and major Russian theatre critics have so far not been able to speak about this wonderful actress.[15]

On 14 August 1916, the liberal Moscow newspaper *Russkie vedomosti* (no. 188) published a report about the beginning of their tour in the Nikitsky Theatre, which at that time was known as the Potopchina's Theatre. It was founded in 1910 by the famous operetta actress Evgeniya Potopchina and her husband and impresario Boris Evelinov (theatrical name of Boris Shteynfinkel, a native of Odessa). Moses Jankowski, the author of the monograph on the history of the art of operetta in Europe and in Russia, stressed the increasing popularity of operetta during the war. On the other hand, it was a period of crisis for the repertoire in Russia because the authorities did not welcome Viennese and German operettas.[16] In a certain sense, this situation also contributed to the rise of interest in American comedy.

On 17 August, the Moscow newspaper *Teatr* (Theatre) wrote about the special temperament of Clara Young, her eccentric style of singing, performance and individual elegant gestures, praised her beautiful appearance and inborn grace. The audience was exalted about an operetta from American-Jewish life.[17] On 27 August, the theatre reporter Rodya (pen-name of Rodion Mendelevich) from the same newspaper published an interview with the following remark: 'Clara Young arrived, and the public rushed to see her art; not only specifically Jewish, but also general public, without distinction of religion.'[18] Judging by this interview, Clara Young on her tour in Russia preferred to be presented as an American actress, not an emigrant one.

On 28 August the chief editor of the *Teatralnaia gazeta* (Theatre Gazette, no. 35) Emmanuil Beskin published the article 'On Clara Young Tours'. He wrote that the talent of the American-Jewish actress resolved all problems and discussions about the so-called crisis of the operetta. Clara Young was 'a virtuoso of the operetta, the greatest master of it in prose and in music'. According to Beskin, she was great in the operetta as Italian actress Eleonora Duse was great in the drama; in the field of frivolous operetta Young created a plastic and psychologically infinitely delicate 'watercolour' that Duse did in drama. Other correspondents wrote about 'endless applause and floral offerings', the newspaper reported about the 'diamond brooch, from which an "admirer" [. . .] did not remove the labels with the price — 5,500 roubles'. The income for the performance reached 7,000 roubles, which was an unprecedented amount for Potopchina's Nikitsky Theatre.[19] Mendelevich joked that ticket speculators were very pleased with Clara Young, because they earned on her tour no less than on Feodor Chaliapin's concerts.

The performances in Moscow were very successful and the actors were rewarded. This success helped them to obtain permission to play in Petrograd. In numerous reviews of this tour, critics mentioned some famous names in the audience, including influential representatives of the Russian aristocracy.[20] For a Russian audience Clara Young personified not the Jewish theatre, but the American theatre and the American style. Theatre reviews of St Petersburg consistently reported on this tour. Information on the performances and the responses to them had been published in the influential liberal newspapers *Rech* and *Birzhevye vedomosti*.

A number of comments reflected a controversy about the national character of the Boaz Youngvitz troupe. Vasily Rappoport from *Birzhevye vedomosti* (5 October 1916) argued that almost all productions of the 'Warsaw's Yankees', as he called them, were missing something specifically national or ethnographic. Rather, it was an American eccentric operetta, which borrowed its scenes and tricks from all over the world. The operettas' music was banal and the libretto included only a few Jewish comic verses and dances. Their language was more American than the language of 'our Pale of Settlement', it was 'the language of the emigre quarters of New York, interspersed with catchwords of American street slang and Odessa patters'. But then this strict reviewer paid tribute to the skill of the comic actress and her partners, who attracted hundreds of viewers.

After the performance of the play *Hanche in Amerika*, Nikolai Volkovussky (*Birzhevye мedomosti*, 6 October 1916) regretted that the actress repeated herself by selecting plays with travesty roles. *Hanche in Amerike* is a jumble of the usual operetta tricks with an admixture of vulgar American responses to sensation that has long been dead, like the performance of a meeting of suffragettes. This piece, he continued, was no worse and no better than anything else from such 'unworthy repertoire' for the talented actress as Clara Young. Another critic, named S. Frid, argued that the play *Alma, vu voynstu?* was not suitable for the Jewish Theatre (*Birzhevye vedomosti*, 8 October 1916).

Two articles by I. Rabinovich in the newspaper *Rech* (29 September and 6 October 1916) contain criticism of Young's repertoire. He argued that not only in Yiddish plays, but even in the European repertoire it would be difficult to find a play matching Young's versatile talent. Not being able to find a suitable art piece, Boaz Youngvitz narrowed her performance diapason and always directed Clara Young in the same genre. Similar regrets were expressed in other articles that appeared in the theatrical periodicals of Petrograd. Jewish theatre critics remembered the tour of Ester-Rokhl Kaminska's troupe and her success in the capital in 1908, and hoped that the American Jewish troupe would show something that could be categorized as a 'serious dramatic play'. The magazine *Zritel* (The Spectator) announced that on September 29 American-Jewish Operetta troupe by Boaz Youngvitz arranged an evening in memory of Sholem Aleichem which included two of Sholem Aleichem's plays, *Tsezeyt un tseshpreyt* (Scattered and Spread) and *Mentshen* (People). Clara Young did not participate in these performances, and the responses reflected the disappointment of the public. L. Annibal wrote in *Obozrenie teatrov* (*Overview of Theatres*): 'Apparently, the Jewish theatre is waiting for its reformers in the light genre, as it found them in the serious dramatic art' (23 September 1916).

Of particular interest are the reviews of Alexander Kugel, the editor of the *Teatr i iskusstvo* (Theatre and Arts), the leading theatrical magazine in Russia, which paid special attention to the problems of national and provincial theatres. Kugel wrote that Boaz Youngvitz's musical comedies portrayed the process of transformation, even conversion, of a traditional East European Yankl into an American Yankee. All performances were smart and cheerful. But where was the 'daughter of Israel', Kugel asked, contrasting the Americanized style to the realistic plays from Jewish life.[21] Such a negative attitude to the American popular culture was rather typical for Russian intellectuals and later for Soviet critics. However, at the end of the tour Kugel changed his sceptical attitude to the art of Clara Young and her partners. Now he raised a question about the distinctive characteristics of Jewish mentality and ways of its representation on the stage, comparing Clara Young's operettas and dramas of Russian-Jewish playwright Semen Yushkevich that were performed at that time in Russian theatres. According to Kugel, they both are able to transmit their 'Jewish accent' in their own way. Clara Young showed that Jews were able to adapt to different environments, but at the same time they preserved their identity.[22]

The weekly *Evreiskaia nedelia* (Jewish Week) noted a paradox: although the Yiddish press was banned by the government, the troupe of American Jews was allowed to stay in Petrograd, 'talking and playing in Yiddish'. The reviewer K. Shneyfal noted

> the enthusiasm of the Jewish Petrograd public that ingested buzzwords and jokes by Clara Young [. . .] You should have seen those impeccably dressed majestic men with massive rings . . . those elegantly dressed ladies [. . .] I have for a long time not seen such a happy Jewish public in a Petrograd theatre. In Clara Young they appreciate not only the talented operetta actress, but also a vivid manifestation of the native *Yidishkayt*, for which their soul yearns secretly.[23]

Liberal Russian reviewers emphasized the international character of Clara Young's repertoire. Thus, Nikolai Shebuev, the editor of the magazine *Zritel* (Spectator), wrote that Clara Young was a beautiful actress who reminded him some of the best features of Russian actresses, such as the intonations of Vera Yureneva, the dances of Vera Shuvalova, the voice of Victoria Kavetskaia and the mischief of Evgeniia Potopchina. Addressing the Jews of Petrograd, he invited them to the theatre to admire their 'Jewish sister', who knew how to laugh and to make people laugh, to rejoice and to gladden. And the prominent theatre critic Iuri Beliaev wrote:

> I do not understand jargon [Yiddish], I could only admire the subtle play of the actress . . . She is a very interesting artist, her style is full of nobility and even in a most risky position she does not descend into caricature. In general, the entire Jewish troupe is full of comic elements.[24]

Boaz Youngvitz wrote that among the admirers of the actress were the Countess Volkonskaia and the influential banker and jeweller Aron Simonovich. Clara Young was invited to a party at the Jewish banker's home with Grigory Rasputin.

Youngvitz described a man in a silk shirt and boots, who proposed a toast 'for the little nation' of Jews.[25] At the party Clara sang in English and in Yiddish. In her memoir article published in New York she mentioned that 'Rasputin was a kind and cunning person'.[26]

The press (for instance, *Zritel*, no. 13, 1916) reported that for the 1917–18 season there were plans to open a Jewish theatre in Moscow with the participation of Clara Young. However, further revolutionary events left these plans unrealized. In the summer of 1917, *Teatralnaia gazeta* published photos and reports about Young's performance in the Nikitsky Theatre. In his article, Beskin (*Teatralnaia gazeta*, no. 20, 1917, p. 10) invited the critics who led theoretical debates about the crisis of the operetta to watch Clara Young. He was convinced that her talent and her ability to be cheerful and elegant would offer a solution to the problem. He stressed that although Clara Young enjoyed travesty roles, her real character was a 'woman in a dress', a women with deep feelings. He noted that the troupe came with a smaller ensemble. Beskin regretted the absence of the talented actor Fishl Kanapov and criticized the male choir. He called upon Youngvitz to 'create a worthy frame and repertoire' for Young's talent. On 20 August 1917 Beskin's newspaper published the photo of Clara with the famous singer Iza Kremer on its cover. Both actresses successfully toured in Russia in 1916 and 1917. It may be noted that the tours of Youngvitz's company in Russia in 1916 became a real triumph of Jewish-American theatre, and to some extent shaped the image of the American scene among the Russian audience.[27]

During the days of the February revolution of 1917 actors stayed in Odessa, and the October Bolshevik *coup d'état* caught them in Gomel. The local Cheka, the new regime's secret police, arrested Youngvitz and detained him for several days as a foreign spy. During the dangerous period of the civil war, the actors had to sell their clothes for bread; they played before and after pogroms, and several actors lost their lives.[28] In the meantime, Boaz and Clara faced a conflict. Boaz created 'the actress Clara Young', but became jealous of her stage fame and professional success. Nevertheless, after a short separation they continued to cooperate. In 1920 Youngvitz managed to leave Russia using his US passport and settled in New York, while Clara continued to play in Vienna and Bucharest, and returned to the United States only in 1921. Then she went to Europe again and performed in Warsaw with her concert programme.[29]

With the beginning of the New Economic Policy (NEP) in 1921, it became possible to organize tours of foreign actors in Soviet Russia. On 27 October 1922 the Moscow central newspaper *Izvestia* published a short announcement about the opening of the Concert Bureau in Petrograd, whose tasks included issuing invitations to foreign artists and sending Russian artists abroad. It also reported that a Jewish troupe of the well-known actress Clara Young should soon arrive in Petrograd. But that tour did not take place. According to Youngvitz, it was in 1924, when they were in Lodz at that time, that they received a telegram with an invitation from the Soviet People's Commissariat of Education. The Soviet authorities offered them a very significant sum of money, and they signed their first six-month contract with the representatives of the new regime. Alexander

Dymarsky, who began his career as a theatrical impresario before the revolution, now became their chief administrator. In June 1925, they came to Moscow to form a Jewish musical company.

At that time Clara and Boaz worked with the composer Ilia Trilling (he left the Soviet Union in 1927), and actors Grigory Spektorov, Iasha Kabak, and others. They had an orchestra, a choir, and a ballet group. This tour took place during the time of sharp debates around the art of operetta in Soviet Russia. The new ideology tended to deem this genre 'bourgeois'. The Nikitsky Theatre, where Clara started her tour in 1916, was closed down by the new authorities in 1919, and in 1920 Evgeniia Potopchina and Boris Evelinov emigrated to Berlin. In the 1920s Soviet officials put forward a programme of reforming this genre. Theatre magazines and other publications were filled with articles concerning operetta as a genre close to political satire, and put forward a demand for 'wide public significance of its social content': 'In our Soviet life we need political satire and political operetta'.[30] At the beginning of 1925 the Private Moscow Operetta Theatre was renamed the Theatre of Musical Comedy.

On 19 July 1925, *Izvestia* announced that the Jewish comedy troupe led by the American director Boaz Youngvitz would begin its performances on 24 July by staging the musical comedy *Dzheykele blofer*. Fifteen performances were planned for the Moscow leg of the troupe's tour, playing *Di amerikanerin* (American Woman), *Dos zekste wibe* (The Seventh wife), *Berel-Sheygets* (Berel-hellion), *Romanian hasene* (Romanian Wedding), and *Hayke in zibetn himl* (Hayke on the Top of the World). After Moscow the troupe was going to perform in Leningrad and in the cities of Ukraine.

On 26 July, *Izvestia* published an article by Sadko (pen-name of the Soviet Russian critic Vladimir Blum), an ardent supporter of Vsevolod Meyerhold and his ideas of revolutionary art. At that time Blum edited the magazine *Novyi zritel* (New Spectator) and headed the Theatrical and Musical section of Glavrepertkom (Chief Repertoire Committee in charge of censorship in the system of *Narkompros*). The article started with a resolute statement that this American-Jewish theatre was 'completely alien to and not interesting for us at all'. Moreover, it was not even Jewish for they performed only one Jewish dance in the *Dzheykele blofer*. In reality, argued Blum, this company played out a 'Jewish internationally petty-bourgeois farce with music'. He ironically mentioned the tune of the *International* in the overture. The use of revolutionary music, as well as certain details in the scenes of strikes and protests on the stage, revealed, according to Blum, the director's desire to reflect the revolutionary spirit of the epoch. However, Blum believed that this troupe was infinitely far from the problems of 'Our Jewish Theatre', such as the Yiddish State Chamber Theatre (GOSET) and the Hebrew Habima. Thereupon Blum's tone suddenly changed and he wrote with sincere admiration about the unique talent of Clara Young, her noble simplicity, elegance, and good 'old-world' tone. At the end Blum came to the conclusion that 'her art belongs to the past'. In her famous song 'Papirosn' he discerned 'a dirge for that kind of art and her old-fashioned heroines'.

On the next day, 27 July, the daily *Vecherniaia Moskva* published an article by the

Fig. 9.2. Clara Young with her colleague.
Courtesy of the RGALI, file 2682

critic Samuil Margolin, who reproduced the conceptual scheme of Blum's article and even reinforced his negative assessments, stating that the actress was far from the origins of Jewish folk theatre, her speech and gestures were not Jewish and even not international; instead, she assimilated American and European Jewish petty-bourgeois narrow-mindedness. He also claimed that Clara was too far from understanding the folk ideas of GOSET.

In the Soviet Union, the actress face an ideologically biased criticism, based on models and clichés of the ideas of the class struggle. In 1924, this approach was applied by Moyshe Litvakov, editor of the Moscow Yiddish daily *Der emes* (Truth) and the pundit of Soviet Yiddish literary and theatre criticism.[31] On the other hand, the critic Mikhail Zagorsky, in the private magazine *Ekho* (*Echo*, no. 3, 1925), paid tribute to her talent. He also wrote, in the journal *Novyi zritel* (*New Viewer*, no. 31, 1925), about the growth of her performing art, comparing her voice and vocal skills in 1916 and 1925. But at the end of the article it was proclaimed that her theatre was 'the translation of European and American operetta pattern into Yiddish'. In all, the attitude of Soviet critics to Clara Yong was very contradictory. They attacked her primitiveness, the lack of ideological message. Like Litvakov, they praised GOSET as a new modern Jewish theatre and disapproved her old-fashioned manner. But all of them admitted her talent.

In 1926, during the Leningrad tour of GOSET, the press debated the problems of the Yiddish theatre. In August 1926, the newspaper *Krasnaia gazeta* (Red Newspaper) published several articles, including ones by Osip Mandelshtam's and A. Kugel's, about GOSET.[32] Clara Young's artists started to perform in Leningrad in September, after GOSET's performances, which made it possible for Kugel to continue his debates with the supporters of leftist art.[33] Aleksandr Kugel (*Krasnaia Gazeta*, nos 218, 220, 224) and G. Romm in the Leningrad magazine *Zhisn' iskusstva* (*Life of Arts*, no. 39, 1926) wrote that operetta could be just for fun and entertainment, not for social propaganda. Meanwhile, Simon Dreiden came to the conclusion — in the official *Leningradskaia pravda* (Leningrad Truth, nos. 215 and 221, 1926) — that this tour of Young's troupe was a feast only for petty-bourgeois philistines. Against the background of Young's operetta, GOSET was praised as the builder of a new Soviet art.

In 1927, in the year of the fiftieth anniversary of Goldfaden's theatre, a brochure about Clara Young was published in Moscow with Mikhail Zagorsky's and Samuil Margolin's articles based on their publications on her tour in 1925. Both critics wrote about the GOSET, Habima, and Belorussian GOSET, presenting them in the Soviet press. Still, the positive responses from Anatoly Lunacharsky and Nikolai Volkov played the main role in this publication. Lunacharsky, the People's Commissar (Minister) of education, wrote an article which became for Clara Young a kind of a 'sgule' (Jewish protecting paper).[34]

For their Moscow tour in 1927, at the time of intensive anti-religious campaigns,[35] Boaz Youngvitz rewrote Boder's play *Dem rebens nigun* (Rebe's Tune) to the new musical comedy *Sha, der rebbe fort!* (Hush, the Rebe is Coming!), mocking the naïve belief of Hasidim in their spiritual leader, *rebbe*. Clara played the role of a fifteen-year-old *rebbe* while riding on roller skates. Akiva Dinner, who was invited to Youngvitz's company as a dancer, describes in his memoirs rehearsals of this play and the success of its premiere. The plot of the play to some extent met the demands of the Soviet theatre, as was noted in I. Kalmen's article in the Leningrad magazine *Rabochii i teatr* (Worker and Theatre, no. 21, 1927).

Clara and Boaz Youngvitz worked in Russia and Ukraine till 1928, and then travelled to Europe and in 1930 to the United States. During the Great Depression they lost their money in financial speculations, as they already had earlier in Warsaw during the First World War. In addition, they had serious problems with repertoire because they could perform only old plays and had no money for new performances. As a result, they decided to return to Europe. Boaz started to think about a stationary theatre, but Clara didn't want to accept this. When in 1934 they received a letter from Narkompros written by A. Dymarsky, she decided to go to the Soviet Union. Clara Young thought that it might be her last chance: her fame didn't make her rich, and new stars such as Molly Picon were appearing on the Yiddish stage in America. She accepted the invitation knowing nothing about the political situation in the country.

In Moscow she became a leading actress of the Jewish Theatre of Musical Comedy, which was opened under the auspices of GOMETZ (State association of music, variety art and circus). Many actors from the previous company of the 1920s, as well as the talented actors Anna Guzik and Mikhail Epelbaum, joined her. Among Clara Young's papers in RGALI there is a notebook where she recorded the list of her performances, from May 1934 till February 1937. The tour of the year 1934 was very intensive. She played her old repertoire with twenty performances per month. There is a note about Sergei Kirov's death in December 1934. Like many other Soviet people, she hardly comprehended the dangerous tendency of Stalin's politics. She continued to act, but Soviet critics became more aggressive with their crude use of the 'class approach'.[36] Em. Beskin wrote that her repertoire was no more than a 'piece of history' (*Vecherniaia Moskva*, 2 July 1934). Again, most of the authors criticized her repertoire, but admired her personal talent.[37]

In 1935 she decided to take Soviet citizenship. She certainly did not realize that, as a result, she would never see her husband and daughter Lucy. In 1936–37 the entries in her notebook changed — now she wrote about concerts, but not comedies or plays. Now she sang folksongs, recited poems by Soviet Yiddish poets such as Itsik Fefer and Peretz Markish, and stories by Sholem Aleichem and Peretz. In 1936 she obtained a flat on Kaluzhskaia Street in Moscow.[38] Liubomirsky described her small room with a large sofa, which she managed to turn into a stage area while speaking with him.[39] From her 1938 autobiography we know that in the summer of 1934, in Odessa, Clara Young joined the Trade Union of Workers of Arts of the USSR. And since that time, with a Soviet *profbilet* (union membership card) no. 176799, she toured numerous cities of the Soviet republics and 'served over 2 million spectators'. On 25 April 1937 in Moscow she received Soviet passport no. 60226.

On 4 January 1937, the English newspaper *Moscow Daily News* published an article titled 'Noted Jewish Actress will stay in USSR':

> Starting her stage career on the Russian stage more than 20 years ago, Clara Young . . . returned to Moscow from the United States two years ago to find

a new audience in a new world . . . Clara Young . . . convinced that this is the only land in the world where her race is developing a genuine Jewish culture . . . 'I find Soviet audience . . . the most stimulating, appreciative and critical I have ever known'.

The article stressed that the actress 'creates her own genre':

Clara Young's solo acting covers a wide range of character portrayal which she infuses with forceful dramatic power. She prefers to act her skits alone without the aid of supporting cast, and utilizing only the barest essentials of scenic effects.

The main event in her life of the 1930s was her concert in Moscow at the Pillar Hall of the House of the Unions (Kolonnyi zal Doma Souzov) in 1937, where she played Argo's vaudeville *Zayt ruik* (Keep Calm), written specially for her.[40] In 1939 the talented writer and the author of libretto of many early Soviet operettas Nikolai Aduev (alias Nikolai Rabinovich) wrote a monologue for the actress under the title *An Answer to the Interviewer* based on the actress's life story.[41]

In 1939, for the twentieth Anniversary of the GOSET, Clara Young's article on the history of Yiddish theatre was published in the Moscow newspaper *Sovetskoe iskusstvo* (*Soviet Art*, 2 April 1939) among the other materials and articles devoted to this event. On 4 February 1940, *Vecherniaia Moskva* published J. Grinvald's positive article about her concerts. On 24 August 1941, she signed the official letter at the meeting of the Jewish representatives alongside with Ilya Erenburg, Solomon Michoels, Itsik Fefer, Perets Markish, and other key figures of Soviet Jewry. This meeting led later to the establishment of the Jewish Antifascist Committee. During the war Solomon Michoels, who highly appreciate Clara's talent, helped her to organize a group of actors and arrange concerts in the rear, in Bashkiria and Uzbekistan.[42] In her archive there are several official letters of gratitude from military hospitals and plants. In April 1946 she received a medal for her activity during the war.

After the war Clara Young travelled on tours with concerts. The Yiddish newspaper *Eynikayt* (Unity), the organ of the Jewish Antifascist Committee, published several short articles about her concerts in Moscow, but on 25 February 1947 an article by A. Movich criticized her repertoire and the lyrical songs by Boris (Borukh) Bergolz. In 1949, she learned about the death from cancer of her only daughter Lucy — she died in New York at the age of forty-five. This family tragedy undermined Clara's health. She died on 27 April 1951.

Akiva Dinner wrote that the administration of the Mosestrada (Moscow Concert Agency) published an obituary in the newspaper *Vecherniaia Moskva*. He could not attend the funeral, but he came to say goodbye in the hospital, where he saw A. Dymarsky and actors Iustina Minkova with her husband S. Zilberblat. The next day he learned that there were a lot of people and last parting words were spoken with warmth by two popular Soviet actors, Leonid Utesov and Vladimir Henkin.[43]

Reading the letters from the wartime audience, preserved in the RGALI archive, we can say that to some extent Clara Young managed to overcome her destiny and prolong her theatre career in the Soviet Union. But she did not succeed in escaping twentieth-century history and took part in its most dramatic changes, though giving the flame of her soul to her audience in big capitals and in small provincial cities.

Notes to Chapter 9

1. Simon Kopelman, *Iung — znachit molodaia* (Springfild: n.p., 1987), p. 32.
2. Klara Iung (Clara Young), Avtobiografiia (1938), RGALI. F. 2663. Op.1. d.110. pp. 81–90; A. E. Dinner, Klara Iung — tri vstrechi, RGALI. F. 2337. Op. 2. d. 3. pp. 136 — 148; Ovsei (Yeshua) Liubomirsky, Biographiia Klary Iung, RGALI. F 2682. Op. 1. d. 60; Yeshua Liubomirsky, *Af di lebnsvegn* (Moscow: Sovetskii pisatel, 1976), pp. 116–31.
3. Boaz Youngvitz, *Mayn lebn in teater* (New York: IKUF farlag, 1950), p. 102.
4. Ibid., p. 94.
5. 'Yong Klara', *Leksikon fun yidish teatr*, II (Warsaw: Farlag Elisheva, 1934), 917.
6. Michael Weichert, *Teatr un drame*, II (Warsaw: Yiddish, 1922), pp. 88–95; Ovsei Liubomirsky, Biografiia Klary Iung, RGALI. F. 2682. Op. 1. d. 60. p. 4 [typescript].
7. A. Mukdoni, *In Varshe un in Lodz: mayne bagegenishn* (Buenos Aires: Tsnetralfarband fun poylishe yidn in Argentine: 1955), II, pp. 256–62.
8. Liubomirsky, Biografiia Klary Iung, p. 7.
9. Youngvitz, *Mayn lebn in teater*, p. 226.
10. Menakhem Kipnis, 'Sha, der rebe fort!', *Haynt*, 22 January 1930, p. 5.
11. Peretz Markish, 'Klara Yong', *Literarishe bleter*, 31 October 1924, p. 9.
12. Mukdoni, *In Varshe un in Lodz*, p. 262.
13. Youngvitz, *Mayn lebn in teater*, pp. 253–59.
14. Ibid., pp. 261–62.
15. [M. D-v], 'Provintsiia. Ekaterinoslav', *Teatralnaia gazeta*, 7 August 1916, p. 12.
16. Moisei Iankovskii, *Operetta: vozniknovenie i razvitie zhanra на zapade i v SSSR* (Leningrad and Moscow: Iskusstvo, 1937), pp. 357–61.
17. 'Gastroli Klary Iung', *Teatr*, 17 August 1916, p. 6.
18. [Rodia], 'Arabeski', *Teatr*, 26 August 1916, p. 27.
19. 'Benefis Klary Iung', *Teatr*, 1894 (1916), p. 6.
20. Evgenii Binevich, *Evreiskii teatr v Peterburge: opyt istoricheskogo ocherka* (St. Petersburg: Evreiskii obshchinnyi tsentr, 2003), pp. 99–110; idem, *Istoriia evreiskogo teatra v Rossii, 1875–1918* (Baltimore: Seagull Press, 2009), pp. 324–30.
21. N. N-ev [Aleksandr Kugel], 'Gastroli evreisko-nemetskoi truppy', *Teatr i iskusstvo*, 39 (1916), 780.
22. Homo Novus [Aleksandr Kugel], 'Zametki', *Teatr i iskusstvo*, 43 (1916), 866–69.
23. K. Shneyfal, 'Yidishkeit u Klary Iung', *Evreiskaia nedelia*, 42 (1916), 26–28.
24. Iu. B., 'Teatr i musika', *Vechernee vremia*, 17 September 1916, p. 3.
25. Youngvitz, *Mayn lebn in teater*, pp. 271–73.
26. Quoted in Kopelman, *Iung — znachit molodaia*, p. 28.
27. See Nina Warnke, 'Going East: The Impact of American Yiddish Plays and Players on the Yiddish Stage in Czarist Russia, 1890–1914', *American Jewish History*, 92.1 (2004), 1–29.
28. Youngvitz, *Mayn lebn in teater*, pp. 297–313.
29. Ibid., p. 332.
30. Valentin Melik-Khaspabov, 'Prekrasnaia bessiuzhetnost', *Vestnik rabotnikov iskusstv*, 1–2 (1926), 9. On Soviet operetta in the 1920s and 1930s, see Iankovskii, *Operetta*, pp. 390–417.
31. Moyshe Litvakov, *Finf yor meluhisher yidisher kamerteatr* (Moscow: Emes, 1924), p. 57.
32. Leonid Katsis, 'Moscow Yiddish Chamber Theater during 1926 (Osip Mandelstam, Alexander Kugel, Khaim Tokar)', in *Around the Point: Studies in Jewish Literature and Culture in Multiple Languages*, ed. by Hillel Weisss, Roman Katsman, and Ber Boris Kotlerman (Newcastle upon Tyne: Cambridge Scholars Publishing, 2014), pp. 541–65.
33. Aleksandr Kugel, 'Gastroli Klary Iung', *Vechernaia krasnaia gazeta*, 17 and 20 September 1926.
34. Anatoly V. Lunacharsky and others, *Klara Iung: Kharakteristika stsenicheskoi deiatel'nosti* (Moscow: Moskovskoe teatral'noe izdatel'stvo, 1927).

35. See e.g. Anna Shternshis, *Soviet and Kosher: Jewish Popular Culture in the Soviet Union, 1923–1939* (Bloomington: Indiana University Press, 2006), p. 4.
36. Albert Gran, 'Ot Ist-Brodveia do Moskvy (k gastroliam Klary Iung)', *Literaturnaia gazeta*, 14 July 1934, p. 4; V. Golubov, 'Gastroli Klary Iung', *Isvestiia*, 15 July 1934, p. 4;. M. Konstantinov, 'Klara Iung i prochie', *Sovetskoe iskusstvo*, 17 July 1934, p. 3.
37. See e.g. the article by the historian of operetta Moisei Iankovskii in *Rabochii i teatr*, 25 (1934), 12.
38. Clara Yung's letter to K. M. Leonidov, RGALI. F. 2682. Op. 1. d. 46.
39. Liubomirsky, *Af di lebnsvegn*, p. 124.
40. [Ia. E.], 'Gastroli Klary Iung', *Literaturnaia gazeta*, 10 January 1937, p. 6; A. Argo, Zayt ruik! RGALI. 2682. Op. 1. d. 1.
41. Nikolai Aduev, Otvet interv'iueru. RGALI. F. 1847. d. 15. p. 47–58.
42. Max Vekselman, *Evreiskie teatry (na idish) v Uzbekistane, 1933–1947* (Jerusalem: Filobiblon, 2005), pp. 114–20.
43. Dinner, *Klara Iung — tri vstrechi*, p. 148.

CHAPTER 10

Yiddish Music and Musicology in Petrograd/Leningrad/St Petersburg through the Prism of the City Archives

Alexander Ivanov

Thanks to the considerable contributions of such scholars as Mikhail Beizer, Benjamin Nathans, and Yvonne Kleinmann, it is no exaggeration to say that St Petersburg has already found its place in academic literature among important centres of Jewish culture in general and Yiddish culture in particular.[1] At the same time it appears that the far-reaching significance of cultural undertakings of Petersburg Jews for the Jewish experience of late nineteenth and twentieth centuries has not been sufficiently comprehended and evaluated. In fact, the St Petersburg-based Jewish public institutions had formed political strategies, ideological patterns, and cultural models that remained relevant to Jewish national movements in different countries throughout the whole twentieth century. The history of Petersburg Jewish cultural institutions, whose sphere of activities included Yiddish-related music and musicology, can serve as a case in point. The concept of a cultural institution is understood here in terms of historical anthropology: as a site of cultural activities, practices, and relationships that are closely connected with national identity formation and are organized and reinforced by the local community. A network of Yiddish-related cultural institutions formed an environment in which Yiddish music could flourish or, at least, survive during periods of changing attitudes to Jewish culture by the authorities.

Several archival collections in St Petersburg, including a few newly discovered ones, can shed a light on this process. The process of identifying such materials and bringing them to the attention of a broader scholarly community has been relatively slow so far, partly due to the lack of information about Jewish archival materials in the Soviet reference sources. The establishment of the Petersburg branch of the research project 'Jewish Documentary Sources in the Archives of Russia, Ukraine, and Belarus' was aimed to solve this problem with regard to the St Petersburg archives. Three volumes of the planned four-volume guidebook of the Petersburg Series came out in 2011, 2013, and 2015.[2] The present article reviews archival sources from official records related to Yiddish music and musicology that have been discovered and described within the framework of that project. These sources can be productively contextualized within the broader Soviet policy regarding Jewish culture, which was marked by contradictions and was fully dependent on the current socio-political situation in the country. The analysis of documents of various Soviet authorities allows us to trace some strategies characteristic of Soviet policy in the field of the Jewish culture in different periods.

After the October 1917 revolution, the Bolsheviks' aim of establishing total control over all spheres of the city's public life gave rise to the growth and bureaucratization of Soviet power structures. As a result, the 50,000-strong Jewish population of Petrograd (as the city was called from 1914 to 1924) found itself in the early 1920s under two authorities. On the one hand, all pre-revolutionary Jewish religious, cultural, educational, charitable, and professional organizations were subordinated to the respective organs of the Soviet state and the Bolshevik party. On the other hand, in keeping with the Bolshevik policy of *nativization*, which was designed to smooth tensions between the central power and the non-Russian population, newly created Jewish organizations acted as communist ideological guides for the Jewish urban population. These new bodies not only controlled the activities of the Petrograd Jewry, but often substituted pre-revolutionary Jewish public organizations. Characteristic in this connection is the history of the Society for Jewish Folk Music (SJFM) during the Soviet period.

Society for Jewish Folk Music in St Petersburg/Petrograd, 1900s–early 1920s

Many researchers rightly see the establishment of SJFM in 1908 as the turning point in the development of Jewish musical activity in St Petersburg, such as professional composition, concert performances, and the study of Yiddish musical folklore.[3] Moreover, according to James Loeffler, 'Intellectually and artistically, the Society remained an influential model for both academic scholars of Jewish music and composers of Jewish concert music throughout the twentieth century.'[4]

The key documentary collection related to this topic is the collection (*fond*) No. 1747 (Society for Jewish Folk Music) in the Central State Historical Archive of St Petersburg.[5] In March 1908 the St Petersburg Special City Office for the Affairs of [Voluntary] Societies registered SJFM, which was founded by the initiative of the pianist Leo Nesvizhskii, the composer Solomon Rosowski, and the opera singer Joseph Tomars. According to the Statute of SJFM, preserved in that documentary collection, the purpose of this institution was to promote 'the study and development of Jewish spiritual and secular music in Russia by collecting pieces of Yiddish musical folklore and its further artistic processing and distribution'.[6] Over the years, among the members of the SJFM Board and the Musical Committee were such prominent Jewish musicians and composers as Mikhail Gnesin, Zinovii Kiselgof, Lazare Saminsky, Joseph Achron, Alexander Zhitomirsky, Moisei Milner, and Lubov' Shtreicher. By 1913, the SJFM membership reached about 900, with its branches opened in Moscow, Kharkov, Kiev, Simferopol, Ekaterinoslav, and Rostov-on-Don. During the first five years of SJFM's activities, it organized 154 concerts in different cities of Russia and published over 100 pieces of music.[7]

Although the *fond* No. 1747 has already attracted scholars' attention and several monographs on Jewish musical culture made use of its materials, it is helpful to make a short review of the collection's content. Among the documents of this collection are various projects of the SJFM Statutes as well as its approved version of 1910; minutes of the general meetings of SJFM members as well as of its Board and Music Committee; financial statements and reports on the activities of SJFM; lists of its members with their home addresses; lists of participants in the general meetings; documents regarding the organization of special courses for the dissemination of Jewish musical repertoire; reports on the activities of SJFM branches in different cities of the Russian Empire; correspondence with the St Petersburg city administration about the organization of concerts of Jewish music; correspondence with Jewish cultural and educational organizations, including the London Jewish National Fund, the Vienna Academic Union for Jewish Culture, the Jewish National Labor Union of America, and the Lublin Society for Jewish Music and Literature Hazomir; posters and concert programmes; reports on concerts; plans of theatres; correspondence with collectors of Yiddish folk songs and melodies and with publishing houses and gramophone record companies, including the Kadima in Vilna, Judischer Verlag in Berlin, and the Mizrakh Partnership in Odessa.

Several manuscript collections and a large number of separate documents related to SJFM and its members are scattered throughout the depositories of St Petersburg.[8] The *fond* No. 536 (Petersburg Noble Deputy Assembly) at the Central State Historical Archive of St Petersburg contains documents on the organization of the SJFM public concert which was held in the assembly hall of the House of Petersburg Noble Deputies on 12 January 1910. It contains copies of the concert poster and programme, which included the performance of musical works by the SJFM members composers Efraim Shklyar, Joel Engel, Aleksandr Zhitomirskii, Pesach Lvov, and Lazar Saminsky; letters and telegrams sent to count Ivan Saltykov, the leader of the St Petersburg nobility, by representatives of the anti-Semitic organization called the Alexander Nevskii Union of the Russian People and by individuals demanding that the concert be banned; clippings from anti-Semitic newspapers with negative reviews on the concert and caricatures of the Jewish musicians. Personal files of SJFM members with important biographical information are preserved in the *fond* No. 361 (St Petersburg Conservatory) at the Central State Historical Archive of St Petersburg. These are also the personal files of conservatory students, such as Joseph Achron, Mikhail Gnesin, Pesach Lvov, Moisei Milner, Leo Nesvizhskii, Solomon Rosowski, Lazare Saminsky, Joseph Tomars, Efraim Shklyar, David Chernomordikov, and Jascha Heifetz. In this connection it is worth mentioning one of the earliest documents on this topic, which is preserved in the *fond* No. 472 (Chancellery of the Ministry of the Imperial Court) at the Russian State Historical Archive: an application submitted in 1900 to the Chancellery of the Ministry of the Imperial Court by Joseph Achron's relatives requesting a 'permission for Achron's residence in St Petersburg and its suburbs with the purpose of preparation for the exams at the Petersburg Conservatory'.[9]

After the October revolution, SJFM was on the edge of a financial crisis. In 1919, in order to receive systematic financial subsidies from the People's Commissariat of Education, SJFM together with the Jewish Society for the Encouragement of the

Arts, Jewish Theatrical Society, and the Leon Peretz Jewish Literary and Artistic Society, made an attempt to join the local Bureau of the Kultur-Lige (League of Culture), which was being organized in Petrograd. Based on this information, the compilers of the archival guide of the Central State Historical Archive in St Petersburg decided that SJFM ceased to exist as an independent organization in April 1920 because of 'joining the Petrograd Kultur-Lige'.[10] But ultimately the Jewish Commissariat of the People's Commissariat for National Affairs in Moscow did not permit the registration of the Kultur-Lige in Petrograd, and the St Petersburg archives have no traces of Kultur-Lige activities in the later period.[11] It is also important to mention that no documents issued by the Bolshevik administration about closing of SJFM have been found in the Petersburg archives.

A letter of 4 May 1922, which was sent by Joseph Achron to the composer Solomon Rosowski who lived in Riga at that time, sheds some light on the situation with SJFM. Achron wrote:

> And now about our common cause, our Society for Jewish [Folk] Music. I am obliged to make a sad confession: our Society has recently ceased to exist legally due to a quite absurd reason: We had to reorganize the Society to ensure its continued existence. The only man who could have done, and was authorized to do this, was Mark Semenovich [Rivesman], but just at that time he had been recuperating in some house of rest [recuperation centre] and was unable to return to the city even for the sake of such an important reason; as a result we do not exist officially any more.[12]

It is worth noting that the Soviet authorities' periodic campaigns to register and re-register 'bourgeois' Jewish societies and organizations served effectively as an instrument of control over their activities. Over time, these campaigns became increasingly severe, forcing the heads of public organizations quickly to prepare and submit registration documents subject to approval by various Soviet institutions, including the local organs of the People's Commissariat for Internal Affairs (*Narodnyi komissariat vnutrennikh del*, abbreviated as NKVD). Some Jewish public organizations of Petrograd, like SJFM, were simply unable to survive the bureaucratic assault of these campaigns, and lost their legal status as a result. Most likely Achron meant in his letter the campaign of re-registration of public organizations, which was carried out by the local authorities in August–September 1921.[13]

At the beginning of the 1920s, the majority of members of SJFM, including Joseph Achron, emigrated from Soviet Russia. Despite this fact, musical works by SJFM members continued to be performed in concerts in Petrograd/Leningrad at least until the mid-1920s. For example, the poster advertising a 'Grand Concert of Jewish Folk, Sacred, and Secular Music', which was held at the Grand Opera Hall of the People's House in Petrograd on 12 February 1922, lists musical works of the former SJFM members Joseph Achron, Solomon Gurovich, Moisei Milner, Solomon Rosowski, Leo Zeitlin, and others, albeit SJFM is not mentioned at all.[14] After the mid-1920s, music of emigrant composers was banned. Sheet music by Engel, Zeitlin, Achron, and other former members of SJFM appears in the lists of publications which the Leningrad Provincial Department of the Main Directorate for Literature and Publishing (abbr. Lengublit) had forbidden to be distributed in the entire territory of the Soviet Union in 1924–27.[15]

Yiddish Music in Leningrad after the Society for Jewish Folk Music, Late 1920s–1930s

Of special interest are documentary sources shedding light on the fates of those SJFM members who remained in the Soviet Union and continued to work there in the late 1920s–1930s. It should be mentioned that Yiddish music played an important role in the cultural and political life of the Soviet Union's several millions Jews at that time. This was a period when the Soviet authorities carried out the ambitious project of Jewish agricultural colonization aimed at the creation of a 'Jewish republic', first in the Crimea and then in the Far East of the country (Birobidzhan). The Soviet Jewish national project, being above all ideological in nature, was extensively and variously represented in visual arts, literature, and music.[16] The highly important task of social and cultural reconstruction of Jewish society was closely connected with the construction of a 'new Soviet Jewry' and a new Soviet Jewish culture based on Yiddish, the language of the Jewish proletarian masses, as opposed to Hebrew, which was condemned as the language of the Jewish bourgeoisie and religion. The construction of Soviet Yiddish culture was carried out at the time of considerable changes in Soviet state policy, which entailed modifications of cultural paradigms. The aesthetics of proletarian avant-garde art with its orientation towards 'the truth of the fact' was gradually replaced by Stalinist socialist realism.[17] As Paul D. Morris remarks, one of the official goals of socialist realism was to incorporate into the Soviet culture 'the best aspects of the folk traditions and fuse them with the new realities of twentieth-century life in a society based on the cultural aspirations of the working class'.[18] Thus, special attention had been paid to Jewish folk production, which was regarded as an inexhaustible source of the present and future development in Soviet Jewish culture. In this climate, the composers Mikhail Gnesin (1883–1957) and Lubov' Shtreicher (1888–1958), both former members of SJFM, organized in 1928 a special 'ethnographic' programme, which included concerts of Yiddish folk music within the framework of the activities of the Leningrad Society for Chamber Music.[19]

Another important figure in the Soviet Yiddish music scene was the composer Moisei Milner (1882–1953).[20] Among various documentary collections that contain materials related to Milner, one can mention two *fonds*: No. 2552 (Department of People's Education of the Executive Committee of Leningrad Provincial Council) at the Central State Archive of St Petersburg, and No. 31 (Leningrad Provincial Department of the Central Administration for Literature and Publishing) at the Central State Archive of Literature and Art. Both collections contain documentary materials concerning the first Yiddish opera in the Soviet Union, *Di himlen brenen* (The Heavens Are on Fire) by Milner.[21] The *fond* No. 2552 contains the following documents: correspondence of 1923 between different Soviet administrative institutions related to the libretto of Milner's opera by Mark Rivesman; reviews by members of the Communist Party Jewish section (known under the Russian abbreviation as Evsekstia) who did not have any objections against staging of the opera; extracts from the minutes of the Repertory Committee of the Department of People's Education with permission for two performances of the opera in the city.[22]

However, in the *fond* No. 31 one can find a list of banned books and publications, which includes the libretto of Milner's opera *The Heavens Are on Fire* of 1923. There is a special note on the list, explaining that the opera was forbidden because of 'its distinct Jewish nationalism and mystical and clerical content'.[23]

Moisei Milner's life circumstances are reflected in two collections of his personal papers, in the Manuscript Department of the Russian National Library and in the Manuscript Division of the Russian Institute of Art History in St Petersburg. The first one, *fond* No. 1067, covers the period from 1912 to the early 1950s. The bulk of the fond contains the following documents: music autographs of Milner, including the 1925 piano piece 'Jewish Dance'; the scores of the operas *Wandering Stars* based on the novel by Sholem Aleichem and *Flavius Josephus* based on Lion Feuchtwanger's Josephus trilogy; the 1927 collection of Jewish songs for children 'The New Song'; songs to Yiddish and Hebrew lyrics by Itzik Feffer, Hayim Nahman Bialik, and others; the songs from the play *Hirsch Lekkert*, etc.; correspondence with the director of the Moscow State Yiddish Theatre (abbreviation: GOSET) Naum Belilovskii, the director of the Odessa State Yiddish Theatre Isaac Fishman, the musicologist Ian Frenkel, and others.

The second, *fond* No. 42, deposited in the Manuscript Division of the Russian Institute of Art History, contains Milner's personal papers from 1906 to 1960, including the following documents: score autographs of the opera *The New Way*; music for the dramatic performances *The Dream of Jacob* at the Habima Hebrew theatre studio and *Wailing Wall* at the Moscow GOSET; piano 'Bar-Kochba' written for the State Jewish Theatre in Kiev; scores, piano sketches, and drafts of music for theatrical performances of *Tevye the Milkman*, based on Sholem Aleichem's work; *The Sisters*, based on Y. L. Peretz's work; works for piano 'Lullaby' and 'Musical Silhouettes'; suites 'Mother and Child' to the lyrics of Y. L. Peretz and 'Sulamith' to the lyrics of Hayim Nahman Bialik; Milner's autobiographical notes and letters to Milner from S. An-sky, Moisei Beregovskii, Leyb Kvitko, and others; posters and concert programmes, articles and reviews of Milner's works; photographs of Milner with members of the Jewish vocal ensemble (Evokans), and actors of GOSET and of the State Jewish theatre in Birobidzhan. These two *fonds* perfectly supplement each other.

In 1926–37, the Jewish National House of Public Education named after Yakov Sverdlov (abbreviation: Yevdomprosvet), an important concert and theatre venue where Yiddish music was often performed, was located at 10 Nekrasov Street. In July 1937, this institution had to move to the building of the Regional Council of Trade Unions (4 Truda Square). Until its liquidation in January 1938, Yevdomprosvet served about 175,000 Leningrad Jews. It housed a theatre workshop (since 1936, the Theatre Studio) and two vocal Jewish ensembles, the Evokans, and a children's vocal group. The Central State Archive of Literature and Art preserves a rich collection — *fond* No. 258 (National Houses of Education in Leningrad) — of documents related to cultural activites of the Yevdomprosvet in the 1920s–1930s.[24]

Yiddish Music in the Soviet Cinema, 1930s

This review of documentary sources related to Yiddish music would be incomplete without mentioning materials on film music, which was one of the most popular genres during the Soviet period. A special mission of the cinema proclaimed by Bolsheviks was not just to entertain, but to enlighten people. The Soviet film industry remained under a close supervision by high-ranking functionaries, including the top officials of Soviet Jewish organizations, and quickly responded to every shift in the Communist Party's ideological requirements.[25] In this respect it is worth mentioning two *fonds* deposited in the Central State Archive of Literature and Art in St Petersburg. The first one, No. 271 (Leningrad Short Films Studio), includes a film script and music notations for a short film, the so-called film-song in Yiddish, *Freylekhs*, produced in 1938 (the director was Pavel Bogolyubov, the author of the song lyrics was Peretz Markish, and the musical compilations were by Aron Roitman, who later became the chief conductor of the Orchestra of the Central Directorate for the Films Production).[26]

The second *fond*, No. 168, contains personal papers of the film director Rachel Milman-Kremer, who made the only Soviet Yiddish sound film, *The Return of Nathan Becker* (*Nosn Becker fort aheym*, 1933). The script was by Peretz Markish, the co-directors were Rachel Milman-Kremer and Boris Shpis, Evgenii Mikhailov was the cameraman, music by Evgenii Brusilovskii, setting by Isaac Makhlis.[27] The film tells the story of a Jewish bricklayer named Nathan Becker (David Gutman) who returns from America to his native shtetl in Soviet Belorussia where his farther Tsali (Solomon Mikhoels), a convinced Soviet enthusiast, lives. Becker, who had emigrated from Tsarist Russia two decades earlier, is eager to put his skills to the service of the grandiose reconstruction of life taking place in the Soviet Union. Together with other inhabitants of the shtetl he starts working at one of sites of the first Five-Year Plan. As a qualified specialist, he is entrusted with training young workers. At first Becker scorns the Soviet methods of training bricklayers, and to demonstrate the advantages of working the 'American way' he participates in a competition in bricklaying with a young Soviet worker but fails to defeat him. Ultimately, Becker's bricklaying system combined with the Soviet technique finds universal approval. Among the documents in that *fond* one can find a short libretto and the script of the film by Peretz Markish as well as musical scores and sketches of Yiddish songs for the film.[28]

Jewish Ethnomusicology in Petrograd/Leningrad, late 1920s–1930s

After the closure of SJFM in 1921, the Music Section of the Jewish Historical and Ethnographic Society (JHES) continued its activities in the field of the study and development of Yiddish music in Petrograd/Leningrad. JHES had started collecting samples of Yiddish musical folklore in 1912–14 during historical and ethnographic expeditions organized by the well-known playwright, ethnographer, and public activist S. An-sky (Shloyme-Zanvl Rappoport; 1863–1920).[29] JHES was established in 1908 on the basis of the Jewish Historical and Ethnographical Commission, which initially belonged to the Society for the Promotion of Enlightenment among Jews in Russia. Three historical and ethnographic expeditions to shtetls in Podolia, Volhynia, and Kiev provinces under the leadership of S. An-sky should be considered as highlights in the activities of JHES. These expeditions collected about 700 ceremonial objects and ritual utensils, more than 100 authentic historical documents, including 50 *pinkasim* (community ledgers), About 2,000 photographs were made, and hundreds of pieces of Jewish folk music were recorded on wax cylinders.[30] The ethnomusicologists and composers Joel (Yulii) Engel (1868–1927) and Zinovii Kiselgof (1878–1939), mentioned above in relation to SJFM, participated in An-sky's expeditions.[31] The expedition materials formed the basis of the JHES Museum, which was operational in Petrograd/Leningrad from 1916 to 1929. Following the Museum's liquidation by the city administration, its rich collections were scattered throughout various depositories and institutions in different parts of the Soviet Union.[32]

The key documentary holding related to the beginning and development of the Yiddish ethnomusicology in Petrograd/Leningrad is the *fond* No. 311 (Museum of the Jewish Historical and Ethnographical Society) at the Central State Archive of Literature and Art. This collection contains the following documents: minutes of the joint meetings of Ethnographic, Artistic and Music Sections of the Museum Commissions of JHES of 1928–29, dedicated to discussions about the organization of ethnographic expeditions to the Caucasus and Belorussia with the participation of ethnomusicologist and JHES member Sofia Magid-Ekmekchi (1892–1954);[33] minutes of the meetings of the Music Sections, containing, in particular, Magid's proposal of an expedition to Volhynia with the purpose of recording Yiddish musical folklore on wax cylinders and her letters regarding the purchase of a phonograph for making these recordings; correspondence with the Berlin-based Committee of the Society for Health Protection of Jews (also known under the abbreviation OSE) concerning delivering the phonograph and wax cylinders to Leningrad; correspondence of 1919 between the Museum director and a former SJFM member Abram Bramson and the SJFM Secretary Mark Rivesman concerning cooperation with the Petrograd Bureau of the Kultur-Lige.

The considerable contributions by Sofia Magid and the prominent ethnomusicologist Moisei Beregovskii (1892–1961)[34] to the study of Yiddish folk music in Russia are well known to scholars of Soviet Jewish history.[35] Suffice it to mention that Magid's expedition materials are stored in the following archival collections: the manuscript collection No. 142 at the St Petersburg Branch of the Archives of the Russian Academy of Sciences; the *fond* No. R-5 at the Manuscript Division of the Institute of Russian Literature; collections Nos. 43, 44, 115, 152, 186, 204 containing wax cylinders with recordings of Yiddish folk songs at the Phonographic Archive of the same institution. Two more manuscript collections contain Magid's papers: the *fond* No. 142 (Museum of Anthropology and Ethnography) in the St Petersburg Branch of the Archives of the Russian Academy of Sciences includes plans and field materials of Magid's 1934 expedition to Volhynia, and *fond* No. 324 at the Manuscript Department of the Russian National Library in St Petersburg contains personal papers of the historian, philologist, and ethnographer Evgenii Kagarov

(1882–1942). This collection also contains Magid's Candidate of Science thesis 'The Ballad in Jewish Folklore' (1939), two reviews of the thesis and substantial comments by Kagarov, as well as an authorized typescript of Magid's thesis with Kagarov's marginal notes.

No contemporary researchers have yet examined the two collections of wax cylinders with recordings of Yiddish folk songs and instrumental music at the Phonographic Archive of the Institute of Russian Literature, which were made in the 1930s by the Leningrad ethnomusicologists Lydia Kershner and Zinaida Ewald. Kershner was born in Kiev in 1905, and in the late 1920s studied the history of music and ethnomusicology at the Leningrad Conservatory. She was also trained as piano player under the guidance of the famous pianist Maria Yudina. After graduating from the Conservatory in 1931, Kershner worked as a music broadcasting editor for Leningrad Radio and a music teacher at the secondary musical school at the Leningrad Conservatory. Since 1927 she had been collecting and studying musical folklore in different regions of the Soviet Union. She died in Moscow in 1968. The collection No. 90, compiled by Kershner, includes 1930 wax cylinder recordings of the Yiddish songs 'Der shney is gegangen' (Snow is falling), 'A sheyner shabes, a fayner balebos' (Good Saturday, Good Host), and 'Ikh ken ruen' (I can relax), and of one Hebrew song 'Menucho' (Rest).

Zinaida Ewald was born in St Petersburg in 1895. In 1926 she graduated from the Leningrad Conservatory and worked as a researcher at the Institute for Study of the USSR. In 1933 Ewald started to work at the Department of Folklore of the Institute of Russian Literature and later became an associate professor at the Leningrad Conservatory. She was one of the creators of the Phonographic Archive of the Institute of Russian Literature. She died during the Leningrad blockade in 1942. Her collection, No. 1111, includes recordings on wax cylinders of the Yiddish songs 'Kinder-yorn' (Childhood), 'Gekumen eyn kazak' (A Cossack Has Come), 'Shoyn draytsn yor' (For Thirteen Years), and a violin performance of the Jewish dance 'Sher'. These recordings were made in the former shtetls of Glushkovichi and Lelchitsy in the Turovsky district of Belorussia in 1932.[36]

'Khrushchev's Thaw' and Yiddish Music in Leningrad, 1950s–1960s

The anti-Semitic campaigns of the late-1940s–early-1950s made research in the field of Jewish culture, including Yiddish musicology, a dangerous occupation. Characteristically, the two-volume bibliographic index *Documents of the Central State Historical Archive of the USSR in the Works of Soviet Researchers, 1917–1962* (Leningrad, 1960–66) lists 3,894 research works, of which only seven are devoted to Jewish studies — six of them published in the 1920s.[37] The 'Thaw' that followed Stalin's death in March 1953 became a period of slow reconstruction of the Yiddish musical culture in the Soviet Union. Several collections of the Central State Archive of Literature and Art testify to frequent appearances of professional performers of Yiddish songs and instrumental music on the stages of Leningrad theatres and concert halls.[38] This can be characterized as a substantial phenomenon. The journals of registration of cultural events in several concert halls of Leningrad (1953–73) mention concerts given by such well-known Yiddish signers as Sidi Tal, Nechama Lifshits (Lifshitsayte), and Veniamin Khayatauskas, as well as performances of the Leningrad Yiddish Music and Drama Ensemble under the direction of Faivish Arones.[39] The archive also preserves financial and logistical documents of 1955–58 related to the organization of tours of Mikhail Epelbaum, Anna Guzik, and other Yiddish singers,[40] and promotional materials and programmes of the concerts (1953–68) of Saul Lubimov, Emil Gorovets, the Yiddish Ensemble of Comedy and Vaudeville led by Ester Roitman (1964–66), and the Yiddish Dramatic Ensemble of Moskontsert (Moscow Concert Organization) under the direction of Veniamin Shvartser. According to these documents, each of the Yiddish concerts was attended by about 300 to 500 people.[41] Besides the Great Choral Synagogue, which continued to operate at that time under the strict control of the authorities and was therefore not considered by many to be a safe gathering place, such concerts of Yiddish music were the only legal meeting place where Leningrad Jews could socialize and communicate.[42]

During the 1950s–1960s, concert activities were supervised by the Department of Arts of the General Directorate of Culture of the Leningrad City Executive Committee. According to several resolutions of the Directorate, all concert programmes had to get the approval of special repertory commissions. Archival collections provide insights into the repertory commissions' decision-making process concerning the programmes of Yiddish music performers. Among them are reports on the concert programme of the cantor of the Leningrad Great Choral Synagogue David Stiskin, who performed Yiddish and Hebrew songs,[43] the programme of Yiddish songs performed by Rosalia Golubeva, and some others. Thus, the repertory commission noted on Golubeva's programme:

> [W]e welcome the searches of Golubeva who revives beautiful and diverse Yiddish folk songs. Everything is modest and restrained, expressive and musically convincing. Comrade Korovin reads good introductions to the songs. The song 'Bronshtele' seems less interesting [. . .] Special mention is due to the very good accompaniment of [the pianist] Shpargel, who played as a full ensemble.[44]

In general, repertory commissions positively assessed the programmes of Yiddish folk songs, and several Jewish singers and ensembles were allowed to perform at Leningrad venues. However, the commissions' conclusions became more censorious following the order of the Ministry of Culture of the Russian Federation No. 638 of 29 October 1957 'On Regulation of Concert Activity', which prescribed regional Departments of Culture 'to verify the ideological and artistic quality of the concerts, to control the repertoire of musical collectives [. . .], to include works by Soviet composers in the mandatory part of the repertoire [. . .], to reflect more vividly the contemporary life in the USSR'.[45] Thus, for example, a 1958 performance by the Leningrad Yiddish Music and Drama Ensemble under the direction of Faivish Arones was criticized by the Department of Culture for 'not touching on contemporary themes'. The report says: 'The programme is quite raw and unpolished. The Department of Culture does not fundamentally oppose the possibility of establishing an interesting Jewish national ensemble, but believes that the programme needs to be expanded.'⁴⁶ However, despite the changes in the programme, the ensemble never qualified for the status of musical collective at the Leningrad Concert Organization (Lenkontsert) because the Ministry of Culture considered it undesirable.⁴⁷ In the early 1970s, with the beginning of anti-Zionist campaigns in the Soviet Union, the development of the Yiddish musical culture in Leningrad was stopped. Anna Guzik's 1973 concert was the final, curtain-dropping event.⁴⁸

Yiddish Music in Leningrad Restaurants, 1950s–1970s

Another type of public space where Yiddish music had been played from the 1950s to the early 1980s was provided by musical venues in Leningrad restaurants. The authors of the booklet for the CD 'Shalom Comrade!' argue that the authorities controlled the restaurant music repertoire less strictly than the state-sponsored concerts in theatres and music halls.⁴⁹ However, documents of various Soviet institutions at the Central State Archive of Literature and Art demonstrate how the authorities tried to control the repertoire of restaurant orchestras and bands. One of them is the list of musical works performed by the orchestra under the direction of K. L. Bernesko-Berneker in 1953.⁵⁰ The orchestra worked at the restaurant Universal at 106 Nevsky Prospekt, which had the reputation of being a Jewish meeting point. The orchestra's repertoire, approved by one of the officials of the Directorate for the Arts of the Leningrad City Executive Committee, includes 'Jewish folk dances' and melodies by Isaac Dunaevskii from the 1936 movie *Seekers of Happiness* (Iskateli schastya) set in the Jewish Autonomous Region.⁵¹

In 1957, a special unit for controlling the musical repertoire of restaurant bands was established at the Department of Musical Ensembles at the General Directorate of Culture of the Leningrad City Executive Committee. In the correspondence between the Department and the Directorate of Public Catering of Leningrad, to which most restaurants were subordinate, one can find instructions that substantially limit the repertoire and activities of restaurant orchestras. For example, according to the established practice, restaurant patrons often requested the performance of their favourite tunes through waiters, or addressed the musicians directly. Significantly, they paid the waiters and musicians for these tunes directly, not the cashier of the restaurant. These tips, deemed 'unearned income', could not be controlled by the state and, therefore, had to be eliminated. The resolution by the Department of Musical Ensembles in 1958 strictly ordered:

> The existing practice of requesting various musical works through waiters and the general intervention of restaurant workers and executives of restaurants in the repertory of ensembles should be prohibited. Typically, the requested music is of low artistic taste.⁵²

Another resolution of the same year required:

> (1). The bandleader has to prepare the programme of a restaurant concert for each evening 7–10 days prior to the performance.
> (2). No less than half of it [the programme] must consist of music by Russian and Soviet authors.

(3). All evening programmes are subject to approval by the Department of Musical Ensembles [. . .][53]

Although those restrictions and prohibitions were often violated, they led to a gradual shift of Yiddish music from the sphere of official culture to informal underground subcultures.

In 1970s, the boat restaurant Koriushka (Smelt) at the Lieutenant Schmidt Embankment became the most popular place for the performance of Yiddish music, or to be more precise, the so-called Odessa-style music with Yiddish flavour. Evgenii Drabkin, one of the band members, remarks that:

> importantly, the Koriushka restaurant was owned by the Leningrad Shipping Company and its ensemble had not been subordinated to any repertory commission [. . .] The songs that we sang there were mostly Jewish Odessa songs, which in those days were an the even greater taboo than real bawdy songs [. . .] When we started to play the Odessa songs [. . .] the restaurant was always overcrowded.[54]

Later these quasi-Yiddish songs with Russian texts which contained Yiddish words shaped the repertoires of many contemporary Klezmer bands.[55]

Yiddish Music in Leningrad/St Petersburg during and after Perestroika

The Perestroika period of 1986–91 brought in a radically new era in the development of Jewish culture in the city. The democratization and ever-increasing openness of society brought about an increase in public interest in Jewish culture including Yiddish music, which for decades had remained under an unofficial ban. In the 1990s, projects related to revival of Yiddish musical culture were taken up by Jewish community organizations such as the Leningrad Jewish Association (since 1992 the Jewish Association of St Petersburg) and the Jewish Community Centre of St Petersburg. The Centre's archive, which was partly processed and described in 2013–14 within the framework of the project 'Jewish documentary sources in St Petersburg archives', contains a significant collection of materials reflecting the process of development of Yiddish music during the late 1980s–2010s.[56] The archive contains the personal papers of the musicologist Marina Goldina (Vainshtein), the author of the first research work on the history of the Society for Jewish Folk Music,[57] which deal with the establishment of the Club of Jewish Music Lovers (later the Society of Jewish Music Lovers) in Leningrad (1986–87); posters, programmes, photographs, audio and video recordings of Yiddish music concerts performed by such prominent singers and musicians as Nechama Lifshits, Adrienne Cooper, Zalmen Mlotek, Arkady Gendler, Leonid Sonts, Michael Alpert, Lorin Sklamberg, Frank London, Shura Lipovsky, Christian Dawid, Psoi Korolenko, as well as music groups Friling, Khaverim, the ensemble of Yiddish Song and Dance of the National Palace of Culture of Trade Unions (Vilnius), Dobranotch, Kharkov Klezmer Band and Kle-Zemer (1989–2007); materials of international conferences and seminars on Yiddish music including programmes, manuscript articles, and correspondace with participant ethnomusicologists, historians, composers, and performers of Yiddish song; clippings from Petersburg magazines and newspapers with reviews of the concerts of Yiddish music (1990s–2010s).[58]

Perhaps the most significant and successful undertaking of the Jewish Community Centre was the annual Klezfest festival in St Petersburg, which included master-classes on Yiddish folk songs and klezmer music by well-known performers, workshops on Yiddish folklore and Yiddish dance, and lectures and concerts of leading singers and musicians from all over the world. This authoritative international music forum, which took place between 1997 and 2008, attracted broad public attention in St Petersburg and became an important event in the city cultural life. *Fond* No. 2 in the archive of the Centre for Jewish Music of the Jewish Community Centre of St Petersburg contains, along with a rich collection of sheet music, records relating to the organization of the Klezfests in St Petersburg, including applications and profiles of participants of the festival, correspondence with musicians regarding the organization of Yiddish music concerts in St Petersburg, announcements of workshops and lectures, photographs, audio and video recordings of the concerts, workshops and lectures organized during the festivals, and clippings from newspapers and magazines with reviews of different festival events.

Throughout the entire Soviet period, Yiddish musical culture was recognized by St Petersburg/Leningrad Jews not only as a part of their cultural heritage, but in a more general way, as an important element of Jewish national identity.[59] Despite the attempts by the Soviet city authorities to exercise a strict ideological control over Jewish musical activities and even to ban Jewish music unofficially, Yiddish songs and instrumental music continued to sound either in private, at Jewish homes, or in the public space of several venues that served as informal meeting points of Jews, such as some restaurants and cafes. The documentary sources relating to more than a century-long history of the performance and study of Yiddish music in St Petersburg, which are surveyed in the current review, describe, to a certain extent, the variety of cultural forms and institutions that enabled Yiddish music activities to survive during the time when the authorities considered Jewish public activities undesirable and to flourish since the beginning of Perestroika, which lifted all previous restrictions.

Notes to Chapter 10

1. See, most notably, Mikhail Beizer, *The Jews of St. Petersburg: Excursions through a Noble Past* (Philadelphia and New York: The Jewish Publication Society, 1989), idem, *Evrei Leningrada: 1917–1939: natsional'naia zhizn' i sovetizatsiia* (Jerusalem and Moscow: Gesharim, 1999); Benjamin Nathans, *Beyond the Pale: The Jewish Encounter with Late Imperial Russia* (Berkeley: University of California Press, 2002); Yvone Kleinmann, *Neue Orte — Neue Menschen: Jüdische Lebensformen in St. Petersburg und Moskau im 19. Jahrhundert* (Göttingen: Vandenhoeck & Ruprecht, 2006).
2. *Dokumenty po istorii i kul'ture evreev v arkhivakh Sankt-Peterburga: putevoditel'*, I: Federal archives, ed. by Alexander Ivanov, Mark Kupovetskii, and Alexander Lokshin (St Petersburg: MIR, 2011); II: Regional archives, ed. by Alexander Ivanov and Mark Kupovetskii (St Petersburg: MIR, 2013); III: Departmental archives, part 1, ed. by Alexander Ivanov and Mark Kupovetskii (St Petersburg: MIR, 2015).
3. See on the history of the Society for Jewish Folk Music: Gershon Svet, 'Evrei v russkoi muzykal'noi kul'ture v sovetskii period', in *Kniga o russkom evreistve*, ed. by Iakov Frumkin, Grigorii Aronson, and Alexander Goldenveizer (New York: Soiuz russkikh evreev, 1968), pp. 254–63; Marina Vainshtein, 'Obschetstvo evreiskoi narodnoi muzyki kak faktor kul'turnoi zhizni Sankt-Peterburga nachala XX veka', in *Etnografiia Peterburga–Leningrada: Materialy ezhegodnykh nauchnykh chtenii*, II, ed. by Nataliia Iukhneva (Leningrad: Nauka, 1988), pp. 29–37;

Galina Kopytova, *Obschetstvo evreiskoi narodnoi muzyki v Peterburge–Petrograde* (St Petersburg: EZRO, 1997); Jascha Nemtsov, *Die Neue Jüdische Schule in der Musik* (Wiesbaden: Harrassowitz Verlag, 2004), pp. 131–47; James Loeffler, *The Most Musical Nation: Jews and Culture in the Late Russian Empire* (New Haven: Yale University Press, 2010).

4. James Loeffler, 'Society for Jewish Folk Music', in *The YIVO Encyclopedia of Jews in Eastern Europe*, II, ed. by Gershon D. Hundert (New Haven: Yale University Press, 2008), p. 1771.
5. In the current paper a fond is defined as a documentary collection, or a record group housed in an archive. See for details: *OAC Best Practice Guidelines for EAD*, ed. by Bradley D. Westbrook and others (Regents of University of California, 2013), pp. 2–3.
6. Central State Historical Archive of St Petersburg (hereafter TsGIA SPb), f. 1747, op. 1, d. 8, l. 5.
7. See the chronicle of activities of the Society for Jewish Folk Music in Petersburg–Petrograd in Kopytova, *Obschetstvo evreiskoi narodnoi muzyki v Peterburge–Petrograde*, pp. 46–61.
8. See also materials on the Society for Jewish Folk Music that appeared beyond the framework of the current review in the following depositories: the Manuscript Department of the Russian National Library in St Petersburg (MD RNB), f. 1308 — Collection of personal papers of Joseph and Isidor Achrons, f. 639 — Collection of personal papers of Andrei Rimskii-Korsakov and Julia Vaisberg, f. 733 — Collection of personal papers of Grigorii Timofeev and Maria Janova; the Archives of the Jewish Community Centre of St Petersburg, f. 2 — Collection of the Centre for Jewish Music.
9. *Dokumenty po istorii i kul'ture evreev v arkhivakh Sankt-Peterburga*, 1, 386.
10. *Tsentral'nyi gosudarstvenyi istoricheskii arkhiv Sankt-Peterburga: Putevoditel'*, 2 vols, ed. by Dmitry V. Nadsadnii et al. (St Petersburg: Archival Committee of St. Petersburg & Central State Historical Archive of St. Petersburg, 2009), II, p. 229.
11. Vera Lebedeva-Kaplan, 'Tri pis'ma iz 1919 goda: Iz istorii evreiskoi kul'tury Petrograda', *Istoriia evreev v Rossii. Problemy istochnikovedeniia i istoriografii*, I, ed. by Dmitry Elyashevich (St Petersburg: Petersburg Jewish University, 1993), pp. 134–65.
12. Phillip Moddel, *Joseph Achron* (Tel Aviv: Israeli Music Publications, 1966), p. 56.
13. See for details: 'O registratsii obshchestv, soiuzov, tserkovnykh i religioznykh ob"edinenii, deistvuiushchikh v gor. Petrograde i Petrogradskoi gub.', *Vestnik Petrosoveta*, 27 August 1921. See also: Alexander Ivanov, 'Petrogradskoe obshchestvo evreiskoi narodnoi muzyki v nachale 1920-kh godov: dokumenty, mneniia, gipotezy', *Iz istorii evreiskoi muzyki v Rossii*, III, ed. by Galina Kopytova and Alexander Frenkel (St Petersburg: Evreiskii obshchinnyi tsentr Sankt-Peterburga, Rossiiskii institut istorii iskusstv, 2015), pp. 114–26.
14. State Museum of Political History of Russia, f. VII, No. 2947.
15. Central State Archive of Literature and Art in St Petersburg (hereafter TsGALI SPb), f. 31 — the Leningrad Provincial Department of the Main Directorate for Literature and Publishing of the RSFSR Commissariat of Education (Lengublit), op. 2, d. 74.
16. On the creation of the Soviet Jewish national culture and its relation to the Biribidzhan project see, for example: Alexander Ivanov, ' "To the Jewish Country!": Representations of Birobidzhan in Soviet Mass-Media, 1920s–1930s', *Promised Lands, Transformed Neighbourhoods and Other Spaces. Migration and the Art of Display, 1920–1950 / Länder der Verheißung, verpflanzte Nachbarschaften und andere Räume: Migration und die Kunst ihrer Darstellung, 1920–1950*, ed. by Malgorzata Maksymiak, Susanne Marten-Finnis, and Michael Nagel (Bremen: edition lumière, 2016), pp. 49–84.
17. See documents related to the Soviet state national policy in the field of Jewish culture in 1920s–1930s in the following archives: Central State Archive of St Petersburg (hereafter TsGA SPb), f. R-2555 — the Leningrad Section of the Main Administration of Research Institutions of the Academic Center of the RSFSR People's Commissariat of Enlightenment, f. R-75 — the Nationalities Section of the Petrograd Provincial Council's Executive Committee, f. R-6962 — the Leningrad Regional Section of the All-Union Society for the Settlement of Jewish Toilers on the Land, LenOZET; Central State Archives of Historical and Political Documents (TsGAIPD SPb), f. R-16 — the Petrograd Provincial Committee of the All-Union Communist Party (Bolsheviks), Leningrad, f. R-2610 — the Primary Organization of the All-Union Communist Party (Bolsheviks) of the Board of the Leningrad Regional Council of the All-Russian Society for the Promotion of the Jewish Toiling Masses', LenOZET etc.

18. Paul D. Morris, *Representation and the Twentieth-century Novel: Studies in Gorky, Joyce and Pynchon* (Würzburg: Verlag Königshausen & Neumann GmbH, 2005), p. 92.
19. TsGAlI SPb, f. 73 — the Leningrad Society for Chamber Music, op. 1, d. 1, l. 104.
20. On Moisei Milner see the biographical materials in the following collected articles dedicated to the composer: *Iz istorii evreiskoi muzyki v Rossii*, II, ed. by Alexander Frenkel and Galina Kopytova (St Petersburg: Evreiskii obshehinnyi tsentr Sankt-Peterburga; Rossiiskii institut istorcii iskusstv, 2006), pp. 15–230.
21. On Moisei Milner's opera *Di himlen brenen* see also Galina Kopytova, 'Opera M. A. Milnera "Nebesa pylaiut"', *Iz istorii evreiskoi muzyki v Rossii*, I, ed. by Leonid Guralnik (St Petersburg: Evreiskii obshchinnyi tsentr Sankt-Peterburga, 2001), pp. 87–100.
22. TsGA SPb, f. 2552, op. 1, d. 1218, ll. 6–9.
23. TsGALI SPb, f. 31, op. 2, d. 3, l. 106.
24. TsGALI SPb, f. 258 — Unified Collection 'National Houses of Public Education in Leningrad', op. 3, d. 25–88.
25. See for example: Aexander Ivanov, 'La participation de l'OZET dans la production du film documentaire Birobidjan (1937)', *Kinojudaica. Représentations des Juifs dans le cinéma de Russie et d'Union soviétique des années 1910 aux années 1980*, ed. by Valerie Pozner and Natasha Laurent (Paris: Nouveau Monde éditions, 2012), pp. 197–219.
26. TsGALI SPb, f. 271, op. 1, d. 5, ll. 1–35.
27. On the film *The Return of Nathan Becker*, see also Miron Chernenko, *Krasnaia zvezda, zheltaia zvezda: Kinematograficheskaia istoriia evreistva v Rossii* (Moscow: Text, 2006), pp. 66–70.
28. TsGALI SPb, f. 168, op. 1, d-d. 13, 14, 27.
29. On S. An-sky, see the recent biographical study: Gabriella Safran, *Wandering Soul: The Dybbuk's Creator, S. An-sky* (Cambridge, MA and London: Harvard University Press, 2010).
30. Benjamin Lukin, 'Ot narodinichestva k narodu: S. A. An-sky — etnograf vostochno-evropeiskogo evreistva', *Evrei v Rossii, istoria i kul'tura*, III, ed. by Dmitry Elyashevich (St Petersburg: Petersburg Jewish University, 1995), p. 140. See also for details: *Photographing the Jewish Nation: Pictures from S. An-sky's Ethnographic Expeditions*, ed. by Eugene Avrutin and others (Waltham, MA: Brandeis University Press; Hanover, NH and London: University Press of New England, 2009).
31. See for instance: Joel Engel, 'Evreiskaia narodnaia pesnia: Etnograficheskaia poezdka', *Paralleli*, iv–v (Moscow: Dom evreiskoi knigi, 2004), pp. 285–305.
32. For example, a collection of wax cylinders with expedition recordings of Jewish folk music is stored now in Vernadsky National Library of Ukraine in Kiev; another collection of wax cylinders No. 45 is deposited in the Phonographic Archive of the Institute of Russian Literature (Pushkin House) in St Petersburg.
33. Several documents related to the early years of Sofia Magid including her photos are stored in the personal documentary collection of her father, the outstanding historian, bibliographer, art critic, and musicologist David Maggid (1862–1942). The collection is preserved in the Archives of the Institute of Oriental Manuscripts of the Russian Academy of Sciences, f. 85. It was partly processed and described in 2012–14 within the framework of the project 'Jewish Documentary Sources in Archives of St Petersburg' by Evgeniia Khazdan, a student of educational programme of the Centre 'Petersburg Judaica'.
34. A collection of personal papers of Moisei Beregovskii No. 45 is preserved in the Manuscript Cabinet of the Russian Institute of the History of Arts in St Petersburg. Although research activities of Beregovskii are primarily associated with Kiev, a considerable documentary collection of his personal papers is stored in St Petersburg now. An archiographical description of the mentioned collection will be included in the next guidebook of the 'Petersburg series'.
35. See for details: Elvira Groezinger and Susi Hudak-Lazić, '*Unser Rebbe, unser Stalin . . .': Jiddische Lieder aus den St. Petersburger Sammlungen von Moishe Beregowski (1892–1961) und Sofia Magid (1892–1954)* (Wiesbaden: Harrassowitz Verlag, 2008).
36. These collections were revealed and described in 2008–09 within the framework of the project 'Jewish Documentary Sources in Archives of St Petersburg' by Dina Gidon, a postgraduate student of the Centre 'Petersburg Judaica' of the European University at St Petersburg. The descriptions of the above-mentioned collections will be included in the next volume of the

'Petersburg series'. It is worth mentioning the collection that contains recordings of Yiddish music No. 46 compiled by Sergei Rybakov from the Phonographic Archive of the Institute of Russian Literature in St Petersburg.

37. Genrikh M. Deich, *Zapiski sovetskogo arkhivista: kollektsiia dokumental'nykh materialov po istorii evreev v Rossii* (Moscow: Obschestvo 'Evreiskoe nasledie', 1996), no pagination.
38. TsGALI SPb, f. 381 — Interregional Public Organization of St Petersburg and the Leningrad Region 'Branch of the Union of Theatrical Figures of the Russian Federation', f. 378 — St Petersburg State Variety Theatre, f. 355 — State Philharmonic and Concert Agency 'Petersburg-Concert', f. 105 — General Directorate of Culture of the Leningrad City Executive Committee. These collections were described in 2009–11 within the framework of the project 'Jewish Documentary Sources in Archives of St Petersburg' by Alexander Frenkel.
39. TsGALI SPb, f. 381, op. 5, d. 9, 12, 13, 15, 18–20, 24, 26.
40. Ibid, f. 105, op. 1, d. 133, 309, 439, 708.
41. See for example: TsGALI SPb, f. 381, op. 5, d. 9, l. 15; d. 12, l. 63. For Yiddish concerts in the post-Stalin period, see also: Gennady Estraikh, *Yiddish in the Cold War* (Oxford: Legenda, 2005), pp. 56–60; Alexander Frenkel, '"Sonim af tsulokhes" — "Vragam nazlo": Evreiskaia estrada v Leningrade epokhi ottepeli', *Iz istorii evreiskoi muzyki v Rossii*, III, pp. 191–242; idem, '"Freyd zol zayn" — "Da budet radost"', ili Khozhdeniia po mukam leningradskoi evreiskoi estrady', *Arkhiv evreiskoi istorii*, viii (Moscow, 2016), pp. 305–39.
42. See for instance the reports of KGB agents about visitors of the Grand Choral Synagogue in the 1960s: Central State Archive of Political-Historical Documents in St Petersburg, f. R-8422 — Leningrad Rural Committee of the Communist Party of the Soviet Union, op. 1, d. 191, l. 12–18, 26–108.
43. Documents related to David Stiskin one can find in the following collections: TsGALI SPb, f. 355; TsGA SPb, f. R-9620 — Plenipotentiary of the USSR Council of Ministers' Council on Religious Cults for Leningrad and the Leningrad Region.
44. TsGALI SPb, f. 105, op. 1, d. 439, l. 29.
45. Ibid., d. 570, l. 102.
46. Ibid., d. 708, l. 7.
47. On Faivish Arones and his ensemble, see also Frenkel, '"Sonim af tsulokhes" — "Vragam nazlo"', pp. 213–27; Idem, '"Freyd zol zayn" — "Da budet radost"', pp. 309–33.
48. On the last concert of Anna Guzik, which was held in February 1973, see Frenkel, '"Sonim af tsulokes" — "Vragam hazlo"', pp. 199, 240.
49. Joel E. Rubin and Rita Ottens, Booklet of the CD 'Shalom Comrade! Yiddish Music in the Soviet Union, 1928–1961' (WERGO, a division of SCHOTT MUSIC & MEDIA GmbH, Mainz, Germany), p. 2.
50. TsGALI SPb, f. 333, op. 1, d. 1100, l. 28.
51. The film *Seekers of Happiness* (*Iskateli schastia*) was released in 1936 at the Sovetskaia Belarus Studio in Leningrad (director: Vladimir Korsh-Sablin; screenplay: Iogan Zel'tser, Grigorii Kobets; cinematography: Boris Riabov; music: Isaac Dunaevskii; setting: Vladimir Pokroivskii; consultant: Solomon Mikhoels; cast: Veniamin Zuskin, Marina Bliumental'-Tamarina, Iona Bii-Brodskii etc.). It is about Jewish resettlers who have moved to Birobidzhan kolkhoz Roite Feld.
52. TsGALI SPb, f. 105, op. 1, d. 708, l. 86.
53. Ibid., l. 107.
54. Evgenii Drabkin, '"We are not from Jazz" (From the History of Underground Music and Soviet Tape-recording)', see: <http://www.blat.dp.ua/legenda/drapkin.htm>.
55. It is interesting to note that a composer of Polish-Jewish origin Juliusz Wolfsohn included in his 'Jüdische Rhapsodie' (1912) and 'Hebräische Suite' (1926) the Yiddish tunes that were late played by the Koriushka restaurant band as Odessa-Jewish songs. See Jascha Nemtsov: Wolfsohn, Juliusz: Paraphrasen über altjüdische Volksweisen / Jüdische Rhapsodie / Hebräische Suite / Franz Liszt: Ungarische Rhapsodien Nr. 3/7/8/13 (Oehms Classics Musikproduktion GmbH, 2008, OC — 572).
56. Archaeographical descriptions of collections stored in the Archive of Jewish Community Center of Petersburg see in *Dokumenty po istorii i kul'ture evreev v arkhivakh Sankt-Peterburga*, III, 1, 347–68.

57. See note 3.
58. The above-mentioned materials are stored in the following collections of the Jewish Community Centre Archive: f. 1 — Jewish Community Centre of St Petersburg; f. 4 — Joint Archive of Private Documentary Collections; f. 7 — Photo-documents Collection; f. 9 — Video-materials Collection.
59. On the relation of Yiddish music to Jewish identity, see for example: Tatyana Gutova, 'Fenomen vozrozhdeniia klezmerskoi muzyki: metamorfozy identichnosti', *Muzyka idishkaita*, II, ed. by Anna Smirnitskaia and Anatoli Pinskii (Moscow: Memories, 2006), pp. 172–85.

CHAPTER 11

Between Ethnography of Religion and Anti-religious Propaganda: Jewish Graphics in the Leningrad and Moscow Museums in 1930s

Alla Sokolova

Introduction

The opening of numerous antireligious museums and relevant departments in existing museums, regardless of their profiles, as well as various antireligious exhibitions began in the mid-1920s under the auspices of the Union of the Godless.[1] Their numbers increased further after the First All-Russian Museum Congress (1–5 December 1930).[2] But, as was noted at the Congress, the majority of those museums 'did not master the methods of organizing [antireligious — *A. S.*] exhibitions' due to the lack of 'serious antireligious work in'.[3] Therefore, the Central Antireligious Museum of the League of Militant Atheists in Moscow (hereafter CAM) was designated as the 'methodical centre of the museum antireligious movement'.[4] According to the decision of the Congress, CAM began to reorganize its own permanent exhibition, which was previously mainly based on photographic material. The CAM staff member Yurii Kogan noted in an article devoted to the development of antireligious museums that CAM had made great efforts to fill its exhibitions with 'authentic artefacts, valuable for antireligious purposes'.[5] It seems that CAM staff members were largely focusing on the experience of their Leningrad colleagues. Referring to 'the exhibition on the history of religion of the Academy of Sciences' which opened on 15 April 1930 in the halls of the Winter Palace, Kogan named Leningrad 'the strong basis of antireligious work'.[6] That temporal 'Antireligious Exhibition' exhibition was prepared under the auspices of the Museum of Anthropology and Ethnography of the Academy of Sciences (hereafter MAE). Its name, trivialized by its frequent use for a large number of other antireligious exhibition projects, did not adequately reflect its grand scale. It included many valuable original objects and a variety of supporting materials. Its scholarly concept had been developed by the prominent Russian ethnographer Vladimir Bogoras, who argued that 'the Antireligious Exhibition should raise the issue of typology and evolution of religion'.[7]

In his article, Kogan also mentioned the Museum of the History of Religion of the Academy of Sciences (hereafter MIR), although its first permanent exhibition in the building of the Kazan Cathedral (that had already been closed for religion services) was still in the stage of preparation.[8] The State Antireligious Museum, located in the building of the former St Isaac's Cathedral (hereafter SAMFIC), occupied the last position in Kogan's list of antireligious institutions.[9] MIR, which grew out of the Antireligious Exhibition, subsequently inherited collections of SAMFIC and CAM. The 'Judaism' collection (*fond*) at the State Museum of the History of Religion (hereafter GMIR) — as the museum is called now — contains original graphic works that had been received from these three sources: MIR, SAMFIC, and CAM.[10] Some of them were commissioned by the museum in the 1930s or selected by its representative with the participation of the artists. In both cases the inclusion of a graphic work in the museum's collection was the result of collaboration between the artist and a staff member. Among these works are twenty-nine drawings by Solomon Iudovin, as well as two drawings of each of the following well-known Jewish artists: Alexander Konstantinovskii, Ilya Maltz, and Manuel Shekhtman. Iudovin's graphic works were used in all of the three Leningrad museum projects of antireligious orientation. Graphic works by Konstantinovskii, Maltz, and Shekhtman appeared at permanent and temporal exhibitions in Moscow CAM.

Isaiah Pulner, Mikhail Shakhnovich, Mark Persits, and Berta Sharevskaia, young specialists in traditional Jewish culture and historians of religion with a sufficiently high level of professional competence, were made responsible for the representation of Judaism in all these museum projects. They oversaw the creation of thematic blocks related to Judaism in permanent exhibitions with a clearly antireligious orientation. They sought to achieve the desired results through scholarly and quasi-scholarly interpretations of religious phenomena rather than satire, which dominated the antireligious museum projects in the 1920s. In this respect, they can be considered followers of Vladimir Bogoras who defended his Antireligious Exhibition from criticism by stressing that 'this stage [satire] of vulgar antireligious propaganda has been long past'.[11] Graphic works by Iudovin, as well as by Konstantinovskii, Maltz, and Shekhtman are treated in this article as two artistic collections that emerged out of that exhibition and other museum projects of the 1930s. In my opinion, by studying these collections that were formed as a result of cooperation between museum curators and artists, recognized experts in Jewish religious rituals, we can better understand certain aspects of the Soviet Jewish culture. I will show in my essay that museum representations of Judaism were addressed primarily to Soviet Jews, focusing on their antireligious education. At the same time, these representations also popularized scholarly study of Judaism. Iudovin's collection consists of composite drawings based on photographs and other visual materials, hand-drawn posters which combined images and texts, as well as life drawings. I will not discuss the artistic quality of the drawings, but only their style and iconography, with the purpose to show how they have reflected the rhetorical formulas of representation of Judaism that determined the character of didactic museum exhibitions in the 1930s.

FIGS. 11.1 and 11.2. Solomon Iudovin, 'The Wedding' and 'The Funeral', drawings of 1930

The Antireligious Project in Leningrad Museums

The creation of the artistic collection corresponds to the major stages of the formation of the entire collection (*fond*) 'Judaism' in GMIR. The eight drawings and seven hand-drawn posters by Iudovin had already existed before the establishment of the museum.[12] These works were inherited by the museum from the Antireligious Exhibition.[13] In 1930, Isaiah Pulner transferred Iudovin's drawings and posters, along with other graphic materials related to 'Judaism', from the MAE collection to the Antireligious Exhibition.[14] In 1929 Pulner graduated from the Ethnographic Department of the Geography Faculty of the Leningrad State University where he studied with Valdimir Borogas.[15] Probably because of that connection Pulner was involved in the preparation of the 'Judaism' section of the Antireligious Exhibition, which Bogoras regarded as 'the nucleus of the future scholarly antireligious museum'.[16] As an employee of MAE, Bogoras initially conceived the exhibition as part of this institution, but soon the exhibition was reorganized into an independent institution, MIR, under his directorship.[17]

Among Iudovin's fifteen graphic works selected for the Antireligious Exhibition, two watercolours, *Wedding* and *Funeral*, are signed and dated 1930 (Figures 1 and 2). Probably, these two works, as well as the unsigned watercolour *Circumcision* similar in technique and style, were prepared especially for the exhibition by Pulner's request (Figure 3). MAE purchased them later together with several other of Iudovin's graphic works and photographs. Among the photographs handed over by Pulner to the exhibition from the collection of MAE, I found some photographs made by Iudovin during S. An-sky's ethnographic expeditions to the Volhynia, Podolia, and Kiev provinces in 1912–14, such as *Torah Scribe* (Figure 4)[18] as well as photographs, that can be attributed to Iudovin on indirect evidence, for example, *Tzaddik's Tomb* (Figure 5). This photograph is mentioned by Bogoras among exhibits of the section on modern Judaism[19] in his article 'The Antireligious Exhibition of the Academy of Sciences of the USSR':

> The following exhibition displays photographs depicting religious rituals of modern Jews connected with birth, marriage, and death. Among them one can notice, for example, the grave of the *tzaddik* (Jewish saint) and *kvitlakh*, petition notes, left by faithful Jews at the *tzaddik*'s grave; the grave of the Torah, which [Jews] also bury in the ground; circumcision, ritual bath, the scene before the Shabbat repast, and the baking of unleavened bread (*matzo*).[20]

Thus, Bogoras included two original items, the *kvitlah*, in the list of photographs.[21] This allowed him to specify an important principle of construction of his exhibition, presenting ritual objects next to a photograph of a religious ritual in which this objects were used. The list also contains the following items: the photograph *Grave of the Torah Scrolls*,[22] Iudovin's drawings *Circumcision* and *Mikvah, the Ritual Bathing Pool*, and the hand-drawn poster *Shabbat Celebration*, with the quotation from the Exodus (31: 13–14) under the watercolour image (Figures 6 and 7). The last item on the list of images is a photocopy of an engraving *Baking Matzo*, dated 1726, which is reproduced in the Russian *Jewish Encyclopaedia*.[23] This list indicates Bogoras's

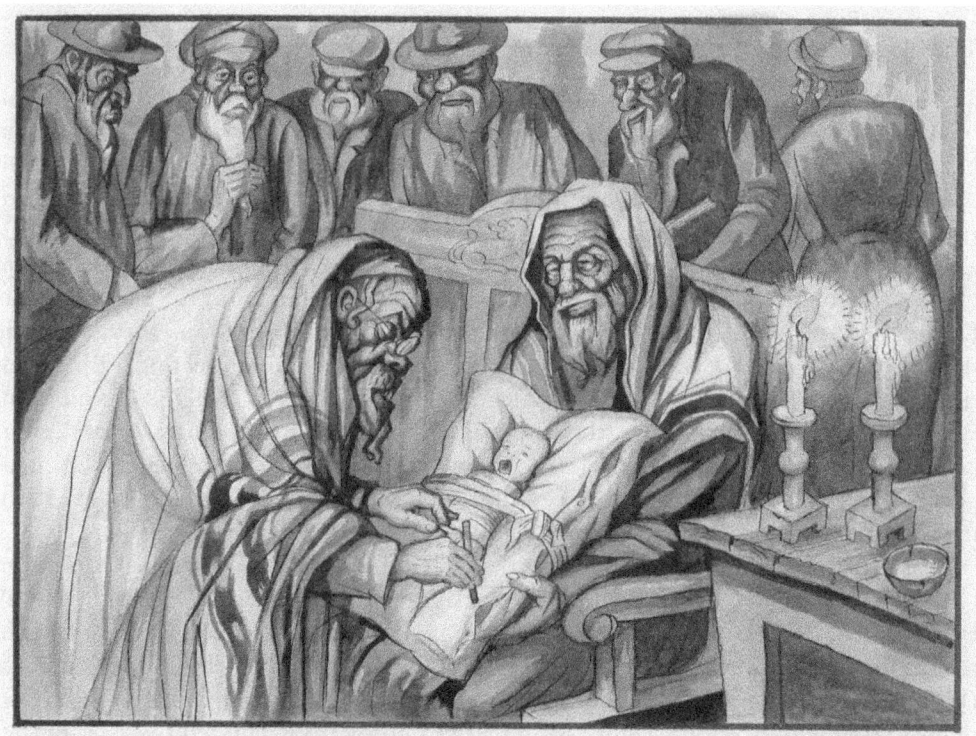

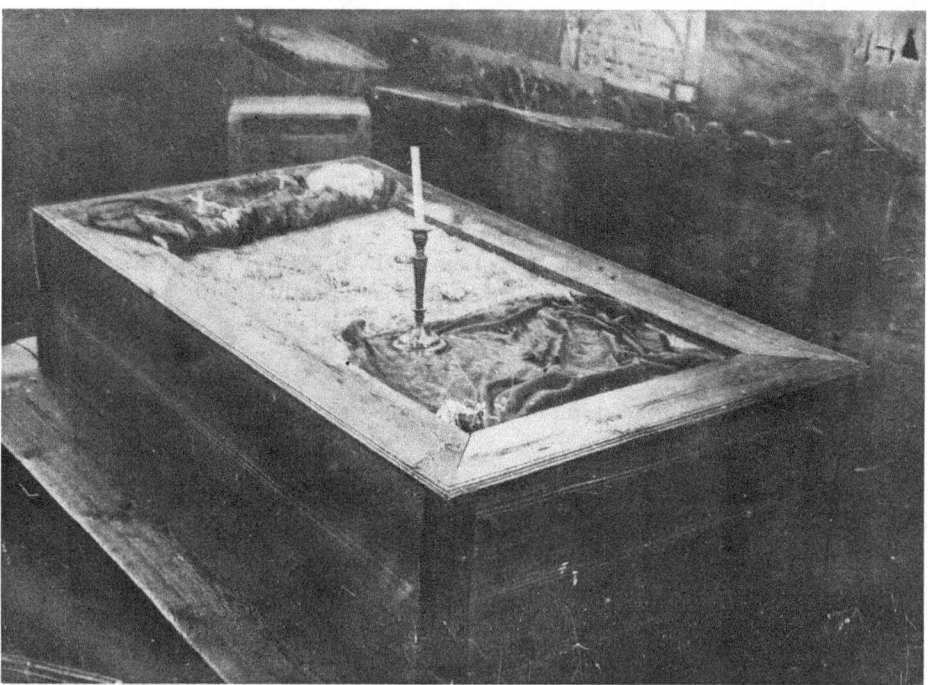

Figs. 11.3 and 11.4. Solomon Iudovin, 'The Circumcision', drawing 1930 (?); Solomon Iudovin, 'Tomb of the Tzaddik', photograph taken during An-sky's expedition in 1912–14 (?)

FIGS. 11.5 and 11.6. Solomon Iudovin, 'Torah Copyist [soifer David Elie. Annopol, Volhynia Province]', photo taken during An-sky's expedition in 1912–14; 'Mikvah, the Ritual Bathing Pool', drawing of 1929

Figs. 11.7 and 11.8. Solomon Iudovin, 'The Sabbath Celebration', hand-drawn poster of 1929 (?); Solomon Iudovin, 'The Slaughterman [Shohet]' drawing of 1930 (?)

indifference to the character of illustrative material presented at the exhibition. His selection disregards the conventional genre hierarchy, according to which original drawings and life photographs have a higher status than mere copies of book illustrations. The exhibition displayed unique artefacts and original works of art side by side with low-quality copies if they were considered realist representations of religious rituals and key events in the history of religions. In all likelihood, Bogoras as well as Pulner considered photographs by Iudovin and his drawings of equal value in terms of adequate reproduction of ethnographic reality.

> Iudovin's graphic works at the exhibition are not stylistically uniform. The drawing *Mikvah, the Ritual Bathing Pool* and the poster *Shabbat Celebration* are neutral, schematic, and dry in their representational style like other posters. By contrast, the watercolours *Circumcision* and *Funeral* are rich in details and have pronounced grotesque features.[24] These graphic works confirm the opinion of the prominent art critic Jeremiah Joffe about Iudovin's woodcut depictions of shtetl everyday life: 'Iudovin rises from realism not towards humour, but towards an amorous mockery over petty poverty and bustle, but [. . .] then he switches towards grim interpretations in which the ghetto life gets apocalyptic, terrible, tragically-screaming expression.'[25]

The watercolour *Circumcision* is described in the records of GMIR as a caricature. But this definition, given when the inventory was compiled at the beginning of the 1950s,[26] is not fully justified. Although the characters are depicted grotesquely, the image as a whole seems devoid of irony or satire. It is consistent with the interpretation of the ritual given on the MIR label in the 1930s: 'circumcision among Jews and Muslims is one of many savage rites preserved in contemporary religions'.[27]

The watercolor *Wedding* — one of the few works by Iudovin, refuting words of Joffe given above, is imbued with friendly irony. Iudovin has depicted a wedding ceremony taking place in the square of a small shtetl. One can see in the background the well and one-storey wooden houses. In such entourage the beardless groom is the only one of the men who wears not a traditional cap but a bowler hat. Beside this the groom is wearing a tie. He looks pretty ridiculous (in my opinion, like Charlie Chaplin in his famous role of a small tramp).

Iudovin's drawing *Ritual Slaughterer [Shokhet]*, based on his photograph,[28] indicates a search for an ethnographically rich and visually accurate representation of religious phenomena. This unique drawing consists of three pictorial fields portraying three stages of the operation *shekhitah* (slaughter according to the rules of *kashrut*). Each one has the figure of the *shokhet* with a chicken in his hands: the first picture shows the preparation for ritual slaughter, the second one captures the crucial moment when the *shokhet* cuts the throat of the chicken, and the third one shows the bleeding chicken in *shokhet's* hands (Figure 8).

Presumably, this drawing was displayed at the Antireligious Exhibition next to the knife for *shekhitah*. The picture of *Feast of Tabernacles* (Sukkoth) was exhibited together with a *lulav* (branch of the date palm tree) which was donated for the exhibition personally by Isaiah Pulner,[29] and the watercolour *Judgment Day* (Yom Kippur), representing a variation on the motives of Jakub Weinles's painting *Yom*

Kippur, was displayed with a *kittel* (a white gown worn on Yom Kippur) and a girding cord that were obtained for the exhibition from a plenipotentiary of the People's Commissariat of Education (Figures 9 and 10).[30] These graphic works by Iudovin were meant to explain to visitors to the exhibition 'what this or that object or a group of objects spoke about', as explained Boris Sokolov, the first director of the Central Museum of Ethnology, at the Meeting of ethnographers from Moscow and Leningrad, in April 1929.[31] Discussing the concept of the Antireligious Exhibition, Bogoras stressed that religious phenomena had to be shown 'in such a form as they are in reality, not leaving out their attractive features, which should be unmasked with the help of clear arguments'.[32]

As I have already mentioned at the beginning of the article, in 1938 the collection of MIR received additional nineteen graphic works by Iudovin, nine hand-drawn posters and ten drawings from the State Antireligious Museum, the former St. Isaac's Cathedral (SAMFIC). In 1931, the first permanent antireligious exhibition was opened there.[33] It included the section 'Judaism', which was prepared with the assistance of Isaiah Pulner.[34] He apparently initiated the establishment of this section in 1930, right after the Antireligious Exhibition in the Winter Palace was completed.

The posters and drawing by Iudovin, as well as his photographs, were delivered to MIR from SAMFIC together with a small Judaic collection, probably with Pulner's assistance.[35] SAMFIC was redesigned as a memorial museum, whereby its main object of display became St Isaac's Cathedral itself,[36] and its non-core collections were transferred to other museums, including MIR.[37] As the set of Iudovin's graphic works demonstrates, Pulner retained the key aspects of the exhibition plan of the section 'Judaism' at the Antireligious Exhibition in his arrangement of the similar section in SAMFIC. Five out of the ten drawings were Iudovin's own copies or versions of drawings that were obtained earlier from the Antireligious Exhibition,[38] and six out of the nine posters were duplicates of posters that had the same origin.

By comparing the duplicate posters we can see that Iudovin prepared the posters for SAMFIC after he had submitted the first set of posters to the Antireligious Exhibition. This assumption is based on the features of drawing the images on duplicate posters. For example, the figure of an old priest (*kohen*) on the poster entitled 'Drawing with Text from Exodus' depicting the performance of the commandment of the firstborn's redemption (Hebrew: *pidyon haben*), which was received from SAMFIC, differs from the similar image on the duplicate-poster 'Redemption of the Firstborn', which was obtained from the Antireligious Exhibition. While mechanically copying the figure from the completed poster to the new one that was assigned for SAMFIC, the artist 'forgot' to depict the priest's hand on the edge of the table (Figures 11 and 12). It is indicative that Iudovin did not put his signature on any of these posters, perhaps because he considered them merely as didactic visual material for illustrating the exhibition theme. On some of those posters images play a secondary role in relation to the text, and all posters are executed in a dry schematic manner so that they do not compete with original religious items presented in the museum exhibition.

Only two watercolours obtained by the MIR collection from SAMFIC, named

FIGS. 11.9 and 11.10. Solomon Iudovin, 'Judgment Day [here, Yom Kippur]', drawing of 1929 (?); postcard with a reproduction of Jakub Weinles's painting 'Yom Kippur'. Russian Empire, Publisher: Lebanon, early 20th cent.

 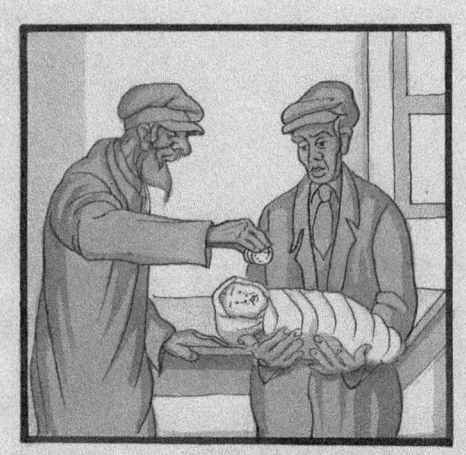

Figs. 11.11 and 11.12. Solomon Iudovin, 'The Drawing with Text from Exodus', hand-drawn poster of 1930 (?); Solomon Iudovin, 'Redemption of the Firstborn', hand-drawn poster of 1929 (?)

'Praying to the Moon' and 'Shabbat Repast', have Iudovin's signature, the monogram 'S. Iu.', at the bottom (Figures 13 and 14). Both works resemble in technique and style two other watercolours of 1930 with the artist's signature 'S. Iudovin', which were mentioned earlier in this chapter. Another watercolour obtained from SAMFIC, 'A Jew Reading the Talmud', does not carry Iudovin's signature, although it is made in a similar manner. This watercolour resembles the photograph 'A Rabbi Reading the Talmud', depicting an old man sitting with his back to the tiled oven in front of an open book in folio, which is presumed to be Iudovin's work (Figures 15 and 16). Apparently, Pulner decided that the photographic portrait of a rabbi was not suggestive enough for the exhibition aimed at presenting the Talmud as a source of harmful religious delusions. Iudovin was able to solve this problem by depicting a gloomy old man reading a book, with yellow candlelight and a large dark shadow behind him. It is possible that Iudovin did not sign the work, as well as the drawing *Circumcision*, because of their pronounced antireligious orientation. The four signed drawings are less aggressive, such as the watercolour *Praying to the Moon*, which depicts merely the 'remnants of worship to the Moon' in the ritual known as 'Kiddush Levana'.[39]

Similarities between the picture *Shabbat Repast* from SAMFIC and the poster *Shabbat Celebration* from the Antireligious Exhibition are quite significant. Although the watercolours are made in different styles, they share the way of forming a combined visual verbal message by placing inscriptions in the pictorial field. Iudovin provided the ritually significant utensils on the table with inscriptions in Hebrew: 'Holy Shabbat' on the napkin, which covered the *challah*, and 'Shabbat' on the glass with wine.[40] Affinity between these works is also visible in the interpretation of the main characters' images, particularly of a child in the foreground. At the same time, the poster *Shabbat Celebration* is rather schematic in comparison with *Shabbat Repast*, which is painted in greater detail and with more expression (see Figures 7 and 14). Possibly *Shabbat Celebration* and other posters from the first set of the Jewish Rituals series were made by Iudovin in 1929 for the Museum of the Jewish Historical and Ethnographic Society (hereafter JHES), but after its closing by the Soviet authorities at the end of that year, Pulner, who then worked as an ethnographer-consultant at the JHES Museum, arranged for the transfer of these graphic works to MAE and the Antireligious Exhibition.[41] As a curator of the JHES Museum, Iudovin was in charge of replenishing the Museum collection and was responsible to the Museum Commission for the preservation of collected items and for the preparation of exhibitions.[42] According to the memoirs of the artist and art historian David Hoberman, the reconstruction of the Museum's permanent exhibition, which started in 1928, was still continuing at that time.[43] It seems that Pulner, a young university graduate, sought to reform the exhibition in accordance with the requirements of the time. He sharply criticized 'Jewish bourgeois museums' in his article 'Organization of Jewish Ethnographic Museums and Jewish Sections in the General Ethnographic Museums'.[44] As Pulner remarked, 'they enclosed Jewish culture into a narrow nationalist framework, separated it from its surroundings, idealized it and made it look noble'; they operated under the slogan 'all Israelites are brothers' instead of demonstrating 'class moments and

FIG. 11.13. Solomon Iudovin, 'Praying to the Moon [here, Kiddush Levana]', drawing of 1930 (?)

FIGS. 11.14 and 11.15.
Solomon Iudovin,
'Shabbat Repast',
drawing of 1930 (?);
Solomon Iudovin,
'The Jew Reading the Talmud',
drawing of 1930 (?)

Fig. 11.16. Solomon Iudovin (?), 'The Graybeard Reading the Talmud', photo taken during An-sky's expedition in 1912–14 (?)

Figs. 11.17 and 11.18. David Hoberman (?), 'From the Morning Prayers', hand-drawn poster of 1929 (?); Solomon Iudovin, 'The Morning Prayer', hand-drawn poster of 1930 with photograph taken during An-sky's expedition in 1912–14.

class contradictions'.[45] This article was published in 1931, a year after JHES and its museum were closed, but undoubtedly Pulner thought about it while working on the above-mentioned text. He stressed that Jewish museums 'should show the people's religious calendar, the life cycle of rituals connected with birth, marriage, and death, with all private and public life, revealing the class origin of festivals and rituals, and exposing them as factors hampering socialist construction'.[46]

In 1928–29 the permanent exhibition at the JHES Museum consisted of two main sections: 'Jewish Everyday Life' and 'Jewish Cult'.[47] In addition, there was a section on the 'Jewish Community', containing portraits of Jewish public figures and writers.[48] Pulner might have tried to give the JHES Museum antireligious orientation according to the strong demands by the representatives of the Soviet institutions of political education.[49] Hoberman recalled that in 1929 he worked in accordance with Iudovin's suggestion[50] 'to make drawings on the theme of Jewish ritual', and two of his drawings were displayed at the permanent exhibition of the JHES Museum shortly before it was closed 'together with the other centres of national [Jewish] culture'.[51] The collection of GMIR contains the hand-drawn poster *From the Morning Prayers*, obtained by MIR from the Antireligious Exhibition. The author of this poster is not identified. Perhaps this is one of the works that Hoberman made under Iudovin's supervision. The watercolour painting at this poster looks like a work of a diligent student. A similar poster by Iudovin, *The Morning Prayer*, also obtained by MIR from SAMFIC, differs from all his other posters because it uses a photograph (of a one-eyed old man, dressed in a *tallit*, with *tefillin* on his forehead), rather than a drawing (Figures 17 and 18).[52] In my opinion, the grisaille watercolour technique — predominantly in shades of grey — used by Iudovin in most of his works, reflects his desire to emphasize photographic accuracy of the images. At the time, photography was recognized as the most appropriate way of representing the reality. In both posters on the theme of the Morning Prayer, the text is placed next to the images. The text is divided into sections according to the structure of the prayer, but this arrangement does not serve to clarify the meaning of the prayer. Of the blessings that begin the morning prayer, there was chosen not the first section in its order, but the fourth one: 'thanks to God for not making one a woman'. These verses are usually evoked for criticizing Judaism as a religion, which 'consecrated social inequalities women'.[53]

In contrast to the posters related to the theme of the Morning Prayer, the poster *Shabbat Celebration* and the drawings *Shabbat Repast* and *Passover* are less clear in their contents. On the one hand, the theme of a festive meal refers to retouched photographs that were reproduced on the early twentieth-century Jewish postcards with the purpose of 'ennobling' the religious tradition.[54] The main characters of these three drawings are the rich and the poor, the owner of the house and the pauper who is invited to take part in the Shabbat repast as a guest. The images of these two persons are opposed to each other in the composition of the picture. In the image of the house owner one can notice signs of idealization of the 'bourgeoisie': he looks like a pious head of a large family rather than a treacherous deceiver. Especially indicative is the drawing *Shabbat Repast* where the interior of the room is drawn in detail: in the background one can see not only the *Mizrakh* and the portrait of Moses Montefiore hanging on the wall, but also a flaky corner of the fireplace. The master of the house can hardly be considered rich. This picture clearly conveyed the idea of the inescapable poverty of large Jewish families that was widespread among the Russian-Jewish intelligentsia.

Antireligious orientation could be added to this picture through the accompanying inscription. The brochure *Whom does the 'Religion of Israel' Serve?* (1929) by Mikhail Shakhnovich (1911–92), who at that time was beginning his scholarly career in religious studies, helps understand how this could be done.[55] Both Shakhnovich and Iudovin worked with Pulner on preparing the Antireligious Exhibition,[56] which could have helped Shakhnovich to compose his brochure. For example, in the chapter 'The Class Nature of [Religious] Festival' Shakhnovich explains how in the days of religious festivals 'the class contradictions were smoothed over'.[57] He exposes the rich man, who has appealed to the poor with the following words: 'Reb Shmuel, let's forget [our] old enmity. All the people are equal before God in such a joyous day — you and me [. . .] We are all children of God [. . .], let's eat what God has sent [us].'.[58] Such explanatory texts could provide unambiguous interpretations of the images in Iudovin's pictures by turning them into compelling visual evidence of how the rich man managed to deceive the poor one, to lure him into his home and to sit him down at his festive table.

Shakhnovich's brochure allows us to reconstruct the contents of three more posters: *From the Prayer Upon Awakening* with the image of a Jew washing his hands in the morning, *From the Prayers before and after Eating* depicting three men at a table with a dish with bread, and *Prayer before Going to Bed* with the image of an old woman lying in bed surrounded by archangels (Figure 19). In the chapter 'Pray and Humble Yourself', Shakhnovich ironically indicates a large number of regulations that an observant Jew must follow:

> Waking up, you have to wash quickly, because you must be washed by the time you accidentally recall the name of God. After washing, it is necessary to give praise to the Lord for he brought you to life. The prayer before breakfast follows the morning prayer, then the time comes for praying after the breakfast, at lunch, in the afternoon, before the evening, before going to bed, etc. The person is supposed to do one thing only: pray.[59]

In the chapter 'The Last Days' one can find the following description of the ritual of *malkot* [lashing]: 'to inspire the faithful's humility, a synagogue servant carried out a punishment by whip for sins: 39 lashes on the back and below'.[60] As Shakhnovich explains, the belief that one cannot resist the blows of fate leads to 'paralysing the class struggle'.[61] Strictly speaking, without an additional text, Iudovin's poster *Punishment for Sins* could not deliver such a clearly antireligious message to the 'target audience' which could have been familiar with a different context of representation of the *malkot* ceremony (Figure 20). Before the October Revolution, studio photographs of the ceremony were often reproduced on the Jewish holiday greeting postcards. Obviously, they had formed a positive context for this kind of image. Iudovin's drawing recalls a studio photograph: the kneeling Jew receives blows by the whip, which symbolized the punishment prescribed by Torah for voluntary and involuntary transgressions. Only the specific explanation on the label

Figs. 11.19 and 11.20. Solomon Iudovin, 'Prayer before Going to Bed', hand-drawn poster of 1929 (?); Solomon Iudovin, 'Punishment for Sins [here, Malkot ceremony]', hand-drawn poster of 1930 (?)

to this poster could give it the antireligious connotation. One of the photographs of the MIR's permanent exhibition, presumably made in 1937, shows the poster *Punishment for Sins* and five of Iudovin's drawings displayed in the section 'Judaism', which was produced by Michael Shakhnovich (Figure 21). He used these graphic works for exposing 'the class essence of the religious doctrine and the practices of Orthodox Judaism against the background of the "shtetl idiocy"'.[62]

It should be noted that the idea of transforming the Antireligious Exhibition into a permanent exhibition was broached as early as 1931. Among other things, it was planned to reorganize the section 'Judaism' by incorporating additional materials that should reveal 'the class nature of Judaism in various periods of its existence, with a focus on the present time'.[63] In the late 1930s more than 200 exhibits related to Judaism were displayed at the permanent exhibition, until it was closed down after the outbreak of the war with Germany.[64] In his manuscript 'Excursions Related to Judaism in the Antireligious Museum of Local History' (Leningrad, 1941), Shakhnovich highlighted 'a large series of Iudovin's drawings on the theme of Jewish religious festivals, rituals and customs, the "Religious Calendar"', as one of the most valuable collections of that profile in the museum holdings.[65]

The Central Antireligious Museum in Moscow

As noted earlier, I have included in the first collection of graphics, along with Iudovin's works, also the drawings by Konstantinovskii, Maltz, and Shechtman, which were transferred to MIR from CAM. This museum emerged from the exhibition 'The Church and Religion', held in 1926 at the Moscow School of Military Engineering. The permanent exhibition of CAM was opened in the building of the Church of the Monastery of the Passion in Moscow in 1929.[66] In 1936 CAM was relocated to the 'specially constructed building' at 23 Kalyaevskaia Street (now Dolgorukovskaia Street) due to the forthcoming demolition of the Monastery.[67] The first permanent exhibition was opened there in 1938–40, and was preserved during the Second World War. In 1942, CAM was renamed the Central Museum of the History of Religion and Atheism (hereafter CMHRA), and in 1946 it was institutionally united with Leningrad MIR.[68] The new director of the merged museum, the prominent Soviet party and state leader, historian, and ethnographer Vladimir Bonch-Bruievich, planned to transfer collections of MIR from Leningrad to Moscow, but the opposite has happened: in 1947, the collection of CAM was transferred to Leningrad MIR, and CAM was closed down.[69]

During the early years of CAM its propaganda activity was directed mainly against the Russian Orthodox Church, but in 1931 the exhibition was reorganized in accordance with the so called 'Marxist scheme' of 'the social formations' in such a way that the main divisions of the exhibition pay attention to different religions. In addition, a special 'Department of National Religions' was set up.[70] In the first quarter of 1932, a section on Judaism appeared in the main exhibition, which displayed predominantly ceremonial objects.[71] In 1932–37, CAM acquired not only objects of Jewish rituals, but also models, paintings, drawings, and photographs for thematic sections on Judaism. The person in charge of this work from 1930 to 1937

178 Alla Sokolova

Fig. 11.21. The print of a glassed negative 'Section 'Judaism' at the MIR exhibition', 1936.

was Mark Persits.[72]

Pictures by Alexander Konstantinovskii *A Whip for Repentance*, *Korobka* (The Tax Box), *The Kiss of Purishkevich*, *The Meeting of Denikin's Soldiers* (the two latter works are known only for their photos from GMIR holdings), and four more drawings that have not been preserved were made in 1932–33 and approved by the Commission of CAM.[73] The Commission found these drawings 'quite satisfactory' in their 'artistic quality', and concluded that 'their ideological consistency is quite consistent with the task which the artist received from Comrade Persits'.[74] Apparently, these works were intended for the thematic section 'Judaism in Tsarist Russia', which appeared in 1936 in the exhibition division entitled 'Religion and Atheism in the History of the USSR'.[75] Persits's article 'Judaism in Tsarist Russia and the USSR', published in 1932, could serve as the introduction to this thematic section.[76]

Konstantinovskii's drawing *A Whip for Repentance* (Figure 22), thematically related to Iudovin's poster *Punishment for Sins*, could be exhibited to demonstrate the use a special 'double-tailed whip (*malkes*) for scourging religious Jews'. This kind of whip, which nowadays is stored in the collection of GMIR, was obtained by CAM in 1931 from the Jewish department of the Museum in Berdichev.[77] It is this whip that the synagogue servant is swinging in the picture *A Whip for Repentance*, depicting the representatives of the Jewish bourgeoisie. One of them, has just been 'relieved from sins', but apparently has not got rid of greed, as he is depicted carefully recounting coins that should be donated to the poor.

This and other pictures by Konstantinovskii are quite realistic, but also ironic. The photograph of the picture *The Kiss of Purishkevich* with the explanatory label 'A rabbi is joyfully kissing participants of pogroms from the "black hundreds" on the occasion of the declaration of the [First World] War, August 1914' (Figure 23), is perceived as a socio-political caricature. The title placed above the photograph states that 'by fanning ethnic and religious strife between nations, capitalists and priests of different nationalities worked together against the working people'.[78] This drawing by Konstantinovskii was particularly in demand: in 1937, CAM transferred coloured photos of two works from its collection to the Museum of Religion and Atheism in Kazakhstan, and the *The Kiss of Purishkevich* was renamed 'Purishkevich at a Meeting with a Rabbi and their Kiss before the Imperialist War in Odessa, 1914'.[79]

In 1938–40, when the division 'Religion and Atheism in the History of the Peoples of the USSR' was rebuilt under the leadership of Persits in the new building of CAM in Kalyaevskaia Street,[80] the Judaism section was noticeably reduced.[81] It was displayed in several exhibition divisions that were combined under the title of 'The Realm Officials, Gendarmes and Priests'.[82] The drawing *Korobka* by Konstantinovskii was presented at the last pre-war exhibition (Figure 24). The artist depicted the scene of levying tax on the purchase of kosher meat, called *korobka* (literally, tax box). In the foreground one can see comical figures of representatives of the 'dark, downtrodden, besotted by religion' Jewish poor.[83] Clearly, Persits considered it important to show that the burden of this tax was carried on their shoulders by the poor. The picture *Korobka* was exhibited, under the name *Korobochnyi sbor* (The Box Fee), next to a colourful table representing the 'scheme of *ḳahal*', also by Konstantinovskii.[84]

A pencil drawing by Ilya Maltz entitled *The Besht Synagogue in Medzhibozh* is

Fig. 11.22. Alexander Konstantinovskii, 'A Whip for Repentance [here, Malkot ceremony]', drawing of 1933.

Fig. 11.23. Photo of the drawing by
Alexander Konstantinovskii 'The Kiss of Purishkevich' (1933)

FIGS. 11.24 and 11.25. Alexander Konstantinovskii, 'Korobka', drawing of 1933; Ilya Maltz, 'The Street in the Shtetl [here, the Yerusalimka district in the town of Vinnitsa.]', drawing of 1934.

part of the same thematic section.[85] This work, probably an enlarged copy of a life drawing, was acquired from Maltz in 1937, shortly after the purchase of his five life drawings made in Yerusalimka, a neighbourhood of Vinnitsa.[86] This area, described as a 'kind of a "chip" of the city from the seventeenth–nineteenth centuries with a disorderly layout and jumble of homes', was widely known as the 'Jewish neighbourhood' where 'the poor huddle'.[87] One of these five drawings is stored in GMIR under the title *A Shtetl Street*, despite the different title by the author, *Vinnitsa. Yerusalimka. 1934* (Figure 25). Persits, who initiated the purchase of Maltz's works, used them for representing Jewish poverty as the specific feature of the shtetls in the former Pale of Settlement. Soviet ideologists saw the traditional way of life in the shtetls as an obstacle for the construction of the new Jewish world.

Persits was in charge of representing Judaism in all divisions and sections of the exhibition except of the division 'Religion and Atheism in the Ancient World', which was supervised by Berta Sharevskaia. In 1938 she prepared a thematic section titled 'Religion of the Ancient Hebrews. Debunking the Myth of Primordial Jewish Monotheism'.[88] She commissioned Manuil Shechtman to make three drawings for the exhibition, among them the watercolour *Scapegoat*, thematically related to ancient Judaism, as well as the drawings *Jewish Passover Meal*, which is known by its photo, and *The Rite of Chametz Removal* (cleaning the house of unleavened bread), which illustrated the section 'Jewish Religious Rituals'.[89] These drawings were displayed at the Anti-Easter and Anti-Passover Exhibition, and then included in the permanent exhibition in CAM.

Characteristic features of Shechtman's drawing *The Rite of Chametz Removal* depicting the ritual 'Bedikat Chametz' (Hebrew: a search for chametz) are lightness and spontaneity, and it is not didactic at all (Figure 26). The stream of light which elucidates the figures seems to be of no less interest to the artist than the scrupulous portrayal of details that are significant from the iconographic viewpoint, such as the last crumbs of bread (*chametz*), found by candlelight, and a goose wing which sweeps them into a wooden spoon so that *chametz* can be put into a prepared piece of fabric and burnt. The figures themselves are devoid of the ethnographic Jewish markers which can be identified, for example, in all of the above-mentioned drawings by Iudovin. While working on the drawings commissioned by the curators of the museum, Shechtman was in the first place concerned with artistic tasks. To a degree, the same conclusion can be made with regard to some of Iudovin's works, particularly for the drawings (most notably, *Funeral*) that carry his signature.

Concluding Remarks

By the mid-1930s the permanent exhibitions in CAM and MIR became thematically repetitive. The similarity among small thematic sections related to Judaism manifested itself most clearly in the use of copies made from reproductions commissioned by the curators. For example, the 'Jewish Section' at the first exhibition in CAM displayed two drawings titled 'The prison cell in the synagogue of Isaac Nakhmanovich in Lviv' and 'The Jew, chained to the wall for disobedience and failure to comply with regulations of the Jewish religion' (Figure 27). Both drawings

FIG. 11.26. Manuel Shechtman, 'The Rite of Removing Chametz [here, Bedikas Chametz]', drawing of 1938.

FIGS. 11.27 and 11.28. 'The Jew, chained to the wall for disobedience and failure to comply with regulations of the Jewish religion', drawing-copy of the illustrations No. 34 in Meir Balaban's book, 1930; 'Prison in the Isaac Nakhmanovich synagogue, in which were kept in chains person who spoke against the power of the rabbis and kagal', photo of the staged scene at MIR exhibition, around 1937

appear in 1930 in the photograph illustrating the article on CAM in the journal *Bezbozhnik u stanka* (*Godless Machine Man*).[90] The following remark of the author is rather significant: 'In the section on the Jewish religion one can see the portrait of the *tzaddik* in chains. For what, by whom, when? It still remains a mystery.'[91] In fact, the 'portrait of *tzaddik*' is a copy of the figure no. 34 in Meir Balaban's book, depicting *kuna* (pillory) in the Great Suburban Synagogue in the city of Lviv.[92] Balaban mentioned only that it was a place for criminals,[93] which means that the explanation of this picture given in the museum was just a groundless speculation by the author of the exhibition. The drawing with the image of a 'prison cell' is not a copy, although it resembles the illustration No. 26 in Balaban's book, titled 'The ground floor room in the house of Solomon Friedman'. Both two rooms have vaulted ceilings and stone floors, but nothing indicates that they are a 'prison cell'.

Both drawings with historically inaccurate labels were on display at the permanent exhibitions of CAM not only in 1930, but also in 1939. Moreover, in 1935, they were photocopied according to the order of MIR.[94] In the same year, the photocopy of the drawing 'The Jew, chained to the wall [. . .]' was included in the permanent exhibition of the museum. The label explained that: 'In Poland, in the seventeenth century, a Jew, condemned for speaking out against the bosses of the synagogue, was chained to a wall in the Jewish prayer house.'[95] In 1938 this plot was presented in the permanent exhibition in a form of a situational scene with figures (Figure 28). Such speculation successfully denigrated religion and its institutions in line with the objectives of the Soviet antireligious project. The same goals set before the antireligious museum in 1930 were briefly mentioned in Shakhnovich's article of 1940 in relation to the activities of MIR. He wrote that museums 'should reveal the social roots of religion, its reactionary role at different stages of development of human society, and the history of atheism and expose the class essence of religion'.[96]

The graphic works by Iudovin, Konstantinovskii, Maltz and Shechtman were considered by curators of the mentioned museum projects as ethnographically adequate images of Jewish religious rituals and, as such, scholarly significant and suitable for use in museum exhibitions aimed at not only for exposing the 'class nature of religious institutions', but also for popularizing the knowledge about them.

At first glance, it may seem that the scholarly educational and propagandist discourses competed in museum exhibitions of 1930s. The former was constructed with the support of original artefacts, items used in religious practices, works of art and historical documents, while the latter relied on various illustrative materials, sometimes of no artistic value, as well as explanatory texts and political slogans. In reality, it was hardly a competition, but rather a symbiosis in which the propaganda component aggressively subdued the educational and scholarly meaning. All items on display, both the works of art made by the orders of the museums and the real objects of cult, served as material evidence in support of the allegations brought within the framework of the antireligious project against religious institutions, including Jewish ones.

Biographical Notes on Artists and Museum Curators

(Listed in order of mentioning them in the article)
Yurii [Uriel] Yakovlevich Kogan (1907–71 or after), a specialist in the field of philosophy and the history of religion. In 1929–39 he was a staff member of CAM. From 1947 Kogan was a junior researcher and in 1959 became a senior researcher at the Institute of History of the USSR. In 1965 he defended his doctoral dissertation. From 1967 Kogan worked as a senior researcher at the Institute of Philosophy of the USSR.
Vladimir Germanovich Bogoras (Bogoraz; before baptism — Nathan Mendelevich; pseudonyms — Tan-Bogoraz or Bogoraz-Tan, in English publications — Waldemar Bogoras; 1865–1936), a historian, the specialist in early forms of religion, linguist, writer, poet, and social activist, a member of the Academy of Sciences, professor of Leningrad University, the founder and first director of the State Museum of the History of Religion.
Solomon Borisovich Iudovin (1892, Beshenkovichi, Vitebsk province–1954, Leningrad), a graphic artist. In 1912–14 he participated as a photographer in ethnographic expeditions of the Jewish Historical and Ethnographic Society, organized by S. An-sky. In 1923–29, he was a curator of the Jewish Museum, organized by the Society.
Alexander Iosifovich Konstantinovskii (1906, Kiev–1958, Leningrad), a theatre designer, the Honoured Artist of the RSFSR. Among his artistic works for theatrical performances were plays staged in the Belarusian State Jewish Theatre (BelGOSET).
Ilya Izrailevich Maltz (1898, Odessa–1973, Moscow), an architect and artist. In 1929 he graduated from the Architecture Faculty of the Odessa Institute of Fine Arts. In 1924–36, he participated in expeditions of the Odessa Museum of Jewish Culture named after Mendele Mokher Seforim.
Manuil (Emanuil) Iosifovich Shechtman (1900, Lipniki in Volhynia province–1941, Moscow), a well-known avant-garde artist. In 1929–34 he was in charge of the Art Department of the Odessa Museum of Jewish Culture named after Mendele Mokher

Seforim. After closing the museum in 1934 (reopened in 1940) he moved to Moscow. In 1935–37 he worked as a designer at CAM; later he made several artworks commissioned by CAM.

Isaiah Mendelevich Pulner (1900, Snovsk in Chernigov province–1942, Leningrad), an ethnographer and bibliographer. In 1930, he headed the Jewish Department at the State Public Library in Leningrad. From 1938 he was the head of the Jewish section at the Museum of Ethnography of the Peoples of the USSR.

Mikhail Iosifovich Shakhnovich (1911, St Petersburg — 1992, Leningrad), a folklorist, an expert in the philosophy of religion and religious studies. From 1932, he was a researcher at the Museum of the History of Religion of Academy of Sciences of the USSR. In 1944–60, Shakhnovich was a deputy director at the same museum. He was the author of the monograph *Zakat iudeiskoii religii* (The Decline of the Jewish religion; Leningrad: Lenizdat, 1965).

Mark Mendelevich Persits (1908 — not earlier then 1964), a historian. From 1929, he was a staff member of the CAM then he worked in the Institute of History of the Academy of Sciences of the USSR. He was the author of the monograph *Otdelenie tserkvi ot gosudarstva i shkoly ot tserkvi v SSSR. 1917–1919 gg.* (The Separation of the Church from the State and Schools from the Church in the USSR, 1917–1919; Moscow: Publishing House of Academy of Sciences, 1958).

Berta Isaakovna Sharevskaia (1904–85), an ethnographer specialized in African studies and a historian of the early forms of religion. In 1937–47, she was a staff member of the CAM.

David Hoberman (1912–2003), painter, graphic artist, photographer, art historian, and ethnographer. Since the late 1930s he was photographing tombstones of the eighteenth to early twentieth centuries at Jewish cemeteries of Ukraine and Moldova. In 1990–2000, several albums with photos of Jewish tombstones and Hoberman's comments were released in Russia and the United States.

List of Items from Collections of GMIR with Inventory Numbers

Artworks by Solomon Iudovin

Hand-drawn posters:

'From the Prayers before and after Eating', watercolour, 32 × 22 cm, obtained from SAMFIC; E-2078-VII, author's copy of E-7588-VII.

'From the Prayer upon Awakening', watercolour, 32.5 × 22 cm, obtained from SAMFIC; E-2158-VII, author's copy of E-7590-VII.

'The Drawing with Text from Exodus', watercolour, 28 × 17 cm, obtained from SAMFIC; E-2160-VII, author's copy of E-7593-VII.

'Rosh Hashanah prayer', watercolour, 42.5 × 18 cm, obtained from SAMFIC; E-7577-VII, author's copy of E-7592-VII.

'Punishment for Sins', watercolour, 23.5 × 21 cm, obtained from SAMFIC; E-7578-VII, author's copy of E-7585-VII.

'Separating Challah', watercolour, 23 × 20 cm, obtained from SAMFIC; E-7579-VII.

'Kosher meat', watercolour, 27.5 × 21 cm, obtained from SAMFIC; E-7580-VII.

'The Sabbat Celebration', watercolour, 20 × 27 cm, obtained from the Antireligious Exhibition; E-7583-VII.

'From the Prayers before and after Eating', watercolour, 33 × 22.5 cm, obtained from the Antireligious Exhibition, E-7588-VII.

'From the Prayer upon Awakening', watercolour, 21.5 × 2 cm, obtained from the

Antireligious Exhibition; E-7590-VII.
'Prayer before Going to Bed', watercolour, 19 × 40 cm, obtained from the Antireligious Exhibition; E-7591-VII.
'Prayer in Judgment Day', watercolour, 43.5 × 16.5 cm, obtained from the Antireligious Exhibition; E-7592-VII.
'Redemption of the Firstborn', watercolour, 31 × 20.5 cm, obtained from the Antireligious Exhibition; E-7593-VII.
'Judgment Day', watercolour, 25 × 32.5 cm, obtained from the Antireligious Exhibition; E-7594-VII.
'The Morning Prayer' photo, watercolour, 28 × 44 cm, obtained from SAMFIC; E-7604-VII.
'Prayer before Going to Bed', watercolour, 24 × 43.5 cm, obtained from SAMFIC; E-7605-VII, author's copy of E-7591-VII.

Drawings

'The Wedding', watercolour, 34 × 40.8 cm; obtained from the Antireligious Exhibition; E-5687-VII.
'Circumcision', watercolour, 36 × 34 cm; obtained from the Antireligious Exhibition; E-5735-VII.
'Shabbat Repast', watercolour, 34.2 × 41.5 cm; obtained from SAMFIC; E-5737-VII.
'Praying to the Moon', watercolour, 34.5 × 25.5 cm, obtained from SAMFIC; E-7576-VII.
'Blessing of the Cock', watercolour, 33.5 x 24 cm, obtained from SAMFIC; E-7581-VII.
'The Slaughterman [Shohet]', watercolour, 25.5 × 35.8 cm, obtained from the Antireligious Exhibition; E-7582-VII.
'Funeral', watercolour, 34.5 x 44 cm, obtained from the Antireligious Exhibition; E-7584-VII.
'Punishment for Sins', watercolour, 24 x 21.5 cm, obtained from the Antireligious Exhibition; E-7585-VII.
'Mikvah, the Ritual Bathing Pool', watercolour, 21.5 × 18 cm, obtained from the Antireligious Exhibition; E-7586-VII.
'Feast of Tabernacles', watercolour, 28.5 × 33.5 cm, obtained from the Antireligious Exhibition; E-7587-VII.
'The Jew Reading the Talmud', watercolour, 36 × 28.5 cm, obtained from SAMFIC; E-7589-VII.
'Shabbat candles', watercolour, 15.8 × 19.8 cm, obtained from SAMFIC; E-7595-VII.
'Passover', watercolour, 24 × 34 cm, obtained from the Antireligious Exhibition; E-7606-VII.

Drawings by Alexander Konstantinovskii

'A Whip for Repentance', ink, 52.5 × 42 cm, obtained from the CAM; E-7491-VII.
'Korobka (The Tax Box)', ink, 52.5 × 42 cm, obtained from the CAM; E-8899-VII, is mentioned in the inventories under the title 'In the Shtetl'.

Drawings by Ilya Maltz

'The Street in the Shtetl' (although the author's own inscription is different: 'Vinnitsa. Yerusalimka. 1934'), pencil, 20.3 × 29.7 cm, obtained from the CAM; E-5698-VII.
'The Synagogue of Beshta in Medzhibozh', pencil, 53 × 69.5 cm, obtained from the CAM; E-8900-VII.

Drawings by Manuel Shechtman

'Scapegoat', watercolour, 36 × 44 cm, obtained from the CAM; E-7629-VII.
'The Rite of Removing Chametz', pencil, 40.5 × 51.3 cm, obtained from the CAM; E-5904-VII.

Photos and photocopies

'Tomb of the Tzaddik', obtained from the Antireligious Exhibition; E-1567-VII.
'Torah Copyist', obtained from the Antireligious Exhibition; E-1067-VII.
'Tomb of the Torah Scrolls', obtained from the Antireligious Exhibition; E-2313-VII.
'Cooking the Matzo', obtained from the Antireligious Exhibition; E-2314-VII.
'The Rabbi Reading the Talmud', obtained from SAMFIC; E-1206-VII.
Of the drawing 'The Kiss of Purishkevich' by A. Konstantinovskii; E-1077-VII.
Of the drawing 'The meeting of Denikin's Soldiers' by A. Konstantinovskii; E-1115-VII.
Of the drawing 'Jewish Passover Meal' by M. Shechtman; E-1116-VII.

Postcards

Jewish postcard depicting the *kapores* ceremony. Warsaw (?), early twentieth century; E-2168/10-VII.
Jewish postcard depicting Rosh Hashanah meals. Warsaw — New York: S. Reznik Publishing, 1910s; E-9823-VII.

Other

Hand-drawn poster 'From the Morning Prayers' by David Hoberman (?) in watercolour, obtained from the Antireligious Exhibition; E-7599-VII.
Kvitlah — notes-petitions on the grave of the righteous person; paper, ink, 18 × 11 cm, obtained from the Antireligious Exhibition; E-2113/1,2-VII.
Double-tailed whip (malkes) for scourging religious Jews, wood, metal, leather, 60 cm, obtained from CAM; E-5048-VII.
Hand-drawn copy 'The Jew, chained to the wall', 38.5 × 29 cm, obtained from CAM; E-7419-VII.

Notes to Chapter 11

1. The Union of the Godless (Russian: *Soyuz bezbozhnikov*), was the All-Union atheistic and anti-religious public organization founded in 1925; in 1929 it was called the League of Militant Atheists.
2. According to Nikolai Matorin, a director of the Museum of Anthropology and Ethnography of the Academy of Sciences, by the beginning of 1931 there thirty-five anti-religious museums had been opened in the Russian Soviet Federative Socialist Republic (see 'Vserossiiskii muzeinyi s"iezd i antireligioznaia rabota', *Antireligioznik*, 2 (1931), 62–64 (p. 63)), and in 1932 there worked more than a hundred of them (see Yurii Kogan, 'Muzei v bor'be protiv religii', *Voinstvuiushchee bezbozhie v SSSR za 15 let, 1917–1932*, ed. by M. Enisherlov, A. Lukachevskii, and M. Mitin (Moscow: OGIZ, 1932), pp. 462–74; 467). On the establishment of anti-religious museums, see for details: Irina Tarasova and Galina Chenskaia, 'Iz istorii muzeinogo dela v Rossii: muzei tserkovno-arkheologicheskii i antireligioznyi', *Trudy Gosudarstvennogo muzeia istorii religii*, II (St. Petersburg: Aktsioner i Co, 2002), pp. 17–30.
3. 'Tezisi dokladov, priniatye [Antireligioznoi] sektsiei', *Trudy Pervogo Vserossiiskogo muzeinogo s"yezda*, II (Moscow and Leningrad: Gosudarstvennoie uchebno-pedagogicheskoie izdatel'stvo, 1931), p. 134.
4. Ibid., p. 135.

5. Kogan, 'Muzei v bor'be protiv religii', p. 465.
6. Ibid.
7. Vladimir Bogoraz-Tan, 'Antireligioznaia vystavka AN SSSR', in Marianna Shakhnovich and Tatiana Chumakova, *Muzei istorii religii AN SSSR i rossiiskoe religiovedenie, 1932–1961* (St Petersburg: Nauka, 2014), pp. 99–109 (p. 101). The current article by Bogoras was initially published in *Antireligioznik*, 8–9 (1930), 87–93.
8. Kogan, 'Muzei v bor'be protiv religii', p. 467. On the creation of the museum in the Kazan Cathedral, see: St Petersburg Affiliation of the Archive of the Russian Academy of Sciences, f. 221, op. 2, No. 1, l. 11, published in Shakhnovich and Chumakova, *Muzei istorii religii AN SSSR i rossiiskoe religiovedenie, 1932–1961*, pp. 30–33.
9. Kogan, 'Muzei v bor'be protiv religii', p. 467.
10. At the present time, the GMIR holdings contain about 2,000 items; among them 1,388 items are registered in the *fond* 'Judaism'. The vast majority of them are Jewish ritual objects of the eighteenth–early twentieth centuries from Central and Eastern Europe.
11. 'Iz pis'ma V. G. Bogoraza nepremennomu sekretariu Akademii nauk, 22 oktiabria 1930 g.', in Shakhnovich and Chumakova, *Muzei istorii religii AN SSSR i rossiiskoe religiovedenie*, pp. 110–11.
12. The images on the posters are accompanied by textual inscriptions, i.e. biblical quotes or excerpts from prayers. These posters have been included in the registration inventories without mentioning the author's name.
13. Documentation and Collections Management Department of GMIR (hereafter DCMD GMIR), Graphic Materials' Registration Book of MIR (1931–1933), l. 1. Initially, the posters and drawings by Solomon Iudovin were taken into account around 1931 in the Collectible inventory No. 3 'Photographs and drawings of Jewish worship (synagogue and household) and mythological images, highlighting the origins of the Jewish cult and life of modern Jewry' (97 objects). Later this Collectible inventory was included in the in the Collectible inventory No. 35, as a part of it.
14. DCMD GMIR, Registration Book of Objects Received for the Antireligious Exhibition from Different Organizations and Individuals, no pagination. In this Book are mentioned the drawings and photos transferred for MAE with special notes that they have been received from Pulner. Separately are mentioned the objects (thirteen items) that have been received from Pulner as of a private person.
15. See Pulner's Curriculum Vitae (1935), Department of Archival Documents of the National Library of Russia, (hereafter DAD NLR), f. 10, d. 3281, l. 9.
16. Bogoraz-Tan, 'Antireligioznaia vystavka AN SSSR', p. 101.
17. See for details: Tatiana Scherbakova, 'Ot vystavki k muzeiu: period stanovleniia Museia istorii religii AN SSSR', *Trudy Gosudarstvennogo muzeia istorii religii*, 1 (St Petersburg: RAN Publishing, 2001), pp. 9–17; Elena Mikhailova, 'Vystavochnyi proiekt Muzeia antropologii i etnografii "Antireligioznaia vystavka v Gosudarstvennom Ermitazhe" i ego sozdatel' V. G. Bogoraz', *Radlovskii sbornik: Nauchnye issledovaniia i muzeinye proekty MAE RAN v 2010 g.*, ed. by Yurii Chistov and Mikhail Rubtsov (St. Petersburg: MAE, 2011), pp. 90–95.
18. This photograph was published by participant of S. An-sky's expeditions Abram Rekhtman under the title "Soifer from Annopol' r[eb] David Eliyahu". See Abram Rekhtman, *Yidishe Etnografie un Folklor* (Buenos Aires: IWO, 1958), p. 349.
19. According to Vladimir Bogoras, the first section was dedicated to 'the ancient period in the history of Israel', and the second — to 'modern Judaism', in which 'the symbol of the god is the torah, a scripture written on parchment and rolled up in a scroll'. See Bogoraz-Tan, 'Antireligioznaia vystavka AN SSSR', pp. 103–04.
20. Ibid., p. 104.
21. DCMD GMIR, Registration Book of Objects Received for the Anti-religious Exhibition from Different Organizations and Individuals, no pagination, list of objects received from Pulner as of a private person: No. 3, 6 'notes-petitions on the grave of the righteous person'.
22. A photocopy of a snapshot of the tombstones at the burial site of 'holy books from the synagogue in the Maryam street which was looted and burned on the 20th of Kislev, 5670 (1909)'.
23. *Evreiskaia entsiklopediia Brokgauza i Efrona*, x (St Petersburg: Brockhaus & Efron Publishing, 1911), p. 719. This engraving illustrates the article 'Matzo'; under the image is placed the following

note: 'Cooking the Matzo' (From the book by Paul Christian Kirkhner, *Jüdisches Ceremoniel* (Nuremberg, 1726).)
24. The watercolour 'Funeral' is a version of the woodcut of 1927 with the same name. See: Jeremiah Ioffe and Erich Hollerbach, *Iudovin, Graviury na dereve* (Leningrad: The Printing house of the Academy of Arts, 1928), p. 30.
25. Ibid., pp. 15–16.
26. This definition was given while inventorying at the beginning of the 1950s.
27. AGMIR, f. 1, op. 2, d. 135, l. 29.
28. The photo is stored in the private collection of Benjamin Lukin and Boris Khaimovich (Jerusalem).
29. DCMD GMIR, *The Registration Book of Objects Received for the Anti-religious Exhibition from Different Organizations and Individuals*, no pagination. It is mentioned there under No. 12 that the 'twig of a palm tree' received from Isaiha Pulner as of a private person.
30. Ibid. The list of items received from a plenipotentiary of the Peoples Commissariat of Education.
31. Boris Sokolov, 'Postroenie i deiatel'nost' sovetskikh etnograficheskikh muzeev. Doklad, sdelannyi na soveshchanii etnografov Moskvy i Leningrada v aprele 1929 g.', in *Sovetskaia etnografiia*, 3–4 (1931), 125–35 (p. 132).
32. 'Iz pis'ma V. G. Bogoraza nepremennomu sekretariu Akademii nauk, 22 oktiabria 1930 g. Ob"iasnenie po povodu zapiski, predstavlennoi direktorom Gosermitazha otnositel'no Antireligioznoi vystavki Akademii nauk', in Shakhnovich and Chumakova, *Muzei istorii religii AN SSSR i rossiiskoe religiovedenie, 1932–1961*, pp. 110–11.
33. The Anti-religious museum was established in 1924 as a result of reorganization of the Museum of Comparative Study of Religions which had been opened in 1923. In 1928, the Antireligious museum had got at its disposal the building of St Isaac's Cathedral. See: Yurii Kogan, Muzei v bor'be protiv religii, 463; Mikhail Shakhnovich, 'Iz proshlogo Muzeia istorii religii Akademii nauk SSSR', in *Muzei v ateisticheskoi propagande* (Leningrad: GMIR, 1982), pp. 20–21; 'Isaakievskii sobor. Istoricheskaia spravka', *Sessiia Leningradskogo Muzeinogo soveta, posviashchennaia gosudarstvennomu muzeiu byvshemu Isaakievskomu soboru, 2–3 marta 1937 g.* (Leningrad: The Leningrad Council of the Workers' Peasants', and Read Army Deputies, 1937), pp. 6–8 (p. 8).
34. See Pulner's Curriculum Vitae (1935). DAD NLR, f. 10, d. 3281, l. 10. I was unable to find any documentary evidence about when and how Iudovin's graphic works and photographs have been received by SAMFIC.
35. Among the photographs mentioned in the Collectible inventory No. 767, one can identify the following photos by Solomon Iudovin: 'Batlan, the beggar, dwelling in the synagogue', 'The Synagogue Boy', 'Heider [Jewish primary school]', 'A group of boys while reading', 'The Rabbi reading the Talmud', 'The Talmud Torah: classes at the Jewish free school for the poor'.
36. Nikolai Fedorovich, 'Proekt tematicheskogo plana ekspozitsii gosudarstvennogo muzeia — byvshego Isaakievskogo sobora v sootvetstvii s ego novym profilem', *Sessiia Leningradskogo Muzeinogo soveta, posviashchennaia gosudarstvennomu muzeiu byvshemu Isaakiyevskomu soboru, 2–3 marta 1937 g.* (Leningrad: The Leningrad Council of the Workers' Peasants', and Read Army Deputies, 1937), pp. 13–14.
37. See for instance: Acts on transferring collections of SAMFIC for permanent use to MIR and to other museums, 1938. Central Archive of Literature and Arts (hereafter TsGALI), St. Petersburg, f. P-330, op. 1, d. 27.
38. These five duplicate-drawings were transferred in 1938 from MIR to the State Museum of Ethnography (since 1992 — the Russian State Museum of Ethnography) in the order of interchange (see: DCMD GMIR, the Book of Acts, no. 10, 1937–38, l. 236. Act No. 1116 of 26 August 1938). Pulner required these drawings of Iudovin's for the exhibition 'Jews in Tsarist Russia and in the USSR', which he organized in 1939 at the Leningrad Museum of Ethnography (see for details about the mentioned exhibition: Alexander Ivanov, 'The exhibition "Jews in Tsarist Russia and in the USSR" and the Closure of the Jewish Modernization Project in the Soviet Union, 1937–41', *East European Jewish Affairs*, 43. 1 (2013), 43–61).
39. Ibid.

40. It should be noted that the same technique Iudovin used for the drawing *Passover*: one can see in hands of the characters glasses with the word 'Pesach', and the table cloth with the inscription 'Matzo'.
41. See Pulner's Curriculum Vitae (1935). DAD NLR, f. 10, d. 3281, l. 9.
42. TsGALI, f. P-311, op. 1, d. 3, ll. 6–12.
43. David Hoberman, 'Khudozhnik o sebe', in *David Hoberman. Zhivopis'. Grafika*, ed. by Valery Dymshits and Irina Mamonova (St Petersburg: European University at St. Petersburg Publishing. 2015), pp. 73–96 (p. 80). It is noted in the 'Report of the JHES Museum for 1928' that: [T]here was carried out considerable changes in the museum collection. Department of everyday life and art was located in separate rooms; a corridor of the Museum was used for exhibiting collections of photographs and portraits of Jewish public figures and writers. Collecting materials for the intended department 'Jewish public calamities' is in progress. See: TsGALI, f. P-311, op. 1, d. 3, l. 12.
44. Isaiah Pulner, 'Voprosy organizatsii evreiskikh etnograficheskikh muzeev i evreiskikh otdelov pri obshchikh etnograficheskikh muzeiakh', *Sovetskaia etnografiia*, 3–4 (1931), 156–63 (p. 157).
45. Ibid.
46. Ibid., p. 161.
47. According to the 'Report of JHES Museum for 1928' the sections of Jewish everyday life and Jewish art were located in separate rooms. TsGALI, f. P-311, op. 1, d. 3, l. 12.
48. Ibid.
49. In 1929, the question of antireligious propaganda in ethnographic museums was discussed at the Meeting of ethnographers of Moscow and Leningrad. Judging by the transcripts of speeches, museum staff members began to follow demands of political education institutions, for example, they discussed the establishment in museums of the special 'anti-religious study rooms'. See *Ot klassikov k marksizmu: soveshchanie etnografov Moskvy i Leningrada, 5–11 aprelia 1929 g*. Series: 'Kunstkamera — Arkhiv', VII, ed. by Dmitry Arzyutov, Sergei Alymov, and David D. Anderson (St. Petersburg: MAE RAN, 2014), pp. 363–405.
50. According to the 'Report of JHES Museum for 1928', Solomon Iudovin was a curator of the Museum; he oversaw the acquisition of objects of the 'Jewish life and worship', as well as works of art. TsGALI, f. P-311, op. 1, d. 3, l. 12.
51. Hoberman, 'Khudozhnik o sebe', p. 80.
52. In the private collection of Israeli art historian Hilel Kazovskii is stored a portrait of an old man made by Solomon Iudovin on the base of this photograph (signed by S. Iudovin in Hebrew letters, paper, ink; 22.8 × 18.3 sm.).
53. AGMIR, f. 1, op. 2, d. 131, l. 318 (labelling for exhibitions in the museum, 1938). The text is written by Mikhail Shakhnovich. See Shakhnovich, 'Iz proshlogo Muzeia istorii religii Akademii nauk SSSR', p. 27.
54. See for example the *Rosh Hashanah* greeting postcard depicting a festive meal from the GMIR collection.
55. Mikhail Shakhnovich, *Komu sluzhit 'religiia Izrailia'?* (Moscow and Leningrad: Priboi, 1929).
56. On the participation of Mikhail Shakhnovich in the preparation of the Antireligious Exhibition I've learned from his daughter, Dr Marianna Shakhnovich. In her article 'Iz proshlogo Muzeia istorii religii Akademii nauk SSSR' on p. 25, Mikhail Shakhnovich is only mentioned as a tour guide at the Antireligious Exhibition.
57. Shakhnovich, *Komu sluzhit 'religiia Izrailia'?*, p. 64.
58. Ibid., pp. 63–64.
59. Ibid.
60. Ibid., p. 59. *Malkot* ceremony is still practised in ultra-Orthodox Jewish communities and consists of thirty-nine symbolic lashes set the mood for true and full repentance.
61. Ibid., p. 60.
62. Archives of GMIR (hereafter AGMIR), f. 1, op. 2, d. 42, l. 73.
63. 'Iz Rabochego plana Muzeia istorii religii AN SSSR na 1931 g.', in Shakhnovich and Chumakova, *Muzei istorii religii AN SSSR i rossiiskoe religiovedenie, 1932–1961*, p. 130.
64. 'Ob"iasnitel'naia zapiska, raz"iasniaiushchaia i obosnovyvaiushchaia printsipy, polozhennye v osnovu ekspozitsii Muzeia istorii religii AN SSSR', in Shakhnovich and Chumakova, *Muzei istorii religii AN SSSR i rossiiskoe religiovedenie, 1932–1961*, p. 241.

65. AGMIR, f. 1, op. 2, d. 108, l. 27.
66. Kogan, 'Muzei v bor'be protiv religii', p. 464.
67. AGMIR. Registration file of the collection No. 31, l. 1 (historical note of 6 September 1952). As the result of construction of the CAM building a part of the closed Church of St Nicholas was demolished.
68. AGMIR, f. 31, op. 1, d. 32.
69. See for details: Shakhnovich and Chumakova, *Muzei istorii religii AN SSSR i rossiiskoe religiovedenie, 1932–1961*, pp. 53–60.
70. Kogan, 'Muzei v bor'be protiv religii', pp. 464–65.
71. AGMIR, f. 31, op. 1, d. 14, l. 6. One can see the section 'Judaism' in CAM's permanent exhibition depicted on the photo by James Abbe. See: http://photochronograph.ru/2013/11/17/sssr-30-x-glazami-amerikanskogo-fotozhurnalista-dzhejmsa-ebbe/. In 1929–31, CAM obtained mainly items confiscated from synagogues closed by the decision of the Moscow City Council, as well as from the collections of the Belarusian State Museum and the Socio-historical Museum in Berdichev. See: DCMD GMIR. The Book of Acts from CAM No. 1 for 1927–1934, l. 81, 89, 126, 132, 168.
72. Ibid., l. 283, 290.
73. The drawing 'The Tax Box' appears in the records of GMIR under the title 'In the Shtetl'. Vladimir Mitrofanovich Purishkevich (1870–1920), a politician in the Russian Empire, was noted for his ultra-nationalist and anti-Semitic views. Anton Ivanovich Denikin (1872–1947) was a leading general of the White movement in the Russian Civil War (1917–20).
74. DCMD GMIR, The Book of Acts from CAM No. 1 for 1927–1934, Act (no number) of 8 July 1933.
75. AGMIR, f. 31, op. 1, d. 36, l. 7.
76. Mark Persits, 'Iudaizm v tsarskoi Rossii i v SSSR', *Voinstvuiushchee bezbozhie v SSSR za 15 let. 1917–1932*, pp. 170–73.
77. DCMD GMIR, the Registration Book of Objects Received by CAM, No. 459.
78. Explanatory labels were glued on the cardboard together with the snapshot, probably for displaying the photograph at the temporary exhibition.
79. DCMD GMIR The Book of Acts from CAM No. 12, Act No. 4 of April, 10, 1937.
80. AGMIR, f. 31, op. 1, d. 329, l. 13.
81. In 1939, after the signing of the Molotov–Ribbentrop Pact, the Jewish theme was hushed up.
82. AGMIR, f. 31, op. 1, d. 87, l. 75.
83. Persits, 'Iudaism v tsarckoii Rossii i v SSSR', p. 171.
84. AGMIR, f. 31, op. 1, d. 87, l. 79.
85. Ibid.
86. DCMD GMIR. The Book of Acts from CAM No. 6, act No. 35 of April, 5, 1937.
87. Oleksandr Birulya, *Arkhitekturna istoriya Vinnitsy* (Vinnitsa: Vecherniy robítnyi universitet, 1930), pp. 44, 47.
88. AGMIR, f. 31, op. 1, d. 68.
89. On fulfilment of the mentioned CAM's order by Manuil Shechtman, see: DCMD GMIR. The Book of Acts from CAM No. 7 of 1938 — Act No. 51 of April, 15, 1938; Act No. 41 of April, 5, 1938; Act No. 44 of April, 8, 1938. Perhaps, the drawing 'Jewish Passover Meal' is not preserved.
90. Eduard Mil'skii, 'V poriadke bezbozhnoi samokritiki', *Bezbozhnik u stanka*, 11 (1930), 11.
91. Ibid.
92. Majer (Meir) Balaban, *Dzielnica żydowska: jej dzieje i zabytki* (Lviv: Rocznik, 1909), p. 86.
93. Ibid., p. 95.
94. DCMD GMIR. The Book of Acts from MIR No. 6 of 1935; act No. 384 of October, 21, 1935.
95. AGMIR, f. 1, op. 2, d. 99: 'The text of labeling . . .' (1938), l. 39. In the permanent exhibition at MIR in 1938 this story was presented as a situational scene with three figures representing 'the prison in the Synagogue of Isaac Nakhmanovich in Poland, in which the persons, acting against the power of the rabbis and *kahal*, were kept in chains'. See 'Ob"iasnitel'naia zapiska, raz"iasniaiushchaia i obosnovyvaiushchaia printsipy, polozhennye v osnovu ekspozitsii Muzeia istorii religii AN SSSR', p. 241.
96. AGMIR, f. 1, op. 2, d. 107, l. 2.

INDEX

Academic Union for Jewish Culture, Vienna 143
Achron, Joseph 142–44, 154 n. 8
Adler, Jacob 126
Aduev (Rabinovich), Nikolay 138
Africa 120, 187
agricultural settlements 56, 59, 61, 71 n. 31, 145
Akhmatova, Anna 74, 82, 87 n. 33
Akselrod, Rokhl 125
Alexander II 25, 80, 97
Alexander III 73, 78–79, 95
All-Russian Writers' Association 60, 62
All-Soviet Union of Associations of Proletarian Writers (VOAPP) 82
All-Union Society for Cultural Relations with Foreign Countries, VOKS 60
Aleksandrovsk 110–11
Almi, A. (Eliahu Chaim Sheps) 24
Alpert, Michael 152
Amalgamated Bank 59
American Jewish Joint Distribution Committee 56
Andersen, Hans Christian 75
Andreev, Nikolai Andreevich 86 n. 14
Andreev, Pavel 107
Annibal, L. 132
An-sky, S. 82, 120, 124, 127, 129, 146–48, 155, 161–63, 172, 173, 186, 190
Antireligious Exhibition 158–61, 165–66, 169, 174–75, 177, 187–92
anti-religious propaganda 4, 158
  see also atheism
anti-Semitism 53, 61, 68
anti-Zionism 151
Antsiferov, Nikolai 87 n. 17
Argo (Goldenberg, Abraham) 138
Arnshteyn, Mark 120 n. 10
Arones, Faivish 150, 156
Aronson, Naum 66
Asch, Sholem 1–4, 5–6, 8, 19–21, 36, 56–72, 74, 82, 109
Assimilationists 22, 28, 29, 48
atheism 4, 77, 100, 177, 179, 183, 186
  see also anti-religious propaganda

Babel, Isaac 59, 66
Bakhtin, Mikhail 84, 89
Balaban, Meir 185
'Bar Kochba' 146,
Baroque 96

Batyushkov, Konstantin 79, 88
Bedny, Demyan 79
Beizer, Mikhail 141
Belarus/Belorussia 2, 22, 30–32, 56, 141, 147–49, 156
Belasco, David 125
Belenki, Moisei (Moyshe) 69
Beliaev, Iuri 132
Belilovskii, Naum 146
Belinsky, Vissarion 75, 80, 86, 87
Belts 115, 116
Bely, Andrey 79
Benjamin, Walter 3, 45–47, 51–55, 61, 84
Berdichev (Berdychiv) 85, 129, 179, 193,
Beregovskii, Moisei 146, 148, 155
Bergelson, David 3, 4, 36, 45–46, 48–55, 61, 62, 71, 86, 99, 103
Bergolz, Boris (Borukh) 138
Bergson, Henri 47
Berlin 3, 20, 51, 52, 58, 61, 62, 86, 119, 128, 133, 143, 148
Berman, Adolf 112, 116
Berman, Herman 112
Bernesko-Berneker, K. L. 151
Beskin, Emmanuel 130, 133, 137
Bessarabia 41, 116
Bialik, Hayim Nahman 124, 128, 146
Białystok 23, 27, 119
Binyomin Shimin's publishing house 19
Birobidzhan 119, 145, 146, 154, 156
Birobidzhan State Jewish Theatre 146
Birzhevye vedomosti 131
Blok, Alexander 80,
Blum, Vladimir 134, 136
Blumental-Tamarina, Maria 124
Blumenthal, Anita 128
Bobruysk 27
Bogolyubov, Pavel 147
Bogoras (Bogoraz), Vladimir 158, 159, 161, 165, 166, 186, 190, 191
Bonch-Bruievich, Vladimir 177
Borges, Jorge Luis 73
Boston 126
Boymvol, Yehuda Leyb 113
Braun, Lev 112, 114–16
Bramson, Abram 148
Braslaver, Nakhmen 82
Brazil 124
Brest-Litovsk 108
Brodsky, Joseph 78

Bronshtein, Yasha 90
Brusilovskii, Evgenii 147
Buenos Aires 119
Bryansk 61
Brutzkus, Boris 13
Bucharest 134
Bund, Bundism 23, 26, 56, 59, 62, 64

Cahan, Abraham 59, 65, 67, 68, 70, 71
Canada 124
Cargill, Oscar 5, 20
Catholics 9, 11, 14, 16, 17, 127,
Central Antireligious Museum (CAM) 158–59, 177, 179, 183, 185, 186, 187, 193
Central State Historical Archive of St. Petersburg 142, 143, 144, 154
Central State Archive of Literature and Art 145–49, 151, 154
Central State Historical Archive of St Petersburg 142–44
Chancellery of the Ministry of the Imperial Court 143
Catherine II 92, 93
Chekhov, Anton 45
Chemerisky, Alexander 65
Cherkassy 119
Chernomordikov, David 143
Chukovskii, Kornei 58, 70
Chicago 126
Civil War, in Russia 1, 51, 53, 93, 99, 119, 134, 193
Clark, Katerina 49, 54, 103
Classicism 96
Cohen, Nathan 36, 37
colonization 61, 63, 65, 70, 71, 145
Committee of Jewish Writers, Artists and Scientists 68
Communism 3, 60, 61, 64, 66, 76, 90, 92, 94, 96, 99, 101, 102, 142, 154, 156
Communist International 61, 65
Communist Party, in: Soviet Union 59, 60, 63, 66, 69, 93, 117, 120, 145, 147; United States 3, 46, 48, 58, 66, 84; Germany 107
Congress Poland, also see Kingdom of Poland 2, 9, 22–24, 26, 28, 29
Conservatory, in:
  St. Petersburg, Leningrad 143, 149
  Warsaw 106
Constructivism 50, 93
Cooper, Adrienne 152
Corrsin, Stephen 9, 10, 20, 31, 32
Courland 24,
Crimea 56, 61, 65, 71, 86, 145
Cylkow, Izaak 28

Dashkevitsh, Nina (Chana) 117
Dawid, Christian 152
Department of Musical Ensembles 151, 152
Department of People's Education 60, 145
Der Fraynd 18, 26, 27, 31, 105, 112, 122
Der Emes, daily 48, 59, 60, 63, 65, 68, 136

Der Emes, publishing house 2, 69
Der Nister 3, 4, 73–102
Der Veg 25, 27
Deutscher, Isaac 68,
Di royte velt 67, 86
Di himlen brenen 145, 155
Dimanshtein, Shimen 63
Dinezon, Jacob 127
Dinner, Akiva 125, 136, 138
Dobrushin, Yehezkel 63, 64
Dorpat (Tartu) 22
Dos yidishe folksblat 19
Dostoevsky (Dostoyevsky), Fyodor 45, 74, 76, 77, 79, 80, 84, 85, 87, 88, 89
Drabkin, Evgenii 152
Dranov, Nathan 116
The Dream of Jacob 146
Dreiden, Simon 136
Dubnow, Simon 28
Dumas, Alexandre 126
Dunaevskii, Isaac 151, 156
Dunets, Khaskl 90
Duse, Eleonora 130
Dvinsk (Daugavpils) 27, 110, 111
Dymarsky, A. 134, 137, 138

Efros, Abram 62
Einhorn, David 62, 67, 71
Ekaterinoslav 110, 129, 130, 139 n. 15, 142
Ekho 136
Elisavetgrad 110, 115
Elizeum theatre, Warsaw 105, 108, 112–17, 122 nn. 40 & 52
Engel, Joel (Yoel, Yulii) 143, 144, 148
Epelbaum, Mikhail 3, 104–23, 137, 150
Epelbaum (Weinstein), Roza 110, 114–16
Eppelberg, Hershl 126–27
Epshteyn, Shakhno 58
Erenburg, Ilya 138
Erik, Max 35, 68
Eisenshtein, Sergei 46
Evelinov (Shteynfinkel), Boris 130, 134
Evreiskaia nedelia 132
Evreiskaia starina 19, 27
Ewald, Zinaida 149
Eynikayt 138

Falconet, Maurice-Étienne 76, 78, 79
Falkovich, Eli 69
famine 66, 75, 93
Fefer, Itsik 67–69, 90, 137, 138
Feinman, Sigmund 125
Feuchtwanger, Lion 146
Feydeau, Georges 128
First Congress of Soviet Writers 68
First General Census of the Population of the Russian Empire (1897) 2, 6–20

First World War 1, 2, 22, 25, 29, 56, 60, 106, 108, 116, 119, 128, 137, 179
Fishelevitsh, Itskhok 116
Fisherman, Jascha 120 n. 3
Fishman, Isaac 146
Fishzon, Abraham 108
Five-Year Plans 77, 147
folklore 23, 82, 114, 121 n. 20, 122 n. 53, 142, 147–49, 153
Forverts 48, 56, 58, 59–61, 63, 65, 66–68
France 56, 67, 68, 124
Frayhayt 46, 48, 58, 60, 66, 69
Frenkel, Jan 146
Frid, S. 131
Fried, Lazar 112, 114
Frishman, David 124, 127, 129
Frumkin, Maria 65
Frumkin, Yakov 23

Galicia 125
Gekht, Semen 59
Gendler, Arkady 152
Genfer, Moisey 108, 110
Germany 61, 124
Gidon, Dina 155 n. 36
Gilbert, Jean (Max Winterfeld) 113, 115, 128
Ginzburg, Saul 83
Glantz-Leyeles, Aron 59
Gliksman, Avrom 35
Glushkovichi 149
Gnesin, Mikhail 142
Godiner, Shmuel 63
Gogol, Nikolai 45, 74–76, 80, 84, 85, 86 n. 14, 96, 97
Goldberg, Samuil 105
Goldfaden, Abraham 110, 111, 113, 125, 127, 136
Goldina (Vainshtein), Marina 152
Golubeva, Rosalia 150
Gomel 134
Gordin, Jacob 108–11, 113, 126
Gorky, Maxim 42, 46, 58, 59, 63, 65, 66, 75, 79
Gorovets, Emil 150
Grand Duchy of Lithuania 2
Granovsky, Alexander 61, 82
Granovsky, Elena 130
Great Choral Synagogue, St. Petersburg 150, 156 n. 42
Great Depression 137
Gretchaninov, Alexander 107
Grigoriev, Nikifor 119
Grinvald, J. 138
Grodno 8, 25
Gruzenberg, Oskar O. 32 n. 44
Gruzenberg, Semyon O. 28, 32 n. 44
Guesnet, François 23
Gulag 69, 120 n. 7
Günzburg, Horace 27
Gurovich, Solomon 144
Gutzkow, Karl 126

Guzik, Anna 137, 150, 151

Habima theatre 133, 136, 146
Halpern, Shmuel 82
Hamburg 86–87 n. 15
Hasidim 23, 25, 30 n. 3, 82, 84, 85, 117, 127, 136
Haskalah 26, 28
Ha-Tsefirah 27
Ha-Zman 27
Haynt 18, 26–29, 112
Hazomir, Lublin Society for Jewish Music and Literature 143
Heifetz, Jascha 143
Heine, Heinrich 73, 74
Henkin, Vladimir 138
Herzen, Alexander 79
Herzen House 62
Higher State Institute for Arts and Technology (VKhUTEIN) 95
Hirschbein, Peretz 109, 110
Hirschhorn, Samuel 30 n. 17
Hitler, Adolf 68
Hoberman, David 169, 173, 174, 187
Hofstheyn, Dovid 82
Hollerith, Herman 6

Iakovlev, Alexander 62
Ianova, Maria 154 n. 8
Imber, Naftali Hirsh 125
Indur 25
Institute for Study of the USSR 149
Institute of Russian Literature 148, 149, 155 n. 32, 156 n. 36
intermarriage 89 n. 61
International Conference of Revolutionary Writers 68
Intourist 58, 59
Iudovin, Solomon 159–61, 162, 164–77, 179, 183, 186, 187
Izraelita 28

Jankowski, Moses 130
Jewish Autonomous Region 151
    see also Birobidzhan
Jewish Antifascist Committee 68, 69, 138
Jewish Commissariat 63, 144
Jewish Community Centre of St Petersburg 152, 153
Jewish Historical and Ethnographic Commission 147
Jewish Historical and Ethnographic Society 18, 148, 169, 186
Jewish Literary Society 18
Jewish Literary and Artistic Society, St. Petersburg 144
Jewish Music Society 18
Jewish National Fund, London 143
Jewish National House of Public Education 146
Jewish National Labor Union of America 143
Jewish Section of the Communist Party 63
Jewish Society of Art and Literature 18

Jewish Society for Development and Education 18
Jewish student union 18
Jewish Telegraphic Agency 63
Jewish Theatre of Musical Comedy, Moscow 133, 137
Jewish Vocal Ensemble 146
Joffe, Jeremiah 165
Judischer Verlag 143

Kabak, Iasha 134
Kachalov, Vasily 124
Kaganovitch, Max (Motl) 81
Kagarov, Evgenii 148, 149
Kadima Publishing Company 143
Kahan, Zalmen 106, 108, 120 n. 10
Kalisz 24
Kálmán, Emmerlich 107
Kalmen, I. 137
Kaminska, Esther Rokhl 19, 113, 114, 126, 128, 131
Kanapov, Fishl 128, 133
Karakozov, Dmitry 80, 97, 101
Katsizne, Alter 35
Kavetskaia, Victoria 132
Kazakhstan 179
Kazan Cathedral 159
Kelter, Jacob 114, 115
Kershner, Lydia 149
Kessler, David 126
Kharkiv/Kharkov 3, 67, 68, 73–75, 81, 84, 85, 90, 92–94, 99, 101, 102, 108, 142, 152
Kharik, Izi 63
Khayatauskas, Veniamin 150
Kherson 65, 107, 110, 111
Khidekel, Lazar 94
Kiev 8, 23, 26, 27, 33, 67, 73, 75, 90, 93, 94, 101, 107, 108, 119, 142, 146, 148, 149, 161
Kiev Opera House 106, 107, 117
Kipnis, Itsik 82
Kipnis, Menakhem 112–16, 122 nn. 53 & 55, 123 n. 56
Kirov, Sergei 137
Kiselgof, Zinovii 121 n. 20, 122 n. 56, 142, 148
Kishinev 115, 116
Kleinmann, Yvonne 141
Kletzkin, Boris 37
Klezfest festival 153
klezmer music 152, 153
Klitenik, Shmuel 68
Knipper-Chekhova, Olga 124
Kobrin, Leon 109
Kogan, Yurii 158
Koidanava 22
Koltsov (Fridlyand), Mikhail 62
Komissarzhevskaya Theatre 56
Kompaneyets, Aba 108, 110–14
Konstantinovskii, Alexander 159, 177, 179–82, 186, 188
Kopelman, Simon 124
Korik, Ilya 108, 110
Koriushka Restaurant 152, 156 n. 55

Korolenko, Psoy (Lion, Pavel) 152
Kremer, Isa 133
Kremlin 46, 59, 75, 85, 99–101
Krivoy Rog 65
Kronenberger, Louis 1
Krutikov, Georgii 94
Krzycki, Julian 28
Kugel, Alexander 132, 136
Kultur-Lige 33, 67, 144, 148
Kurier Warszawski 27, 29
Kushnirov, Aron 63, 64
Kvitko, Leyb 67, 69, 82, 146

Lacis, Asja 51, 52
Ladovskii, Nikolai 94
Landau, Adolf 26
Landau, Samuel 112
Lateiner, Joseph (Latayner, Yosef) 112, 122 n. 41, 126
Latvia 30 n. 6
lawyers 17, 18, 22, 23, 112
Lehar, Franz 105, 112, 113, 115
Lenin, Vladimir 47, 52, 53, 74–77, 84, 96, 100, 101
Lenin Mausoleum 100, 102
Leningrad (St. Petersburg) Conservatory 143, 149
Leningrad Jewish Association (since 1992 the Jewish Association of St Petersburg) 152
Leningrad State Musical Comedy Theatre 120 n. 7
Lengosestrada state concert agency 106
Leningrad blocade 149
Leningrad Region Department of Ministry of State Security of the USSR 212 n. 18
Leningrad Provincial Administration of the Central Administration for Literature and Publishing 145
Leningrad Provincial Department of the Main Directorate for Literature and Publishing 144
Leningrad Society for Chamber Music 145
Leningrad State Musical Comedy Theatre 120 n. 7
Leningrad State University 161, 186
Leningrad Yiddish Music and Drama Ensemble 150
Leningradskaia Pravda 136
Leonidov (Volfenzon), Leonid 129
Leonov, Leonid 62
Levin, Vladimir 26
Libert, Yankev 112, 114
Libin, Zalmen 109, 111
libraries 14, 18, 27, 35, 38, 39, 41, 60, 146, 148, 154 n. 8, 156 n. 32, 187
Lidin (Gomberg), Vladimir 56, 62, 66
Liebknecht, Karl 107
Liebknecht State Academic Opera House 107
Lifshits, A. 110
Lifshits, Mikhail 98
Lifshits, Nechama 150, 152
Linezky, Yoel 128
Lipovsky, Naum 108
Lipovsky, Shura 152
Lissitzky, El 75

Literacy 2, 6, 13, 14, 19
  in Hebrew 13, 15, 16
  in Polish 3, 14–16
  in Russian 14–17
  in Yiddish 13–16
Literarishe bleter 33–43, 125, 127
Litvak, A. (Khayim Yankl Helfand) 36
Litvakov, Moyshe 59, 62–67, 136
Litvaks 2, 23–29, 30 n. 5, 6, 32 n. 51
Liubimov, Saul 106, 120 n. 6, 150
Liubomirsky, Yeshua (Ovsei) 125, 137
Lobel, Malvina 116
Lodz 23, 24, 27, 110, 113, 116, 126, 127, 134
Loeffler, James 142
Loewenberg, Jakub 28
London 126, 128, 143
London, Frank 152
Lotman, Yuri 53 n. 1, 75
lottery 60, 61
Lublin 91, 143
Lugansk 110, 111
Lukács, Georg 98
Lunacharsky, Anatoly 124, 136
Lvov, Pesakh 143

Maggid, David 155 n. 33
Magid-Ekmekchi, Sofia 148, 149, 155 nn. 33 & 35
Maizel, H. 126
Makhlis, Isaac 147
Maltz, Ilya 159, 177, 179, 182, 183, 186, 188
Mandelstam, Osip 79, 81, 82, 136
Margolin, Samuil 136
Marina Roshcha Yiddish school 60, 61
Mariupol 110
Markish, Peretz 35, 40, 59, 128, 137, 138, 147
May Day 45–47
Mayzel, Nakhman 33–35, 37, 39–41, 43
Mendele Moykher-Sforim 124, 128
Mendelevich, Rodion 130, 131
Mendelsohn, Stanislaw 31 n. 38
Meyerhold, Vsevolod 134
Miedzyrzec 24
Mikhailov, Evgenii 147
Mikhoels, Solomon 61, 62, 66, 68, 138, 147, 156 n. 51
Milman-Kremer, Rachel 147
Milner, Moisei 120 n. 3, 142–46, 155 nn. 20 & 21
Ministry of Culture of the Russian Federation 150, 151
Minkova, Iustina 138
Minsk 8, 22, 25, 27, 90, 116
Miron, Dan 46
Mishurat, Meyer 108, 109, 121 n. 23
Mizrakh Partnership 143
Mlotek, Zalmen 152
Moment 19, 28, 112, 127
Montefiore, Moses 175
Morrison, Moritz 126
Moscovitch, Maurice 126

Moscow Art Theatre 129
Moscow Central Telegraph Office 50
Moscow Conservatoire 106
Moscow Pedagogical Institute 2
Moscow State Yiddish (Chamber) Theatre 2, 133, 146
Moskvin, Ivan 124
Movich, A. 138
Mukdoni, Alexander 31 n. 27, 112–15, 121 n. 39, 122 n. 45, 127, 128
Muranov Theatre, Warsaw 111
Museum of Anthropology and Ethnography 148, 158
Museum of Religion and Atheism in Kazakhstan 179
Museum of the History of Polish Jews 32 n. 51
Museum of the History of Religion 159
Museum of the Jewish Historical and Ethnographical Society 148, 169
musicology 120 n. 2, 141, 146–49, 152
Mussorgsky, Modest 107
Myodovnik, Mark 121 n. 23

Nadina, N. G. 110
Natanzon, Charles 115
Natanzon, Sonia 115
Nathans, Benjamin 7, 141
nativization policy 142
Nekrasov, Nikolai 80
Neroslavskaya, Nadezhda (Esther) 111–14
Nesvizhskii, Leo 142, 143
Neue Freie Presse 67
New Economic Policy 134
New York 7, 40, 48, 56, 59, 113, 114, 116, 119, 125, 126, 129, 131, 134, 138
Niger, Shmuel 36, 82, 85
Nikitsky Theatre, Moscow 130, 131, 133, 134
Nomberg, Hersh David 36, 59
North-Western Region (*krai*) 2
Novaia Odessa 110
Novosti Theatre, Odessa 117
Novyi voskhod 27
Novyi zritel 133, 136
Nusinov, Isaac 62, 63, 67, 98

Obozrenie teatrov 132
Odessa 26, 56, 106, 108, 110, 111, 114–17, 124, 128–31, 134, 137, 143, 152, 156 n. 55, 179, 186
Odessa State Yiddish Theatre 146
Olgin, Moyshe 3, 45–49, 53
Olshvanger, Aba 28
Opatoshu, Joseph 36, 40
opera 104, 106–08, 111, 113, 114, 117, 120 n. 10, 142, 144–46
operetta 107–15, 117, 122 n. 39, 124, 125, 127, 128, 130–34, 136, 138
Orlenev, Pavel 110
orphanages 99
Orshansky, Ber 90
Orthodox Christianity 11, 14, 15–17, 48, 50, 80, 83, 177

Orthodox Judaism 177, 192 n. 60
  see also Hasidim
Orzeszkowa, Eliza 24

Pale of Jewish Settlement 1, 6, 8, 25–27, 30 n. 6, 109, 129, 131, 183
Papernyi, Vladimir 45
Paris 29, 62, 66, 119
Parush, Iris 11
Passover 174, 183, 192 n. 40
pedlars 17, 18
PEN clubs 67, 68
People's Commissariat for Internal Affairs (NKVD) 144
People's Commissariat of Education 60, 134, 143, 166
Peretz, Yitskhok Leibush (Isaac Leib, Leon) 19, 26, 91, 114, 115, 124, 127, 128, 137, 143, 146
Perezhitoe 19
Persits, Mark 159, 179, 183, 187
Peter I (the Great) 76, 78, 79, 87 n. 33, 95
Philadelphia 126
Picon, Molly 137
Philipp, Adolf 128
Pilnyak, Boris 54 n. 22, 62, 75, 82
Piłsudski, Józef 59, 64
Pinsk 27
Pisarev, Dmitry 101
Pobedonostsev, Konstantin 77
Podolia 148, 161
Pokrovsky, Mikhail 95, 99
Poland 2, 3, 7, 9, 22–24, 26–27, 30 n. 6, 34, 37, 41, 43, 46, 50, 56, 59, 64, 65, 68, 91, 106, 108, 109, 114, 116, 124, 128, 185
Popov, Nikolay 124
Potopchina, Evgeniia 130–34
printers 17
Prokofiev, Sergei 107
prostitution 17, 20, 80
Prylucki, Noah 18, 112, 113, 115
Prylucki, Zvi 18, 24, 25, 27, 29
Przeglad Codzienny 27
publishing houses 2, 19, 56, 59, 67, 69, 73, 143
Pulner, Isaiah 159, 161, 165, 166, 169, 174, 175, 187, 190 n. 14, 21, 191 n. 29, 38
Pultusk 28
Pushkin, Aleksander 45, 74–76, 78, 79, 94, 99, 130

Rabin, Joseph 69, 70
Rabinovich, I. 131
Rabochii i teatr 137
Rachmaninov, Sergei 107
Radek, Karl 124
Radin, Pyotr 110
Radomsk 28
Rakov, Nahum 125
Rakovsky, Puah 23, 24
Rappel, Lazar 108, 112, 115, 116
Rappel, Max 115, 116

Rappel, Zina 115, 116, 123 n. 58
Rappoport, Vasily 131
Rasputin, Grigory 80, 124, 132, 134
Rassvet 26, 27
Ravitch, Melekh 35, 37
readership 2, 19, 26, 33, 35, 37, 40–43, 44 n. 12
Rech 131
Red Army 93
Red Square 46, 48, 51, 58, 59, 66, 92, 100, 102
Reed, John 84
Reinhardt, Max 58
Reisen, Avrom/Abraham 22, 26, 60
Rekhtman, Abram 190 n. 18
Remenik, Hersh 87 n. 28, 89 n. 70
Renaissance 78
Repertory Committee, Department of People's Education 148
revolution in Russia 1, 5, 9, 26, 51–53, 67, 68, 70, 75–77, 79–81, 84, 85, 92, 94, 97, 99, 102 n. 10, 109, 133, 134, 142, 143, 175
Reznik, Lipe 82
Riga 27, 119, 144
Rivesman, Mark 144, 145, 148
Roitman, Aron 147
Roitman, Ester 150
Romania 124, 128
Romm, G. 136
Rosenberg, Israel 124
Rosenfeld, Shloyme
Rosh Hashanah 187, 189, 192 n. 54
Rostov-on-Don 142
Rozowski, Solomon, 142
Rubinstein, Anton 106
Rumshinsky, Joseph 124, 125, 127
Ruppin, Arthur 13
Russian Academy of Sciences 148
Russian National Library 148
Russian Orthodox Church 177
Russian State Archive for Literature and Art in Moscow, RGALI 125
Russification 12, 28
Rybak, Yisakhar Ber 66

Sabbath 69, 82, 127, 164
Sabsay, David 110
Saltykov, Ivan 143
Samberg, Aizik 116
Saminsky, Lazar 142, 143
Sandler, Peretz 112, 114, 122 n. 39
Schildkraut, Rudolph 58, 126
Schiller, Friedrich 126
schools: Hebrew 23; Yiddish 60, 61, 66
Schwartz, Sholem (Shalom Ben-Baruch) 116
Second Moscow State University 60
Second World War 177
Segalovich, Zelig 36
Seekers of Happiness 151

Semashko, Nikolai 61
Semenov-Tian'-Shanskii, Petr P. 6
Shakhnovich, Mikhail 159, 175, 177, 186, 187
Shapiro, Lamed 93, 94
Sharevskaia, Berta 159, 183, 187
Shatzky, Jacob 10
Shebuev, Nikolai 132
Shekhtman, Manuel 159
Sherman, Joseph 48
Shipovnik Publishing House 56
Shklyar, Ephraim 143
Shneyfal, K. 132
Sholem Aleichem 6, 27, 115, 131, 137, 146
Shomer, Abraham 124
Shor, Anshl 124
Shor, Moyshe 124, 127
Shpits, Boris 147
Shtreicher, Lubov', 142
Shulman, Zinovy 104, 106, 107, 117, 120 n. 6
Shumlky, Volf 110
shund 19, 109, 110, 111, 114, 122 n. 43
Shuvalova, Vera 132
Shvartser, Veniamin 150
Siberia 49
Simferopol 142
Simonovich, Aron 132
Singer, Bernard 11
Singer, Israel Joshua 35, 40, 59, 60, 67
Sklamberg, Lorin 152
Sliozberg, Genrikh 22, 24, 25, 30 n. 3
Slonim 27
Smolar, Boris 63–65
Smolar, Hersh 65
Smolenskin, Peretz 24
socialist realism 49, 75, 82–85, 90, 101, 145
Society for Jewish Folk Music, St. Petersburg/Petrograd 18, 120 n. 3, 142, 144, 145, 152, 153 n. 3, 154 nn. 4, 7 & 8
Society for the Protection of the Health of the Jewish Population 18, 148
Society for Settling Toiling Jews on the Land, OZET 59
Society for the Spread/Promotion of Enlightenment among the Jews of Russia 18, 148
Sokolov, Boris 166
Sokolov, Nahum 25
Sonts, Leonid 152
Soviet Union 2–4, 48, 50, 56, 58, 59, 61, 62, 64–68, 81, 82, 85, 87 n. 17, 90, 91, 104, 108, 119, 120, 124, 125, 128, 133, 136–38, 144, 145, 147, 148, 149, 151
Special City Office for the Affairs of Societies, St. Petersburg, 142
Spector, Mordechai 124
Spektorov, Grigory 134
St Isaac's Cathedral 159, 166, 191 n. 33
Stalin, Josef 2, 58, 59, 67, 69, 81, 84–86, 93, 120, 137, 145, 149

State Institute for Theatre Arts (GITIS) 106
State Jewish (Yiddish) Theatre in Birobidzhan 146
State Jewish (Yiddish) Theatre in Kiev 146
State Museum of the History of Religion (GMIR)
Stiskin, David 150
Strindberg, August 126
Sudermann, Hermann 126
Svirskii, Aleksei 62
Symbolism 3, 73–75, 77, 79, 80–83, 85, 90, 91, 92, 99, 101, 127

Tal, Sidi 150
Talmud 169, 171, 172
Tantsman, Josef 128
Teatr 130
Teatr i iskusstvo 132
Teatralnaia gazeta 130, 134
Thalia Theater, New York 126
Timofeev, Corigorii 154 n. 8
Tobenkin, Elias 68
Tolstoy, Lev 45
Tomashevsky, Boris 126
Tomars, Joseph, 142
Toporov, Vladimir 53 n. 1, 75, 87 n. 17
Torah 161, 175
Trade Union of Workers of Arts 137
translations, into: English 5, 74; Polish 28, 42; Russian 28, 56, 67, 69; Yiddish 39, 73, 107, 112, 122 n. 39
travelogues 59, 86 n. 12, 91
Tribuna evreiskoi sovetskoi obshchestvennosti 59
Trilling, Ilia 134
Troinitskii, Aleksandr G. 6
Trotsky, Leon 59, 79
Trubetskoi, Paolo 76, 95
Turkow, Zygmunt 122 n. 45

Ukraine 1, 2, 56, 61, 62, 65, 73–75, 90, 92–94, 99, 108, 119, 122 n. 53, 133, 137, 141, 187
Union of the Godless 158
Universal Restaurant 151
United States of America 3, 48, 50, 61, 124, 127, 128, 130, 132, 134, 137, 143, 147, 187
Utesov, Leonid 138

Vaykhert, Mikhl 35
Vaysenberg, Itshe Meyer 36
Vecherniaia Moskva 66, 133, 137, 138
Vernadsky National Library of Ukraine 155 n. 32
Vetrova, Maria Fedosyevna 79
Vienna 128, 134
Vienna Academic Union for Jewish Culture 143
Vilna 8, 23, 27, 32 n. 51, 116, 127, 143
Vilnius 152
Vinaver, Maxim 29
Vinnitsa 182, 183, 188
Vitebsk 27, 107, 110, 111
Volhynia 8, 24, 27, 30 n. 6, 85, 148, 161, 163, 186

Volkov, Nikolai 136
Volkovussky, Nikolai 131
Voskhod 26, 28, 82

Warsaw Conservatory 106
Warsaw Institute of Music 106
Weichert, Michal 127
Weinles, Jakub 165
Weinstein, Aaron (aka Rachmiel) 64 n 11
Weinstein, Roza, *see* Epelbaum (Weinstein), Roza
Wendroff, Zalman 60–62, 64
Wiadomosci Literackie 35
Wloclawek 24
Wolfsohn, Juliusz 156 n. 55
World War I, *see* First World War
World War II, *see* Second World War

Yampolsky, Mikhail 57
Yatzkan, Shmuel Yankev 26, 29
Yerusalimka 182, 183, 188
Yiddish Dramatic Ensemble of Moskontsert 150
Yiddish Ensemble of Comedy and Vaudeville 150
Yiddish literature 3, 20, 34–36, 38, 39, 42, 48, 49, 50, 63, 67, 74, 76, 81, 84, 91
Yiddish opera 145
Yiddish operettas 114, 115, 117
Yiddish songs 3, 104, 106, 117, 119, 122 n. 56, 147, 149, 150, 152, 153

Yiddishism 33, 48, 111, 112
YIVO 38, 42, 119
Yom Kippur 165–67
Young, Clara (Shpikolitser, Khaya-Risye) 114, 124–39
Youngvitz, Boaz 124 -134, 136, 137
Yudina, Maria 149
Yureneva, Vera 124, 132
Yushkevich, Semen 109, 132

Zagorsky, Mikhail 136
Zajka, Vital 23
Zak, Avrom 25
Zandberg, Yitskhok 113, 127
Zdunska Wola 28
Zeitlin, Arn 35
Zeitlin, Hillel 28
Zeitlin, Leo 144
Zhitomirsky, Alexander 142, 143
Zhitlovsky, Khaim 36
Zilberblat, S. 138
Zionism 23, 25–27, 56, 58, 91, 120 n. 3
Złoczew 125
Zoshchenko, Mikhail 82
Zozulya, Efim 62
Zritel 131, 132, 134
Zuskin, Benjamin 61, 62, 66
Zycie Zydowskie 27

www.ingramcontent.com/pod-product-compliance
Lightning Source LLC
LaVergne TN
LVHW061251060426
835507LV00017B/2009